Contents

Foreword

This book represents perhaps the first attempt on the part of the West to enter deeply into the heart of the problems that have become the focal point of the contemporary discussion between Christianity and Buddhism. As for its value and significance in this regard, the reader will find proof enough in the pages that follow.

I should like here only to draw attention to two points that, as part of the background of the subject matter treated, may contribute to our understanding of it. First: Why is it primarily the philosophers of Japan who have undertaken to confront the two cultures and two religions with each other? And second: Why are these philosophers for the most part close to Zen?

In contrast to life in European countries that until quite recently was defined exclusively in terms of Christianity, in Japan Shintoism, Buddhism, Confucianism and Christianity all exert an influence. Consequently a worldwide crisis evoked by the clash of different religions and cultures manifests itself in a particularly clear way in Japan. The task of the philosophers is to inquire into life and into the religion that lies behind it. Hence, given their situation, a number of Japanese philosophers have felt impelled to direct their concerns with religion mainly toward the question of the encounter between Buddhism and Christianity. But, we may ask, is this not also the situation of the world at large? How long will Europe be able to go on disregarding the non-European intellectual world?

Regarding the second point, we consider it necessary for our philosophical inquiry to maintain a fundamental religious attitude that accords with the spirit of free and critical thought of philosophy. Since Zen has no dogmatics, and wishes to have none, it is easy to understand why many of us keep rooted in the experience of Zen practice. The age-old questions, "What is religion?, What is philosophy?", need to be posed anew in our times.

The experience the author has gained through extensive stays in Japan, the astonishing amount of material he has brought together, and his discussion of the topic in Germany have led to results that go a long way toward fulfilling the expectations he has engendered. In deep gratitude I can only express my further hope that his work will inspire new beginnings for a deeper encounter between Christianity and Buddhism.

Kyoto   Keiji Nishitani
October 4, 1976

Author's Preface to the English Edition

In his first encyclical, *Redemptor hominis*, dated 4 March 1979, Pope John Paul II wrote: "True ecumenical activity means openness, drawing closer, availability for dialogue, and a shared investigation of the truth in the full evangelical and Christian sense" (Sec. 6). Not only does the Holy Father ask this attitude of Christians in dialogue among themselves, but he extends it to the wider reaches of ecumenism in which representatives of all the religions of the world seek to come closer together.

After an initial phase of euphoria, those engaged concretely in improving mutual understanding among religions have come to realize that there is simply no such thing as a dialogue between *religions* in the abstract sense. There is only dialogue between *people* of like or different background, mentality, nationality, culture and faith. Like all dialogue, then, it requires a basic *openness* to listen to one another, and this in turn promotes a *drawing closer* to one another. Only then can we speak of an *availability for dialogue* through communication, mutual esteem, an exchange of thoughts and approaches, and a sharing of visions about the road that all men seek or are called to seek. Only then, in the exercise of such communication, can we speak of a *shared investigation of the truth* in the broadest sense of the term.

In the case of the present study, this "truth" which the Holy Father goes on to characterize in its full biblical and Christian sense, no longer has any name at all. To write such a book, about "absolute nothingness," may not be the usual thing. The very title lends itself to misunderstanding and ridicule. But the subject matter has nothing to do with nihilism or apparent meaninglessness and nonsense. It breaks through the superficially meaningless and the menace of nihilism into the realm of speechlessness—of open hands and open hearts and a new kind of communication without words.

In general, training in the experience of wordless communication occurs through the practice and mastery of silence and meditation. The great religions of Asia have provided Western man with new incentives and assistance in this regard. Yet the world in which we all live, orientals and occidentals, is one that has come more and more to bear the stamp of rationality. The quest for *wordless* communication in such a setting, therefore, can only avoid being an escape from the world if it can present itself in *worded* communication as something reasonable and meaningful.

That such an undertaking is not impossible is something I have learned, with increasing enthusiasm, from my encounter with Japanese philosopher Keiji Nishitani. Professor Nishitani, who will celebrate his eightieth birthday on 27 February 1980, is a thinker who stands at the very cutting edge of the manifold spiritual tendencies of our times. This is something that is treated in detail in the text. I should only like to add here that he is above all a man who teaches by personal example what it means to pursue the truth right into one's old age. Several years ago he spoke of himself as "a Buddhist in the making who has found his home in Buddhism" and at the same time as "a Christian in the making who has not yet found his home in Christianity." As a philosopher he is concerned with erecting bridges of understanding through the awareness that everything that is said is only meaningful if spoken out of the ultimately unspeakable, in whose service it must remain. I myself see in him a fellow traveler of Karl Rahner, whose thought shows a sense of duty to the *reductio in mysterium.* It is in gratitude to Professor Nishitani that I offer this English translation, even as three years ago I was privileged to dedicate to him the original German text.

The present English edition would not have been possible but for two fortunate circumstances. First, I was approached by Jan Van Braght, with whom I had studied in Kyoto some years ago and who is currently director of the Nanzan Institute for Religion and Culture in Nagoya, for permission to prepare and publish a translation of the book for a monograph series being planned by their Institute. Second, I have found in James W. Heisig an able translator who rendered my text into English in a very short time. To both of them I should like at this time to extend my special thanks.

This book is offered as part of the continuing dialogue among world religions, more specifically the dialogue between Christianity and Mahāyāna Buddhism. If it succeeds in laying down a few "building blocks" to that end, I shall consider it to have fulfilled its purpose.

Bonn
6 August 1979.

Hans Waldenfels

Translator's Note

The reader of these pages will no doubt notice occasional irregularities of usage and grammar in certain of the passages quoted from articles published in the East in English. While such unevenness of editing in English texts is not uncommon in Japanese publications, even in scholarly essays, neither is it by any means limited to those whose native language is not English. I have only taken liberties in putting some uniformity into orthography and punctuation, without drawing any particular attention to the fact.

I have consulted English translations of works published originally in Japanese, where they are available, and have made corrections in translation and grammar where necessary. Where no such translation exists, the renditions are my own. In either case, certain minor differences from the author's German translations have been unavoidable.

An exception has been made, however, of Professor Nishitani's *What is Religion?* which I cite faithfully according to the periodical publication of its English translation, since a fully re-edited edition of this work is being planned for future publication in the Nanzan Studies in Religion and Culture with the kind cooperation of Professor Nishitani.

Amendments to existing standard English translations of German works have been indicated each time in the notes.

Finally, I should like to express my thanks to Jan Van Bragt for reviewing this translation in its entirety.

J. W. Heisig

Introduction

In 1959 the Japanese philosopher of religion Yoshinori Takeuchi wrote in a Festschrift dedicated to Paul Tillich:

> Whenever discussion arises concerning the problem of encounter between being and non-being, Western philosophers and theologians, with hardly an exception, will be found to align themselves on the side of being. This is no wonder. The idea of "being" is the Archimedean point of Western thought. Not only philosophy and theology, but the whole tradition of Western civilization has turned around this pivot.
>
> All is different in Eastern thought and Buddhism. The central notion from which Oriental religious intuition and belief as well as philosophical thought have been developed is the idea of "nothingness." To avoid serious confusion, however, it must be noted that East and West understand non-being or nothingness in entirely different ways.[1]

Heidegger's question, "Why are there beings rather than nothing?"[2] is focused here on an aspect that he himself did not fully appreciate. Tillich, one of the few significant Christian theologians to carry on a dialogue with Asian thinkers, stated in his *Systematic Theology* that the question of being is produced by the "shock of non-being,"[3] and yet that this shock produces an anxiety that must be lived through. This led him in turn to inquire after the courage to accept the anxiety of non-being and to conclude that "the question of God is the question of the possibility of this courage."[4] God is therefore seen as "being-itself, in the sense of the power of being or the power to conquer non-being."[5] Here the thesis of Takeuchi finds its confirmation. For what in the last analysis remained hidden to Tillich was the realization that what the Mahāyāna Buddhist tradition, from early times up to the present, has termed "nothingness" cannot be encountered from a posture of anxiety.

The Catholic theologian and philosopher of religion Bernhard Welte has recognized more clearly than Tillich that there is a nothing-

1

ness that is not empty and meaningless, and that does not therefore summon in despair:

> Nothingness is not empty nothingness. In times of basic ethical decision we are given to see how it carries us along, how it safeguards and decides, how it sends out the challenge to trust, to step onto the fathomless and the still of nothingness, and to believe. Its mute power is greater, uncontestably greater than all that otherwise appears great and powerful.[6]

These words form bridges and throw open doors. But someone is bound to take exceptions: Is not that which is called "nothingness" in Buddhism—particularly when it is addressed by its other, and for the Asians themselves its less ambiguous, designation of "emptiness" (Skt., śūnyatā Jap., kū)—in fact an "empty nothingness"? Here we come up against the helpless impasse that burdens so much of the dialogue between Asia and the West. Obviously similar words do not always carry similar meanings.

The goal of the present work is to make some contribution to a better understanding on this point. On the one hand it is concerned with what is meant by the Asian-Buddhist formula "absolute nothingness" or "emptiness." On the other hand it aims to clarify what kind of response is possible within the horizons of Western-Christian thought. For this reason we do not propose here to trace a detailed picture of the many-faceted history of "absolute nothingness." Instead we shall make the focal point of our exposition the understanding of "nothingness" as it has unfolded, ever more clearly, in the thought of the still active Japanese philosopher Keiji Nishitani, and as it is presented today among students and colleagues who, like him, stand in the tradition of Zen Buddhism.

The advantage of approaching the problem from the viewpoint of the living representatives of the so-called Kyoto School which began with Kitarō Nishida, the father of modern Japanese philosophy, lies in the very way they themselves view their task. From the outset they see it not as a mere reverential backward glance to an aged tradition, but as an existential and dialogical engagement with the modern world characterized as it is by secularization, science and atheism. In this way it can be shown how a one-dimensional view of man[7] presents a distortion of true humanity; and how a radical experience of man that is finally subsumed into the unspeakable, in both its positive and negative meanings, cannot be said to be in contradiction to an equally radical promotion of rationality.

For the Western reader, however, this standpoint needs to be presented, at least in general outline, in its relationship to the heritage of Buddhism. For this reason an initial section on the Buddhist tradition has been included by way of preparation. This should help make clear how the Mahāyāna tradition of nothingness, which derives from Nāgār-juna, the southern Indian philosopher of the second to third centuries A.D., and which found its most intense expression in the Zen tradition, can be spoken of as genuine Buddhist tradition back to the Buddha himself.

The final section of the book is intended to demonstrate both to the Western reader and to Japanese colleagues that dialogue on questions like those which animate the current discussions of the Kyoto School has recognizable parallels in the Christian West. To point these out to each side as stepping stones to further dialogue can only be a mutual benefit. For Asia is seeking an encounter with the Western world as well, and that precisely as a world which bears the stamp of Christianity. But all too often possible participants for the dialogue go unrecognized. Europe, on the other hand, is in danger of sinking, after a long period of world hegemony, into a kind of self-enclosed provincialism vis-à-vis the rest of the world. Nishitani's reproach is very much to the point here:

> . . . If the various components of our daily life are traced historically, one finds that our present situation is inseparably bound to European history. This is because European history has become a part of our own history. At the same time, it means that Eastern history, which formerly meant all of history from a Japanese standpoint, is now seen as only part of our history. In other words, when we look at ourselves historically, we are now aware of the fact that we belong to a united and larger world comprised of both East and West. And precisely the same thing could be said, to one degree or another, about all non-European nations. However according to Toynbee, in spite of the world having changed in this way, it was Europe alone which was unable to free itself from a Europe-centered outlook. The Europe which, through the dynamic of its civilization, led various other countries to a consciousness of being part of a larger world, was the Europe whose viewpoint remained self-circumscribed. This is what Toynbee calls the "contradiction of the present age."[8]

It is also a question for us then of making some small contribution to the overcoming of this contradiction. The world as a whole can only become a more human and more peaceful place to live if all the parts cooperate in seeking to understand one another and to enter into the kind of meaningful rivalry with one another that will bring it closer to the common goal of a new world, a new society and a new humanity.

Part One

BACKGROUND

1. The Buddha

The thought of Keiji Nishitani and his colleagues bears the stamp of an alert sensitivity to the problems of the contemporary world as they present themselves in a highly industrialized Asian land. But in the final analysis their reading of the times takes place in the light of Buddhist tradition as it has developed up to the present day in the schools of the Great Vehicle.

The influence of Buddhism is more apparent in the thought of Nishitani than it had been with Nishida. In the first decades after the Meiji restoration of 1868 the spirit of Japanese nationalism reawoke, and with it came more to the fore an ideology of a Shintoistic stamp. Only after the breakdown of this ideology at the end of the Pacific War in 1945 was Japanese Buddhism allowed to make a contribution to modern society and its spiritual vacuum. Christianity was not in a position to give the decisive answer the Japanese were seeking to their questions, and this made the opportunity all the greater. This is not to say that Buddhism was altogether in such a position either. Still, one cannot in fairness overlook the Kyoto School in whose circles rational philosophy was being pursued all along without denying an intrinsic relationship to Buddhism. From these efforts a characteristically Japanese philosophy has been able to emerge that at once opens up a workaday secularized society to the realms of deeper experience and offers liberation to a society that is seen as closed in on itself.

The ability of Buddhism to disclose man in his depths resides in its operational realization of what is called "absolute nothingness" or "emptiness." In order to show that this concerns an attitude fundamental to Buddhism, a number of key points in the history of what is called "absolute nothingness" must first be highlighted.

It is not of course a question of offering here any contribution to Buddhology or to questions related to the history of Buddhism. That Nishitani himself—at least for the period covering his major work—has rather opted to follow a commonly accepted understanding of Buddhism without any intention of making a direct scholarly contribution, relieves us of that obligation. In line with present-day discussion, then,

7

the history of the Buddhist understanding of nothingness can be said to admit of stages that will determine our exposition. First, the story of the Buddha himself will serve us as a point of departure. We shall then focus on the discussion of "emptiness" (Skt., *śūnyatā*) revolving about the Indian philosopher Nāgārjuna. The preeminent place where "absolute nothingness" is practiced, in Japan, is in Zen Buddhism, which will be taken up next. And finally, we shall show how it was through the practice of *zazen* that Kitarō Nishida, founder of the Kyoto School, found his way to "absolute nothingness."

*   *   *

The origin of the stress later put on "emptiness" can be traced back to the life of the Buddha himself, and to his choice of homelessness and his silence on metaphysical questions, or at least to his talk of the non-self and "dependent origination" which is intimately bound up with his life experience. In any case these points all lead to the same conclusion: that every Buddhist system can be represented as a doctrine of the Middle Way.

Homelessness and Silence

In the course of an address delivered on July 22, 1962, on the occasion of the 700th Jubilee of his hometown Messkirch, Martin Heidegger remarked:

The possibility persists, and is confirmed more and more each day, that the situation will soon be upon us in which man will no longer know, and no longer need, what is called a home, because he can get along without it.[1]

And later on he adds:

Perhaps man is settling into homelessness. Perhaps the ties to home and the pulls to home will disappear from the Dasein of modern man. But perhaps, too, amidst the pressures of not feeling at home, a new relationship to feeling at home is in the offing.[2]

He concludes:

Presumably the sense of not being at home in the technological world and of a profound tedium go together as a kind of hidden pull towards a home which is being sought. For no amount of technological apparatus and none of its achievements and aids, none of

its ever increasing inventiveness nor even all of its limitless indus-
triousness can make a home for us—that is, the sort of thing that
sustains us in the core of our Dasein and defines it and brings it to
bloom.[3]

Commenting on this address, Nishitani has shown that from its
very beginnings Buddhism has known about homelessness. For Buddha
and his disciples had freely chosen the life of homelessness:

Then I, monks, after a time, being young, my hair coal-black, possessed of radiant youth, in the prime of my life—although my un-
willing parents wept and wailed—having cut off my hair and
beard, having put on yellow robes, went forth from home into
homelessness.[4]

This experience of the Buddha himself was then turned into a challenge
for all those who followed him on the road:

A householder or a householder's son or one born in some respect-
able family hears that *dhamma* [Skt., *dharma;* = teaching]. When
he has heard that *dhamma* he acquires a faith in the *Tathāgata* [a
name for the Buddha, literally meaning "he who has thus come"].
Possessed of this faith he has acquired, he reflects thus: "Confined
is this household life, a path of dust, while going forth is of the
open air. Yet it is not easy for one who has lived in a house to fare
the Brahma-faring completely fulfilled, completely purified, pol-
ished like a conch-shell. Yet suppose I were to have my hair and
beard shaved, to don saffron robes, and go forth from home into
homelessness?" After a time, getting rid of his mass of wealth,
whether large or small, getting rid of his circle of relations, whether large or small, having had his hair and beard shaved, having
donned saffron robes, he goes forth from home into homelessness.[5]

Nishitani takes up Heidegger's phrase to give his view of the voca-
tion of the Buddhist:

On the one side, a Buddhist must seek, amidst the uncanny homelessness of the present technological age, amidst the widespread situation of man's estrangement from himself, the way back to the
Heimat or, as Heidegger has put it, to that which sustains us in the
core of our Dasein. On the other side, he must essay to recover, in
and through the same situation of estrangement, his own authentic
way of Awakening and to revive Buddhism for the present age . . .
As the Buddhist way of Awakening itself signifies the return to and
repose in the *Heimat,* it is clear that these two sides are united in
one and the same task.[6]

For the Buddha himself wordlessness or silence is a special kind of "homelessness."[7] The parable of the poisoned arrow is well known in this regard. Just as it is senseless for a man who has been pierced with a poisoned arrow to trouble himself first of all with who the archer is, what is his caste, from which family he comes, what he looks like, etc., so is it also senseless to say (as the Buddha tells a disciple):

I will not fare the Brahma-faring under the Lord until the Lord explains to me either that the world is eternal or that the world is not eternal, either that the world is an ending thing or the world is not an ending thing; either the life-principle is the same as the body or the life-principle is one thing, the body another; either that the Tathāgata is after dying or the Tathāgata is not after dying, or else the Tathāgata both is and is not after dying. This man might pass away, Mālunkyaputta, ever it was explained to him by the Tathāgata.[8]

To the question why he has not explained this, the Buddha answers:

It is because it is not connected with the goal, is not fundamental to the Brahma-faring, and does not conduce to turning away from, nor to dispassion, stopping, calming, super-knowledge, awakening nor to *nibbāna* [Skt., *nirvāna*].[9]

Takeuchi sees the reason for the silence of the Buddha connected, in the final analysis, with meditation:

The silence of the Buddha is not only the exclusion of metaphysical opinion, but also its conquest and elevation to the higher dimension of absolute nothingness.[10]

Buddhism has to do with "reaching beyond the beyond," and this it "finds in the 'here and now' of real human existence." Takeuchi adds: "The obscurity of phrases like anātman and śūnyatā are due to this phenomenon." He then goes on to locate the ambiguity that modern man finds in talk of homelessness and wordlessness in the levels of meaning comprehended by the Buddhist notion of "ground" or "fundamental principle." In reference to Hegel and Heidegger, he summarizes the Buddhist treatment of ground as threefold: "the ground of origination, the going-to-ground [*zu-Grunde-gehen* = to be destroyed] of all beings, and finally the sublation (*Aufhebung*) of the ground itself."[11] For Nishitani this same ambiguity is involved in talk of "nihilism," as we shall see. It is also present in Buddhism in talk of "*anātman*" and in the doctrine of "dependent origin" (Pali, *paticcasamuppāda;* Skt., *pratītyasa-mutpāda*).

Anātman and Pratītyasamutpāda

In commenting on this complex but basic Buddhist notion, we must of course keep the fact clearly in mind that it is a notion heavily laden with ʰistorical, exegetical and philosophical ambiguities.[12] We shall touch on some of these only insofar as it is relevant to an understanding of Nishitani.

Our troubles begin already with the translation of the word "*anāt-man*" (Pali, *anattā*). Edward Conze proposes "non-self" in English so as to avoid having to decide whether it is best rendered as "not the self," "not a self," "not-I", "not the Self," "is without self," "unsubstantial" or something else again.[13] Oldenberg translates it into German as "Nicht-Ich"; von Glasenapp elaborates it as "Ohne 'Selbst,' i.e. without a persistent, autonomous being."[14] Murti clarifies *anātman* as "the denial of substance (*ātman*)," that is to say, "of a permanent substantial entity impervious to change."[15] In this quest for the right translation the question of the Indian understanding of *ātman* and *anātman* shifts around to the question of the Western understanding of "I," "self," "substance" and—let it be added—of "soul."

It can no longer be said with certainty how far talk of *anātman* is to be linked verbally to the figure of the historical Buddha, and in any case falls outside the scope of our concerns here. The question "Is this the life-principle, this body, or is something else life-principle, something else the body?" asks after the *jīva*—the "soul," the life-principle of man—and thus comes close to the question of *ātman.*[16] The Buddha leaves the answer open, as we have seen, affirming neither a dualism nor a monism. This leads Conze to conclude that talk of *anātman* should be taken as "a guide to meditation and not as a basis for speculation."[17] Frauwallner stresses in turn that

> the Buddha rejects the question of a present, existing self, since he treats it as one of those questions which end up in sterile discussion and debate, and distract from the proper goal of salvation . . . No actual denial of the soul is made; rather, when an expressed statement is wanting, it is simply characterized as incomprehensible.[18]

Strictly speaking, it is obvious that the Buddha is dealing with teaching man "that one ought not take the self to be something that is not the self (*ātma;* Pali, *attā*)." For salvation consists in "one's recognizing that everything that is falsely assumed to be self is non-self (*an-ātmā;* Pali, *anattā*) and thus letting go of the desire for it."[19] In this sense the Buddha invites man to a radical "shift of thinking" (metanoia), to a "turning about," a "conversion." It is precisely here that Heinrich Dumoulin sees the core of truth contained in the doctrine of the *anātman:*

> I refer to the truth that man must undergo a conversion, a breakthrough or awakening, in order to become his true self and gain access to what is authentically real. Zen Buddhism names this conversion the "great death" [Jap., *taishi*]—the sole way by which man can enter true life.[20]

Thus talk of *anātman* comes close to the challenge to "selflessness" within Western understanding, even if the courage to embrace its full radicality is often wanting. Cornelis correctly observes:

> ... it is as if the Buddha had grasped, six centuries beforehand, the message of Jesus: "Anyone who tries to preserve his life will lose it; and anyone who loses it will keep it safe" (Lk. 17:33). In my view it is the sense of this passage from the gospels that lies at the root of the Buddhist doctrine of *anattā,* i.e., of "non-self" or the renunciation of all egocentric activity.[21]

This brings us closer to the understanding of *anātman* that we might also presuppose to be operative in the work of Nishitani. In any event, we find in the second chapter of his book *What is Religion?* the following clarification that he added in reviewing the English translation: "*anātman* or *muga,* that is, non-ego or selflessness."[22]

The difficulties that Western man encounters with the doctrine of *anātman* result not so much from any opposition it entails to Christianity as from the theory of the modern image of man. We are dealing here with a disorder whose symptoms have long since become manifest: the self-reliant, self-conscious, autonomous, individual-personal man who at the same time differentiates himself from others or wishes to assert himself before them, effectively isolating himself and cutting himself off. W. L. King, who knows both sides well (he has been in direct contact in Kyoto with the representatives of the Kyoto School), has summarized well the problem of self, non-self and selflessness. We quote at length:

> A basic clarification might be found in the fact that the Christian-Western view of self-hood has been predominantly *conceptual* and the Buddhist-Eastern *existential.* For the West, therefore, selfhood has become a tightly-packaged individuality which is to be sharply separated from, and protected against, all invasions of the impersonal or non-personal. Hence it has strongly emphasized specific self-consciousness, i.e., the consciousness of the personal self as separate from other selves and from things, and tended to identify

this self with what Fingarette calls the "anxiety-generated" subjectivity, that subjectivity resulting from intra-psychic conflict; or we might call it the self of consciousness-in-emotional-tension-with-its-existential-situation. The West has also tended to soften the call of its own predominant faith (Christianity) to "self-denial," or to give such denial narrow and obvious forms; and above all to fearfully reject the mystic witness and call to the achievement of an *un*-self consciousness or *im*personal awareness.

The Buddhist pattern in contrast has been to adjure *all* conceptual selfhood whatsoever as intrinsically evil, and to glory in its precise opposite—the destruction of the sense of self-hood, the denial of the reality of the self, the illusory quality of self-consciousness, and so on. . . . But we may ask, *which* self (or self in *what* context) does Buddhism desire to rid humanity of? For the non-self language of Buddhism should not blind *any*one, either non-Buddhist *or* Buddhist, to overwhelming *existential* vitality of some sort of selfness in Buddhism. . . . Indeed throughout the Buddhist spiritual discipline in all its varieties and history, a persistent feature strikes the attention: The increasingly "non-selfed" or "de-selfed" self acts increasingly like what the West has sought to designate by its terms autonomous, integrated, liberated, spontaneous, enlarged, or redeemed self, i.e., the achievement of genuine self-controlled, acting-from-within selfhood—though it may be argued that Buddhism achieves a deeper level of subjective spontaneity and integration.[23]

In this connection brief mention should also be made of the notoriously difficult doctrine of *"pratītyasamutpāda"* (Pali, *paticcasamuppāda*). While there is no uniformally accepted translation of the concept, two elements contained in it come clearly to the fore: the idea of the origin of all worldly beings or of all being, and the idea of origination in dependence. Accordingly it is variously referred to as "conditioned co-production,"[24] "dependent co-origination,"[25] "dependent origination," "origin in dependence,"[26] "reciprocal dependency" or "causal chain."[27] Perhaps one could also offer a kind of paraphrase: "pure relationality, pure 'existing from-and-in relation to.' "[28]

Frauwallner rightly calls this doctrine "the most meaningful thing that ancient Buddhism has had to say concerning the theoretical foundations for a doctrine of salvation . . . the most worthwhile thing it has contributed to philosophical thought."[29] Its fundamental principle, variously articulated in many different formulas,[30] may be put briefly:

> If this is, so is that;
> if this begins, so does that;
> if this is not, neither is that;
> if this passes away, so does that.[31]

It embraces the entire realm of what is, what comes to be, and what passes away. Takeuchi sees in it "the logical and ontological grounding of our painful existence . . . Taken together or individually, the many faces of *pratītyasamutpāda* reveal the entire world in its full assemblage."[32]

Taking the two doctrines of *anātman* and *pratītyasamutpāda* in correlation to one another, this latter can then be seen to underline the idea that there is no such thing as an independent, self-supporting world substance; instead all beings in the world, in virtue of their dependency, have their being from and in dependency on one another. Thus the doctrine offers at the same time a starting point for inquiring into its relationship to the Western doctrine of the contingency of all beings in the world. To be sure, the Buddhist authors as a rule are skeptical of the Judaeo-Christian doctrine of creation. But even as one must warn the West against a hasty rejection of the doctrine of *anātman,* must one not also warn the East against a too hasty rejection of the doctrine of creation?

The language of *"creatio ex nihilo"* does not facilitate the dialogue between Buddhism and Christianity on this point.[33] Nonetheless, the Buddhist must be called upon, as the Buddha himself had insisted, not only to set himself free from all false affirmation, but also to be cleansed completely of all false and ungrounded denial.

2. Nāgārjuna

One of the key figures in the struggle for the true Middle Way in imitation of the Buddha is Nāgārjuna, the founder of the Mādhyamika School[1] who lived from 150 years after Christ. His deep and thoroughgoing reflections sprang from a posture of silence and freedom from all metaphysical standpoints, like the Buddha, and returned to the service of that silence. This posture also accounts for the stimulus he has given Nishitani, so much so that we may safely assert that in his own way Nishitani is seeking the selfsame thing that Nāgārjuna had aimed at in the early years of our era.

Although Karl Jaspers has listed Nāgārjuna among the "great philosophers,"[2] Nāgārjuna is in the first place a Buddhist. Whatever he has had to say philosophically all has to do with clearing the way for enlightenment and with the radical liberation of man from all false attachments that obstruct that way. Whether, like Plato, his teaching was grounded in personal mystical experience remains a moot question.[3] But in any event one can hardly overlook the religious undertones of his argumentation and the clear affinities they show with the language of the mystics. Dumoulin rightly emphasizes the point:

> It is not a matter here of mere metaphysical speculation but of a mysticism to be reached in particular, immediate experience. It is a philosophy that ends in silence, for the enlightened has nothing more to say about being and non-being.[4]

In contrast to the historical Buddha, who left behind no writings, a number of the writings of Nāgārjuna can be established today as historical.[5] For a long time his conceptual outlook was considered nihilistic, or in any case purely negative, until Stcherbatsky and Schayer uncovered its ontological and logical dimensions.[6] In the last decade or so since then the religious and psychological motivation of his argumentation has become increasingly clear.

The history of the influence of the great Indian thinker is even today far from over. His importance for the development of Mahāyāna

Buddhism in Tibet, China and Japan—above all in Shingon and Zen Buddhism—is beyond dispute.[7] The history of his influence in the West remains an open question. As is well known, Nāgārjuna lived in a part of southern India that had already for a long time been engaged in vital commercial and intellectual exchange with the Near Eastern Mediterranean countries. S. Radhakrishnan has pointed out the similarities and conceivable connections between Indian and Western thought.[8] Schlette, who has pursued the "Indian in Plotinus," is forced to admit that historical arguments can only be advanced with difficulty, but observes at the same time: "If there is any analogy at all between Indian and Plotinian thought that comes clearly to the fore, it is to be found in negative theology."[9] If one recalls that the search for the author of the writings attributed to Dionysius the Areopagite has yet to reach a commonly accepted conclusion,[10] one realizes that an important thread in the origins of Western negative theology fades away into the dark shadows of history. Rudolf Otto has tried to work out a comparison between Meister Eckhart and Shankara, which Nishitani has taken as a lead for his book on *God and Absolute Nothingness*.[11] Even a witness as far above reproach as the Christian theologian and philosopher of religion Tetsutarō Ariga has made the claim that both Nicholas of Cusa and Nāgārjuna seem to find a common ground to stand on in the doctrine of the Middle Way.[12]

All this should in fact have been reason enough to pay more attention to this important figure from the history of Mahāyāna Buddhism. But the decisive impact of Nāgārjuna has been rather in his radical working out of a view of the Middle Way, and in his assignation of a more central role to the doctrine of *śūnyatā* in this regard than had previously been the case. And so when, in the course of the development of his own thought, Nishitani comes to replace "absolute nothingness" (Jap., *zettai mu*) with "emptiness" (Jap., *kū*; Skt., *śūnyatā*), he does so "in memory of" Nāgārjuna.

The Middle Way

Between the lifetime of the Buddha and the time of Nāgārjuna lay the development of an extensive doctrinal system fashioned alternatively from exegesis of the original preaching of the Buddha and from efforts to set off the way of the Buddha from the metaphysical doctrines of Hinduism. In this latter regard, the development of its own metaphysic was in a certain sense unavoidable. At the same time, the danger it presented to the original intention of the Buddha cannot be gainsaid.

Against the background of this development we can appreciate Murti's remark that the doctrine of the Mādhyamika School represented a critique of all philosophy, indeed a sort of Copernican revolution in Indian philosophy.[13] The critical method taught by Nāgārjuna and his students was the *reductio ad absurdum* (Skt., *prasaṅga*) of all opposing theories. It consisted in convincing an opponent of the falsehood of his own thesis, without at the same time offering a counter-thesis.[14] The conversion of the opponent was of course only possible if it succeeded in convincing him by means of his own logic, on the basis of his own principles and procedures.[15] The goal of the conversion was hence merely to liberate the defender of a particular thesis from false attachment to it.

This goal needs to be defined still more precisely. Nāgārjuna was not so much concerned with a radical *negation* in the realms of logic and ontology as he was with a radical, self-composed *letting go* as the way to full enlightenment. Here his thought is close to the Greek notion of *apatheia* or to the Ignatian notion of "indifference." Conze correctly remarks:

> If selfless renunciation is the essence of the religious life, then these teachings reach the highest possible summit of unworldliness. If non-attachment is a virtue, then the negation of the multiplicity of all *dharmas* is the intellectual counterpart to the desire "to abandon all the points to which attachment could fasten itself." If our basic anxiety is merely perpetuated when we rely on something, and is rooted out only when we give up searching for a firm support, what could be more conducive to depriving us of any stable support than a perpetual concentration on the self-contradictory nature of all our experience? And if a peaceful attitude to others is the test of religious zeal, it must be greatly furthered by a doctrine which tells us not to insist on anything, nor to assert anything. Where it is actually believed to be true, this kind of ontology must lead to calm and evenmindedness.[16]

With this doctrine Nāgārjuna aligns himself on the side of the Buddha, whom he thanks expressly at the end of *Mūlamadhyamakakārikās:*

To him, possessing compassion who taught the real *dharma*
For the destruction of all views—to him, Gautama, I humbly offer
    reverence . . . (27:30).[17]

The freedom striven for with great self-composure is reached with the aid of the so-called tetralemma, i.e., the four alternatives that are involved in the discussion of any problem.[18] These may be reduced to combinations of the four elements of being and non-being, affirmation and negation:

1. Being is affirmed; non-being is denied.
2. Non-being is affirmed; being is denied.
3. Both being and non-being are at once affirmed and denied.

4. Both being and non-being are at once neither affirmed nor denied.

The Mādhyamikas are thus concerned with taking up a position equidistant from all positions. As their name indicates, they seek a middle way between all extremes. This "position," however, must then cease to speak of itself as a "position" in the proper sense of the word, for it does not simply wish to become one more position among so many others. The "middle" is rather located, according to Murti, "beyond concepts or speech; it is the transcendental, being a review of all things."[19]

How serious Nāgārjuna is in assuming this attitude becomes clear in the *Mūlamadhyamakārikās,* the "Dialectical Songs of the Original Mādhyamaka," in which he resolutely refuses to use "emptiness" (*śūnyatā*) for purposes of argumentation:

Whoever argues against "emptiness" in order to refute an argument,
For him everything including the point of contention [*sādhya*] is known to be unrefuted.
Whoever argues by means of "emptiness" in order to explain an understanding,
For him everything including the point to be proved [*sādhya*] is known to be misunderstood (4:8–9).

Emptiness is proclaimed by the victorious one as the refutation of all viewpoints;
But those who hold "emptiness" as a viewpoint—[the true perceivers] have called those "incurable" [*asādhya*] (13:8).

And as for the key notion that concerns us in these pages, the text reads:

One may not say that there is "emptiness" [*śūnya*], nor that there is "non-emptiness."
Nor that both [exist simultaneously], nor that neither exists; the purpose for saying ["emptiness"] is for the purpose of conveying knowledge (22:11).

The knowledge that is meant here, however, is no longer mere conceptual knowledge, but that wisdom (Skt., *prajñā*) and ultimate truth[20] (Skt., *paramārtha satya*)[21] that stands silent and unspeakable behind and within all apparent and relative truth (Skt., *samvṛti satya*):

Perfect wisdom, in its indifference to all (empty) forms, does not assert a teaching; the only "answer" one can receive from wisdom (*prajñā*) is silence.[22]

In his apologetics, the *Vigrahavyāvartanī* or "Subsumption of Discussions," Nāgārjuna accordingly dismisses the critical demand that he himself offer still further arguments for his case:

> If I would make any proposition whatever, then by that I would
> have a logical error;
> But I do not make a proposition; therefore I am not in error (v.29).

> Since anything being denied does not exist, I do not deny anything;
> Therefore [the statement]: "You / deny"—which was made by
> you—is a false accusation (v.63).
> Regarding what was said concerning what does not exist: "The
> statement of denial is proved without a word,"
> In that case the statement expresses: "That [object] does not exist";
> [the words] do not destroy that [object] (v.64).

In short, the key concept that stands behind all the various forms of "non-" and assures obedience to the Middle Way is nothing other than "emptiness."

Śūnyatā

By Nāgārjuna's time, the word *śūnyatā* (emptiness) or *śūnya* (empty) already had a long history behind it. Etymologically, the Sanskrit word derives from the root "*śvi*" meaning "to swell." The idea of swelling was then further tied up with that of hollowness. "Something which looks 'swollen' from the outside is 'hollow' inside."[23] This relationship is made still clearer by the fact that the mathematical symbol for zero was originally none other than the symbol for *śūnyatā*.[24] The root word can be shown to extend still further into the Indogermanic realm in the Greek words "*kýō*" (to become pregnant) and "*koilía*" (the body cavity, the inside of man), and in the Latin words "*cumulus*" (heap), "*caulis*" (stem) and "*cavus*" (cave).

When employed in Buddhism, *śūnyatā* is always related to the process of the salvation and liberation of man:

> "Emptiness" has its true connotations in the process of salvation,
> and it would be a mistake to regard it as a purely intellectual concept, or to make it into a thing, and give it an ontological meaning.
> The relative nothing ("this is absent in that") cannot be hypostatized into an absolute nothing, into the non-existence of everything, or the denial of all reality and of all being. Nor does
> "emptiness" mean the complete indeterminate, the purely potential, which can become everything without being anything, the
> "mass of matter" of which Jeremy Taylor spoke as "having nothing in it but an obediential capacity for passivity."[25]

In this regard, Nāgārjuna considers himself to be imitating the Buddha, as he expressly states in the *Kārikās:*

"If that which has deceptive basic elements is vain, what is there which deceives?"[26]
This was spoken by the glorious one to illuminate "emptiness" (13.2).

It is so written already in the *Majjhima-Nikāya:*

"Friend, Visākha, when a monk has emerged from the attainment of the stopping of perception and feeling three impingements assail him: impingement that is void [empty], impingement that is signless, impingement that is undirected."[27]

André Bareau has given a clear résumé of the main developments of the doctrine of emptiness that is worth citing in full:

Original Buddhism had recognized that all composite things (*samskṛta*) are empty (*śūnya*), inconstant (*anitya*), impersonal (*anātman*) and full of pain (*duḥkha*), but this emptiness was only empty of the "self" (*ātman*) or the person (*pudgala*). In Mahāyāna things are taken not only as empty of self and person, but in addition empty of "things" (*dharma*), i.e., empty of their own nature (*svabhāva*). To take a classic Mahāyāna example: ancient Buddhism compared things to empty vessels, while Mahāyāna rejects the existence of the vessels themselves and thus arrives at a total absence of substance. Everything is empty, everything is dissolved in universal emptiness. It should be borne in mind that this new conception did not mean a total upheaval for Buddhist doctrine. It rather sharpened and systematized a very old and persistent tendency that had long found its expression in the ideas of inconstancy and ephemerality, and of impersonality.[28]

Bareau's description directs our gaze to the crucial point of the doctrine of *śūnyatā* found in Nāgārjuna and the Mādhyamika School. Just how difficult it is to verbalize this doctrine and at the same time avoid causing misunderstanding or misinterpretation, becomes apparent when we look at the relationship between the adjective *śūnya* and the noun *śūnyatā*. On the one hand "empty" is being predicated of "something" which, as "something," is simply not there, if "something" refers to what is unchangeable, "self-sufficient," "self-supporting," and in this sense "substantial." Of what is it predicated then? On the other hand, "empty" may not be understood either in an objective, substantial sense as "something" that man can "imagine" to himself. What is it then if it is "nothing" of any kind, i.e., if it is "not any thing" at all? At this point we are faced with a verbal paradox, with the evaporation of all talk of "nothingness" into mystery. At least that is what must be said if the "nothingness" that is meant here is not to be identified with "nothing" in the vulgar, nihilistic sense.

Thereby the starting point of the doctrine of *śūnyatā* takes another step closer to the doctrines of *anātman* and *pratītyasamutpāda*. Murti even goes so far as to call the entire Mādhyamika system "a reinterpretation of *pratītyasamutpāda*." [29] But whereas these latter doctrines give rise to philosophical positions, Nāgārjuna seeks to prevent that from happening by unmasking such positions as new "standpoints" to which man mistakenly seeks to cling. In this way, anything that can become an occasion for a new attachment is spoken of as "*śūnyatā*." As an insight into *pratītyasamutpāda* this means that not only what appears as a momentary occurrence in the temporal sphere, but also the very process of coming to be and passing away itself is foresworn as part of the general renunciation of every form of reity and reality. *Pratītyasamutpāda* is *śūnyatā:*

The "originating dependently" we call "emptiness";
This apprehension, i.e., taking into account [all other things], is the understanding of the middle way.
Since there is no *dharma* whatever originating independently, no *dharma* whatever exists which is not empty.
If all existence is not empty, there is neither origination nor destruction. You must wrongly conclude then that the four holy truths do not exist (24:18–20).

Streng thus concludes that *pratītyasamutpāda* can be said to become "the form for expressing the phenomenal 'becoming' as the lack of any self-sufficient, independent reality." [30]

To the question of true reality, Nāgārjuna replies in the *Kārikās* to the effect that it is

"Not caused by something else," "peaceful," "not elaborated by discursive thought,"
"Indeterminate," "undifferentiated": such are the characteristics of true reality (*tattva*) (18:9).

David Casey summarizes these attributes in two points as "without a relation to anything else" and "unique." [31] Murti defines true reality as "something in itself, self-evident and self-existent." Accordingly it follows that:

Only the Absolute as the unconditioned is real, and for that very reason it cannot be conceived as existence (*bhāva*) or non-existence (*abhāva*) or both, etc. [32]

Since reality as one can neither be a mere link in the causal chain nor be fully separated from it, absolute reality and the union of *saṃsāra* and *pratītyasamutpāda* are in the final analysis one; and *saṃsāra* and *nirvāṇa* are likewise one:

> If *nirvāṇa* is neither an existent thing nor a non-existent thing,
> Who can really arrive at [the assertion]: "neither an existent thing nor a non-existent thing"?
> It is not expressed if the Glorious One [the Buddha] exists after his death,
> Or does not exist, or both or neither.
> Also, it is not expressed if the Glorious One exists while remaining [in the world],
> Or does not exist, or both or neither.
> There is nothing whatever which differentiates the existence-in-flux (*saṃsāra*) from *nirvāṇa,*
> And there is nothing whatever which differentiates *nirvāṇa* from existence-in-flux;
> There is not the slightest bit of difference between these two (25:16–20).

With this Nāgārjuna repudiates even the last remaining differentiations in the realm of ordinary conventional thought. It should be observed, however, that his identification of *saṃsāra* and *nirvāṇa* is a negative identity aimed at freeing man from images of *nirvāṇa* that would only make it the reverse of *saṃsāra* and so leave it within the reach of conceptual comprehension.[33] Nāgārjuna refuses to give a positive description of final reality, aware as he is that "emptiness" can as well refer to "fullness." Thus the negation expressed in a " 'no views of the real' attitude" must not be confused with a " 'no reality' view."[34] And this confirms the thesis that Nāgārjuna was concerned, through his concept of "emptiness," with the radical liberation of man in the process of salvation:

> ... The Mahāyāna dialectics will stop at nothing in its efforts to deprive us of all and everything and to prevent us from hugging and cherishing even the tiniest reward for all our renunciations and sacrifices. In fact the teachings become quite logical and unavoidable when regarded as the ontological counterpart to a completely selfless and disinterested attitude.[35]

Streng makes use of terminology long familiar to Christian spirituality in speaking of "purity, i.e., the non-attachment." We may take his words by way of conclusion:

> Emptiness is nonsubstantial and nonperceptible. As "nonsubstantiality" does not indicate non-existence, but a denial that things are

real in themselves, so "nonperceptibility" does not mean a state of unconsciousness; rather, it serves to check the inclination to substantialize phenomena through conceptualization. Thus, "emptiness" itself is empty in both an ontological and an epistemological sense: "it" is devoid of any self-sufficient being, and it is beyond both designations "empty" and "non-empty."[36]

3. Zen Buddhism

The "place" where contact between the starting point of Nāgārjuna's thought and the philosophy of Nishitani is to be established is the theory and practice of Zen Buddhism. At first this might sound contradictory. For more than any other form of Buddhism, Zen is known for its enmity towards theory and tradition in deference to the absolute primacy of actual practice.

The words attributed to Bodhidharma have become famous in this regard:

A special tradition outside the scriptures;
No dependence upon words and letters;
Direct pointing at the soul of man;
Seeing into one's own nature, and the attainment of Buddhahood.[1]

Strictly speaking, however, these words do not prescribe a radical doing away with all tradition, but only with a particular way of handing tradition on. Accordingly already at this point we may make the claim: just as it is impossible for the most sublime forms of human self-realization to be contained as such in pure theory, it is equally impossible to take man seriously without seeing him as an intellectual, rational creature. Masao Abe has argued emphatically that the encouraging of *non*-thinking extolled in Zen Buddhism (Jap., *hi-shiryō*) is often falsely understood in the sense of a purely negative denial of thought or "*not*-thinking" (Jap., *fu-shiryō*).[2] Thus the Buddhist idiom, as rich in negation as it is, can fall into the danger of missing the positive role that thought, and words, and indeed the modern scientific world as a whole have to play. This is one of the current themes met with again and again in the Kyoto School, chiefly in Nishitani.

To turn our focus to Zen Buddhism, our first priority must be given to a further understanding of "absolute nothingness" (in its preferred Western formula) or "emptiness" (in Asian terms). It is a well known fact that both the word "Zen" and the practice itself came to Japan from China, where it can be traced back to the Chinese word "*Ch'an*," which in turn derives from the Sanskrit word "*dhyāna*" (Pali, *jhāna*) meaning meditation. This linguistic chain is only one indication of the wide-reaching process of translation that was involved in transplanting Buddhism from its place and circumstances of origin in India to China and Japan. The final outcome, of course, is well enough known; but the full story of how this came to be remains as much as ever a mystery.

The point is important insofar as within the Kyoto School as well concern with the outcome of the transmission process has been given precedence over concern with the process itself and the unreflected, uncritical way tradition was once elaborated and passed on. We can thus limit ourselves to a few general contextual remarks and then turn to Japanese Zen Buddhism and its efforts at "emptying" or "emptiness."

Theory and Praxis in Zen Buddhism

Zen Buddhism, as it is understood today in its Japanese form, represents a particular development of an originally much more comprehensive meditation-oriented form of Buddhism. To be sure, the practice of meditation is characteristic of all discipleship of the Buddha. Hearkening back to the enlightenment and silence of the Buddha as his central point of reference, every true Buddhist must aspire fundamentally to become silent and to attain enlightenment.

On the other hand, the idea of silence is quick to arouse curiosity. Already at the start of its history we find in the various schools of ancient Buddhism a steady stream of disputation. Nāgārjuna emerges here as the thinker who, with the aid of logic and clear insight, sought to advance the case for silence in order to stress the practice of *dhyāna* and thereby also to reassert the primacy of praxis. In so doing he can be said to have pushed his doctrine of the middle way to its outermost limits. As was the case with the Buddha, and perhaps even still more intensively here, disputes arose among his followers concerning the meaning of "emptiness" to the point that Nāgārjuna himself was even accused of nihilism.[3]

The same dialectic of praxis and philosophy, of experience and reflection, shows up unmistakeably in the second great Mahāyāna school, the Yogacāra,[4] which goes back to Maitreya (270–350) and his students, the brothers Asaṅga and Vasubandhu (both around the middle of the fourth century).[5] This school includes both a theoretical, philosophical side—whence its adherents are called "*Vijñānavādin*" or "those who teach awareness"—as well as a practical side—whence originated their other title of "*Yogacārin*" or "those who practice yoga."[6]

It is important for our purposes to note that while among the Yogacāra themselves the doctrine of *śūnyatā* is accepted, the Mādhyamika interpretation is altered to identify "emptiness" with pure consciousness (Skt., *vijñāna*). In so doing it becomes empty of all its duality but at the same time takes a step back in the direction of substantiality.[7] The influence of Nāgārjuna and the interpretations of the Yogacārin have both been at work in Japanese Zen Buddhism. This holds true also for the Kyoto School's philosophy where Shin'ichi Hisamatsu in particular has given consideration to the " 'mind in itself' nature of Oriental nothingness."[8] In his discussions of "mind" and "consciousness" not only the influence of German idealism but also of the Buddhist theory of mind cannot be overlooked.[9]

The mediation of ontological-logical statements and of psychological thought processes through the aid of texts is found also in Zen Buddhism. The most important of these we may mention, with Dumoulin, as: (1) the Prajñāpāramitā Sūtras, "The Sūtras of Perfect Wisdom," which number among the oldest Mahāyāna texts; (2) the Avatamsaka Sūtras whose contents cannot be firmly established since the full text has survived only in Tibetan and Chinese versions, and only fragments of the Sanskrit original remain; (3) the *Vimalakīrtinirdeśa;* (4) the Laṅkāvatāra Sūtra, which originated in the first centuries after Christ and is especially dear to the Yogacārin.[10] D. T. Suzuki has condensed the content of the Prajñāpāramitā texts into the following fundamental formulation:

rūpam = *śūnyatā*
śūnyatā = *rūpam*

In Chinese the formula is: *shih* = *k'ung, k'ung* = *shih;* in Japanese: *shiki* = *kū, kū* = *shiki;* in English: form = emptiness, emptiness = form. Literally it is: "Form is not different from emptiness, emptiness is not different from form; what is form is no other than emptiness, what is emptiness is no other than form." This is the basic philosophy of the "Prajñāpāramitā" group of Buddhist sūtras.[11]

This reciprocal equation which Japanese expressed by means of the conjunction *soku* belongs to the basic statements of the philosophy of the Kyoto School as well and will be met with again and again not only in Nishida but also in Nishitani. In this one example alone, we can see the way in which the Chinese formulation of the texts has played a considerable role in not only the selection of but also in the emphasis placed on certain points of view in preference to others.

There is no doubt that the philosophy of the Avatamsaka Sūtras is of great importance, particularly for an understanding of the cosmic, total oneness of Buddha-realization and of the notions of the interchangeability and mutual permeation of each and every thing that is. The doctrinal text of the Vimalakīrti (Jap., *Yuimagyō*), whose first commentary in Japanese was composed by no less a personality than Shōtoku Taishi (574–622), stresses both that the road to awakening stands open to all men, and that enlightenment comes to term in the existential realization of the non-word. In the text, Vimalakīrti, a layman, answers the question about the attainment of the unequalled truth of Buddhism. After having asked thirty-two Bodhisattvas for clarification on the doctrine of non-duality, he finally receives the answer from Mañjuśrī:

Where there is neither word nor speech, neither revelation nor consciousness. Such a state of mind is called the attainment of the unequalled truth of Buddhism.[12]

When Mañjuśrī then asks Vimalakīrti to give his own view, he remains silent, whereupon Mañjuśrī exclaims:

Well done! I have spoken of "non-word," but you have revealed it with your body.

The renunciation of the word, or at least the preference for paradox, remains one of the basic elements of Zen praxis and one in which it attains its goal and maintains a distance from reflection.

Dumoulin sees in the obscure answers of the Laṅkāvatāra Sūtra (Jap., *Ryōgakyō*) a function similar to that of the *kōan*, which we shall discuss later on, namely "to unmask the inadequacy of reason and hence point the way to pure experience."[13] This sūtra forges ahead, beyond all words, to the point where expression can occur in a mere gaze, in the twinkling of an eye, in laughter, in clearing the throat.[14] It speaks also of the immediacy and the suddenness of enlightenment.

The Mahāyāna texts important for the development of Zen Buddhism show that theory and its traditions are not to be separated from praxis, but instead that all theoretical debate finds its ultimate reference in a wordless silence. Alongside the tradition of words stands the tradition of the masters. One of the most significant examples of the "surrender of the mind," the selection of the sixth patriarch in line after Bodhidharma by the fifth patriarch, illustrates impressively how little the doctrine of "emptiness" has to do with metaphysical considerations.

As the "Sūtra of the Sixth Patriarch" recounts, Hung-jēn challenges his students to make manifest through verse the state of their enlightenment. A quarrel breaks out as Hui-nēng (638–713), a young man who could neither read nor write and was allowed to do only kitchen work, composed his verse in opposition to that of Shēn-hsiu (606–707), one who because of his education and experience was held in high esteem by the others and occupied the first place among the young disciples in training. The two verses read:

Shēn-hsiu:
"The body is the Bodhi tree [enlightenment],
The mind is like a clear mirror standing.
Take care to wipe it all the time,
Allow no grain of dust to cling."

Hui-nēng:
"The Bodhi is not a tree,
The clear mirror is nowhere standing.
Fundamentally not one thing exists;
Where then is a grain of dust to cling?"[15]

The story ends with the paradoxical reaction of the old patriarch. He praises Shēn-hsiu openly, but tells him privately that he has not reached enlightenment. On the other hand, he erases the verse of Hui-nēng and openly declares that he has not yet reached enlightenment, but at nighttime seeks him out and bestows on him the honor of patriarch and then counsels him to flight.

No doubt partly as a result of his interest in D. T. Suzuki, Thomas Merton has pursued the conflict between these two personalities with great sympathy and insight. He attributes the conflict to a difference in understanding of mind (Chinese, *h'sin*). This would mean that according to Shēn-hsiu a final state is reached in which " 'the mind' will be in 'emptiness' and 'poverty.' But in reality, *'emptiness' itself is regarded as a possession, and an 'attainment.'* "[16] For Hui-nēng, on the other hand, the attainment of enlightenment is a non-attainment since

... the "purity" of *śūnyatā* is not purity and void considered as an object of contemplation, but a non-seeing, a non-contemplation, in which precisely it is realized that the "mirror" or the original mind (of *prajñā* and emptiness) is actually a non-mirror, and "no-mind" ...

... For Hui-nēng there is no primal "object" on which to stand, there is no stand, the "seeing" of Zen is a non-seeing, and as Suzuki says, describing Hui-nēng's teaching, "The seeing is the result of having nothing to stand on." Hence, illumination is not a matter of "seeing purity" or "emptiness" as an object which one contemplates or in which one becomes immersed. It is simple "pure seeing," beyond subject and object, and therefore "no-seeing."[17]

In opposition to the *apophatic* position of Hui-nēng, the verse of Shēn-hsiu also works positively, *cataphatically.*[18] On the other hand, the negativity of Hui-nēng serves to aid the radical letting go of his own ego and false self, and of everything that can become an "other" or object for him.

The overcoming of a dualism born of false insight and false points of view will concern us later on. At this point, before turning to Japanese Buddhism as a patch of the native soil in the Kyoto scene, it remains for us to give some consideration, however brief, to the distinctive mark left by the process of translation into Chinese.

The Role of China as Mediator

To draw a straight line from the original Buddhism of India to Japanese Buddhism is to overlook the fact that, as a rule, intermediary cultures not only bridge but also stimulate and check. This is true as well for the part that Chinese culture has to play in the development of Buddhism.[19]

Hajime Nakamura, who has done some of the most significant research in the field of intercultural Asiatic relations, mentions several facts that illustrate the nature and extent of the divergencies between Indian and Chinese Buddhism.[20] To begin with, the Chinese did not adopt Sanskrit and Pali as sacred languages, but undertook to translate the Buddhist texts into their own language. Frequently, of course, the translations were modified both with regard to content and literary style, and even supplemented with interpolations that can only be isolated by comparison with the original texts. Later Chinese scholars found themselves in the position that they were unable, due to improficiency in foreign languages, to compare translations and even, not uncommonly, to understand them. As a result, many Chinese Buddhist texts struck out on a path of their own differing from Indian traditions. All of this only confirms the fact that while translations in any language are something to be welcomed, one must at the same time keep in mind the possibilities and limitations of particular languages. Since the Japanese language is related in many ways to Chinese, together they can be said to offer an important reference point for our interest in Far Eastern texts on the whole.

Nakamura cites from a study on the Chinese language:

> Whereas primitive languages are characterized by the extreme variety of verbal forms, Chinese is extremely poor on this point. It uses uninflected monosyllabic words; there is no distinction of parts of speech. However, the flavor of concreteness—provided by various forms in other languages—is shown by the extreme abundance of Chinese words which convey concrete phases of things with unparalleled power . . .[21]

The strength of the language, then, is its concreteness. What may appear abstract in other languages is concrete in Chinese, and thus also in Japanese, for reasons of the particular way in which its characters are composed and juxtaposed. Therefore, that the way linguistic expression in Zen Buddhism floats between concreteness and abstractness should result in a curious blend of nearness and distance, is hardly to be wondered at.

But the language's very strength is also its weakness. Where it is a question of the precise translation of abstract, logical thought processes as in philosophy, it is easily given over to misunderstandings and misinterpretations.[22] And where no general laws and rules are acknowledged as such, such things as the precedence of authority take over. The difficulties multiply when the abstractness of Western concepts like "being," "non-being," "emptiness," and the like come up against the concreteness of the Sanskrit notions of "*bhāva*," "*abhāva*," "*śūnyatā*" and their equivalents in Chinese and Japanese.[23]

Nakamura correctly identifies the influence of the Chinese language as a contributing factor in the Zen Buddhist repudiation of the written word.[24] The development of the characteristic Zen dialogue, and the deliberate promotion of the non-logical through *kung'an* (Jap. *kōan*) provide still further links here. The passage that stands at the beginning of the collection known as the *Wu-mēn-kuan* (Jap., *Mumon-kan*) or *The Gateless Gate,* which dates from the year 1228, is well known:

> A Monk asked Jōshū, "Has a dog the Buddha Nature?" Jōshū answered, "Mu." [In Japanese, *mu* means nothing(ness).][25]

Dialogues of this sort do not lead on to further reflection and speculative advance, but rather as a result of the very words themselves, lead to the point that the logic of immediate perception collapses and that words are repudiated. Not infrequently, it is worth noting, memories of events and persons from the past provide the catalyst for such a leap beyond logic. The Chinese word *kung'an* originally means "public notice," or "public announcement," and later took on the sense of a "model" or "example of the elders," and finally came to denote the "law of old."[26]

W. Bauer has described convincingly what a great force the relationship to the past, to its preservation and transmission, has exerted on Chinese history, so that every attempt at stabilization in modern revolutionary China is traumatic and becomes suspect of inaugurating a new period of stagnation.[27] Further questions concerning China's understanding of history, development, progress and free expansion, as well as the relationship of freedom to necessity, and of culture to nature, are also of interest, particularly as they have been given new stress by the renewal of contact with the Western world.

For the Chinese, "tradition" and doctrine always stand midway between the acceptance of a clearly recognizable, given world, i.e., a pragmatic world-affirmation on the one hand, and the throwback to belief in another world of a higher order, a world accessible through magic and ecstasy on the other. Hence the attitude of the Chinese, even where it is a matter of adapting to a natural or social order, remains basically pragmatic.[28] As mutually conditioning factors, Chinese modes of thought and language and modes of living turn out to be rather unsuitable for the development, elaboration and recreation of a distinctive rational philosophy.[29] A language that has no copulae and no way of working out logically a distinction between substance and attribute does not allow so much for the recognition of a deepening of logical structures through a realm beyond logic—even in the case of a doctrine like that of Nāgārjuna's—as simply for a reconfirmation of what is already contained in its own structures. In China, too, praxis and experience enjoy primacy over theory and reflection; of this there is no doubt. But the question remains whether or not an experience and praxis that has not been tested by the fires of rational critique can be compared *tout court* with something that seems to have such a critique already behind it.

On the Japanese scene this question comes to a head in a double form. First, does the adoption of Buddhism in general, and of Zen Buddhism in particular, mean that the same situation that obtained for ancient China obtains also for Japan for reasons of similar linguistic conditions? The answer, at least in a limited sense, is in the affirmative.

The second question follows upon the first: Does not the encounter of Zen with philosophy and philosophy with Zen in the Kyoto School perhaps bring Zen that fire of rational critique—albeit, in this case, from the West—which pushes enlightenment and experience further into their depths? This question forms the backdrop to the second part of this book.

Japanese Zen Buddhism

At this point a number of remaining remarks dealing with Japanese Zen Buddhism can be gathered together. A thorough historical exposition of its development can be foregone here in view of the adequate scholarly publications on the subject already at our disposal.[30] Whether the Asians themselves have always given sufficient weight to the exact study of historical connections is another question altogether.[31] Even D. T. Suzuki himself needed the incentive of historical studies done in the Western world to arrive at maturity in his role as a bridge between East and West in the name of the Way of the Buddha—a role for which his name has come down in history today.[32]

At any rate it cannot be denied that up to the present day a satisfactory synthesis of guidance in the practice of Zen and presentation of its historical conditions has yet to be worked out.[33] This lacuna in turn keeps alive the troublesome question whether and under what circumstances the practice of Zen can be separated from its foundations in a particular culture, history and *weltanschauung* so as to be transplanted in a completely other world. On the one hand, to use such language as *"foundations* of Zen" seems to those actively engaged in its practice contradictory. On the other, the practicer and his master, if they do not want to be accused of lack of communication or a refusal to communicate, must allow, at the risk of falling into dangerous and perhaps even ultimately impossible objectification, that what to the observer outside the Asiatic world and its cultural currents and historical developments appears as Zen and Zen Buddhism seek to be as comprehensible as possible. Not *wanting* to speak and not *being able* to speak are often so close as to be indistinguishable, and yet the one who actually can*not* speak cannot forbid the one who *wants* to speak from doing so, as long as he has not yet reached the point where he too can no longer speak either.

Accordingly, the following fundamental points to be observed and borne in mind throughout the rest of this study may be listed seriatim:

(1) In contrast to the Chinese who translated the Indian texts immediately, the Japanese expounded on and disputed Buddhism in the Chinese language during the first 700 "classic" years of its expansion.[34] The intellectual dependence of Japanese Buddhism continued consistently, in many respects, right up to the dawn of the modern era. And this openness for manifold cultural influences went hand in hand with the lack of a corresponding distinctive critical sense.[35]

(2) Buddhism was brought to Japan mainly by Japanese who traveled through China, settled in Buddhist centers there where they practiced and learned, and then, as enlightened, returned to their homeland bearing the classical texts of the school with them. The introduction of Buddhism in Japan is usually dated 552; its later promotion is attributed to Crown Prince Shōtoku (574–622), who himself composed commentaries to the Lotus Sūtra (Skt., *Saddharmapuṇḍarīka Sūtra;* Jap., *Myōhōrengekyō* or simply *Hokekyō*) which even today is greatly revered in Japan, to the Vimalakīrtinirdésa (Jap., *Yuimagyō*) and to other texts.[36]

(3) Although a wide range of well-known intellectual currents from India were brought to Japan during the Nara period (710–794), Buddhism was received principally in the form of the Great Vehicle. In 625 the Chinese *San-lun* School was founded as the Japanese *Sanron-shū*[37] in which "The Three Treatises"[38] of Nāgārjuna, the Mādhyamikas, were handed on. In 654 came the *Hossō-shū,* which belonged to the tradition of the Yogacārin. The founder of this school, *Dōshō* (628–700) erected the first Zen Hall in Nara at a time when Zen was experiencing its full blossoming in the T'ang Dynasty in China.[39]

(4) The uniqueness of the Zen sects or schools that grew up in the twelfth to thirteenth centuries lay in their claim to preach more or less exclusively the way of meditation as the way of the Buddha. In China at this time the full blossoming of Buddhism was already over, after a period of persecution, but the Zen schools survived and came to life again in

the southern regions of China in the so-called "Five Houses" or lines of tradition.⁴⁰ Even if these schools belong to the world of southern Zen and if the antagonisms are less noticeable, the old quarrel over the naming of the sixth patriarch is still reflected somewhat in the two strongest schools: the gradual, progressive attainment of the goal in the Ts'ao-tung School—named after the two founders Ts'ao-shan (840–901) and Tung-shan (807–869)—and the sudden enlightenment achieved with the aid of the *kōan* in the Lin-chi (Jap., *Rinzai*) School—named after Lin-chi (died 867). Adherents of these two schools in Japan are found in the Rinzai sect founded by Eisai (1141–1215) and the Sōtō sect founded by Dōgen (1200–1253).

(5) "It may well be that Dōgen is the strongest and most original thinker that Japan has so far produced."⁴¹ He studied and practiced at the Hiei-zan in Kyoto, was later in the School of Eisai, and then went to China where he took up the orientation of Ts'ao-tung. He returned to Japan in 1227 without a new sūtra. In contrast to Eisai he taught pure *zazen*, "sitting in meditation" without *kōan, shikantaza,* "merely sitting with all one's strength." Consequently he refused any contact with other forms of Buddhism and in 1236 erected the first self-supporting Zen monastery. Yet even if he went his own way, Dōgen was well-versed in ancient Buddhist literature, cultivated its criticism and offered reinterpretations.⁴² His own works, *Fukanzazengi*, "General Teaching for Zazen," and the *Shōbōgenzō*, "Treasury of Knowledge of the True Dharma," are numbered today among the classical Japanese texts on Zen, and as such have been the subject of renewed interest among Nishitani and his colleagues.⁴³

(6) The most significant Zen master after Dōgen is Hakuin (1685–1768) who belonged to the Rinzai Sect.⁴⁴ He lived through the "great doubt," practiced the *kōan "mu"* (Nothing/nothingness) that he had found in the *Mumonkan,* a work which he treasured above all others, and achieved the "great enlightenment" in the experience of the "great death." Again and again we find his influence at work. What sets him off is the fact that as a Japanese Zen Buddhist he painted and composed verses, and so brought his experience to artistic expression as well.

(7) Through Zen the translations of the two great collections of *kōan* of the Lin-chi sect, the *Wu-mēn-kuan* (Jap., *Mumonkan*) dating from the year 1228 and already referred to several times earlier, and the older *Pi-yen-lu* (Jap., *Hekiganroku*) dating from the year 1125, continue to be influential up to the present day.⁴⁵ The spirit of Zen is also detectable in the wider milieu in the several skills or "ways" (Jap., *dō*) such as the way of tea (*sadō, chadō* or *cha-no-yu*), the way of flowers (*kadō* or *ikebana*), the way of the sword (*kendō*) and others that are still practiced in Japan. The eloquence of Zen painting from the Ashikaga period and above all from the Muromachi period (1393–1573) associated with such artists as Nōami (1397–1471) and the great Sesshū (1420–1506),

and still later with Masanobu (1434–1530), is still as vital and impressive today as ever. The same can be said of Zen poetry whose spirit is embodied most dramatically in Bashō (1644–1694).[46]

We conclude our remarks on Japanese Zen Buddhism with a reference to the arts not least of all because in Kyoto itself speechlessness, concreteness and experience, the concern for the whole and for every individual thing in it, never achieves as clear an expression as it does in art. Its influence must therefore be seen as a permanent part of the background of the Kyoto School.[47]

4. Kitarō Nishida (1870–1945)

Near the end of the Second World War Robert Schin-
zinger, a long-time resident and teacher of philosophy in Japan, published for the first time, in German, three representative chapters from
the philosophical work of the great Japanese philosopher, Kitarō Nishida.[1] In the period following the war he came out with an English
translation under the clearer title *Intelligibility and the Philosophy of
Nothingness.*[2]

With his death at the end of the war in 1945, Nishida went down in
Japanese history as the most important philosopher of modern Japan,
indeed the first true philosopher of Japan in the modern Western sense
of the word. He initiated a trend that in turn gave rise to a school of
thought among whose adherents are to be counted such thinkers as Hajime Tanabe, Keiji Nishitani and Yoshinori Takeuchi. Together with
Kōichi Tsujimura, Shizuteru Ueda and many others in Kyoto and outside of Kyoto, they make up what is called the Kyoto School.[3] In spite
of this activity, Nishida remains to the present day relatively unknown
in the Western world.

D. T. Suzuki (1870–1966), a school companion and friend, nevertheless described Nishida's mission as "to make Zen intelligible to the
West."[4] In fact, of course, it was not Nishida but Suzuki himself who
succeeded in bringing Zen closer to Western man. There are a number
of reasons for this.

To begin with, Suzuki wrote in English, the language of those to
whom he wished to communicate his thought, and he wrote about what
he wanted to communicate, namely Zen Buddhism. Nishida was different. He wrote in Japanese, and hence in effect primarily for his own
countrymen; and he wrote about Zen in a way that tended to keep it
cloaked from Western eyes, namely by presenting it through philosophical patterns, thought processes and authors familiar to those con-
versant in Western—and in particular, in German—history of
philosophy.

In this regard I have remarked elsewhere:

Nishida quotes a great number of Western authors and alludes occasionally to Buddhism. Thus it is only after the reader becomes

35

aware of what Nishida does *not* say rather than of what he says that for the first time there is some sort of true insight. And here I agree that some psychological preparation is required for the Western reader, some basic knowledge of Buddhism and its understanding of Zen, some knowledge of Nishida's personal background and, finally, some guidance in the study even of the translations of Nishida. For there are, besides the rare cases that Buddhism, the teaching of Shinran etc., are mentioned directly, some quotations, short sayings as they are used by Zen masters in their instructions,—sayings that after some time become dear and familiar to their disciples in the same way as Scripture sayings become dear to the Christian. Often enough these short sayings are not marked as Zen sayings, and since they are not really quotations, they are not indicated as such, and, finally, in translations they are hardly to be recognized as Zen sayings at all.[5]

Moreover, as Suzuki observes:

Nishida's philosophy of absolute nothingness or his logic of the self-identity of absolute contradictions is difficult to understand, I believe, unless one is passably acquainted with Zen experience.[6]

Secondly, we may observe that Nishida's Western contemporaries were quick to associate the idea of "nothingness" not so much to the tradition of "nothingness" found among the mystics of the late Middle Ages, both Spanish and Rhinelander, as to the nihilism found in various forms in modern thought inimical to religion, to Nietzsche's critique of Christianity and to the French existentialism of Sartre and his colleagues. At all accounts, Buddhism remained for them a book with seven seals.

In the third and final place, we need only mention the most obvious obstacle of all: the language barrier that blocks the entrance to those who cannot read Japanese and are limited to the few exact translations at hand.[7]

Portraying the problematic in this way also helps explain why our inquiry here must reach so far back. A certain degree of understanding and sympathy for Zen and its native Buddhist soil must be presupposed for entering into the concerns of the Kyoto School. But once one has entered, it becomes plain to see that there may be no other place in all of Asia where a Buddhist-Western dialogue can be carried on, comparatively speaking, with such deep ties to the contemporary scene as in Kyoto.[8]

To return to where we left off, Suzuki's remark about Nishida's mission may not in fact be fully correct inasmuch as Nishida did not dialogue directly with the West but with his own country which, since the Meiji restoration of 1868, had given itself over to the challenge of

Western civilization and culture as well as its ideologies and thought. In so doing he had to face the question of the relationship between tradition and development, experience and reflection, East and West, Christianity and Buddhism, and also the question of many competing ways and interpretations, and of an ultimate One. From the very first for Nishida, as for Suzuki, the question of a "mission" was secondary.

Suzuki's claim for Nishida properly applies only with the contemporary representatives of the Kyoto School: they seek dialogue with the West, or rather can be found right in the thick of it. Therefore, Nishida cannot be said to be a *current* participant in this dialogue. That role falls to Nishitani and his colleagues, friends and students. All of them share this in common, that they have gone beyond Nishida. For some this means that since 1945 they have brought modern questions of a unifying world culture fully into their realm of concerns. For others, it means deepening their understanding of tradition with a view to impending problems. This entails an understanding of Asiatic traditions, above all of Buddhism; an appreciation of modern Western traditions, and above all those of philosophy; an understanding of mystical experience and modern theology, and of the preoccupations of theology with the unity of faith-experience and interpretation.

The vision and the stimulus for this East-West dialogue that has only today become possible was already present in Nishida. Therein lies his importance and the reason why we must include him as part of the background of the scenario. Some remarks on his religious commitment and his philosophical concerns should clarify this still further.

Nishida and Zen

Anyone seeking a deeper insight into Nishida's work through first-hand acquaintance with his publications, gathered together now in eighteen volumes,[9] cannot but be impressed by the abundance of allusions to James, Bergson, Kant, Fichte, Hegel, Cohen, Dilthey, Husserl and Heidegger, to Plato and Aristotle, Plotinus and Augustine, and to mystical authors ranging from Dionysius to Eckhart and Boehme. Yet one is likely to overlook, at least in the case of the Western reader, that the relatively few allusions to Buddhism, Zen and Amidism[10] that occur in fact sketch the essential horizons of Nishida's thought.

In his very first work, *Zen no kenkyū* ("A Study of the Good"),[11] Nishida ties his opening theme, "pure experience" (*junsuikeiken*) to the thought of William James and other psychologists, and not with Zen Buddhism—a fact that his own later remarks confirm. On the other hand, in speaking of "intellectual perception" in the same opening section, he writes as follows:

... Intellectual intuition is nothing more than a further deepening and enlargement of our state of pure experience, that is, it refers to the manifestation of a greater unity in the development of a system of consciousness. A scholar's acquiring of new thoughts, a moralist's acquiring of new motives, an artist's acquiring of new ideals, a sage's acquiring of new insights—all are based on the manifestation of this kind of unity, i.e., they are all based on mystical intuition.[12]

This provides Matao Noda with justification for writing:

He accepts, from the first, the position of a mystic. His metaphysics has its characteristic motif in his mystic religiosity.[13]

That in fact it is mystical experience or Zen experience that lies behind his notion of "experience" becomes clear only when we have seen Nishida's own religious orientation. Nishida came from a Jōdo-shin-shū family. In a short essay dating from 1911 entitled "Gutoku Shinran," which was included as a contribution to a Festschrift marking the 650th anniversary of the death of Shinran, he mentions that while his mother was a pious Amida believer, he himself neither truly believed in nor knew very much about his religion.[14]

We come to know of his own religious orientation from early diary sketches.[15] These begin in the year 1897 and describe the year immediately preceding the appearance of *Zen no kenkyū*. Although we have only hints to go on, the development is clear. His growing concern with Zen is reflected throughout. Masters and temples, the days of practice, the thoughts and concerns he carried around with him, are all noted down. In 1901 Nishida became a *koji* or lay practicer of Zen, receiving on the occasion the name of "Sunshin." For ten years, nearly without exception, he spent the time around New Year's in Zen halls and took part frequently in *sesshin* (Zen "retreats"). His academic reading, including Western material as well, came to show a clear relation to the practice of Zen. He corresponded with Suzuki regarding this point.

On August 3, 1903, during a *sesshin* in Kyoto's Daitokuji, he received from his Master the *kōan* "*mu*" (nothing/nothingness) that we have met already in the *Mumonkan* and which is among the most preferred of *kōan* in Japan.[16] Nevertheless, it is interesting to note, he expressly remarks that he was not particularly overjoyed with it. In the practice of Zen, Nishida's concerns revolved about the "heart" and life. Thus he wrote on July 19, 1905:

I am neither a psychologist nor a sociologist; I shall be a researcher of life. Zen is music, Zen is art, Zen is movement; apart from that there is nothing wherein man may seek peace of soul ... If my heart can become pure and simple like a little child's, then I believe there can be apparently no greater fortune than this. *Non multa sed multum.*

Prior to attaining *kenshō,* enlightenment, he had no desire to think of religion and philosophy.[17]

Thus it is a fundamental option that Nishida associates with the way of Zen that is responsible for the fact that his life work as a philosopher is to be understood as a struggle with the relationship between religion and philosophy, East and West, reality and interpretation. As Noda says of him:

> . . . Nishida never lost sight of his central problem, namely the confrontation of Oriental Buddhistic ideas with Western philosophy . . . This central concern with Buddhism can be detected at every stage of his thought.[18]

As late as 1936 Nishida wrote in a letter to Hisamatsu of his attempts to labor over a philosophy that would never cut him off from the standpoint of Zen. Ueda, who cites the letter, goes on to describe the problematic which Nishida set in motion with the catch phrase "reality and interpretation" regarding the confrontation of religion and philosophy.[19] The struggle with the unity of these two apparently differing standpoints runs through Nishida's life work, from *Zen no kenkyū* up until his last treatise, "*Bashoteki ronri to shūkyōteki sekaikan*" ("The Logic of Locus and the Worldview of Religion") which he finished shortly before his death.

Since philosophy however meant Western philosophy, and since the characteristic religion of the West was Christianity, Nishida's search for connecting links between the West and modern Japan had to be concerned at once with developing a logic that would make sense of talk of the "experience" of "reality as it is," and at the same time with finding in a somewhat different system of thought a mode of expression for a reality that is ultimately beyond expression. The result was the statement in Western categories, as they were understood in Japan, that that which (or the one who) is addressed in Christianity as ultimate principle, namely God, be drawn into the discussion, while that which in Buddhist tradition is addressed as *śūnyatā* be named in a terminology closer to the West—though not also, for reasons stated earlier, thereby easier to understand—as "absolute nothingness" (Jap., *zettai mu*).

In this vein Nishida writes at the end of *Zen no kenkyū,* in a chapter that apparently was not originally intended for the book:

> God is not to be known through analysis and inference. If we grant that the essence of reality is something personal, God is that which is most personal. Our knowing God is possible only through the intuition of love or faith. Therefore, the one who says, "I do not know God but only love Him and believe in Him" is the one who is most capable of knowing God.[20]

In this way Nishida demonstrates how clearly he saw the limits of his own endeavor. The drawing together of logic and nothingness calls to mind Nāgārjuna but at the same time hails an altogether new stage of historical development. The drawing together of nothingness and God gives the discussion an entirely new accent that has since become a challenge for Christian theology as well.

Absolute Nothingness

Zen no kenkyū opens with the statement: "To experience means to know the facts just as they are." "Pure experience," Nishida continues, is "direct experience":

> When one has experienced one's conscious state directly, there is as yet neither subject nor object, and knowledge and its object are completely united.[21]

All of Nishida's work revolves about the understanding and realization of this "pure experience."[22] The unity prior to the distinction and separation into subject and object, wherein consciousness is still in the state of unconsciousness, where event is still without reflected meaning, is the starting point. And the unity wherein subject and object are no longer distinct and separated, wherein consciousness and event no longer confront one another objectively but conscious occurrence and occurring consciousness are identical, is the goal. Nishida wrestled with the oneness of reality.

If this reality is given only through surrendering the self—"the selfless man, i.e., he who has destroyed the self, is the one who is greatest"—[23] then we are left with the question of the reality of nature, mind and God. In the case of the reality of God, Nishida cannot but point up a contradiction whenever he finds God conceived as an "object" that is "cut off" from self-consciousness, as the transcendent God was in fact conceived by him.[24] But here, as he understood it, thinkers like Nicholas of Cusa come to his aid:

> In what form does God exist? Seen from one side, God, as Nicholas of Cusa and others have said, is all negation; for what may be specified and affirmed, i.e., that which may be grasped, is not God, for if He is something that may be specified and grasped, He is already finite, and is unable to perform the infinite function of unifying the universe (*De docta ignorantia*, cap. 24). Seen from this point, God is absolute nothingness [*mattaku mu*]. However, should one wonder whether God be merely nothingness, this is certainly not so ... God is the unifier of the universe. He is the ground of reality, and precisely because He is able to be nothing-

ness, there is no place whatsoever where he is not present, no place where he is not at work.[25]

In Part IV of the book that treats the relationship of "God and World," Nishida offers a similar formulation:

There are those, like Nicholas of Cusa, who claim that God transcends both being and nothingness, and that if God is being, He is also nothingness. When we try to reflect deeply on the inner recesses of the consciousness of the self, we both find profound meaning in terms like those which Jacob Boehme once used—God is a "quiet without anything," or "abyss" (*Ungrund*), or again "will without object" (*Wille ohne Gegenstand*)—and we are struck by a kind of sublime, mysterious feeling.[26]

Somewhat later on he adds:

Nothingness separated from being is not true nothingness; the one separated from the all is not the true one; equality separated from distinction is not true equality. In the same way that if there is no God there is no world, if there is no world there is no God.[27]

In this way Nishida set the tone for his own point of view and in many ways for that of his successors as well.

The locus of nothingness, taken here in the context of a basically Buddhist perspective, is sought on the Christian side in the direction of God. The understanding of God in turn is criticized whenever God *is* an object, where he *has* attributes, and where he does not unite but separate because he is not immanent but transcendent. Thus the doctrine of a *free* creation of the world through a transcendent God also becomes a stumbling block precisely because the link between God and the world is described by him as necessary.[28]

The option for a relationship between nothingness and God that is one of mutual definition (nothingness⇆God), has consequences for two definitions of nothingness in the Western world: (1) the "nothingness" out of which God creates the world (*creatio ex nihilo*); and (2) the "nothingness" that as "nothing"—in the nihilistic sense of the word—becomes a counterresistance to a God who gives meaning and promises fulfillment.

Further analysis of these various points of contact makes it plain that the concern of Nishida and his successors is no longer the "mere transmission" of a Buddhistic *depositum* and the erection of apologetic philosophical safeguards, but with bringing about a dialogue between positions that have not come together in such a way for a long time. Hence follows the further question of how matters stand regarding the logic and intelligibility of what Nishida has to say later of "locus" (Jap., *basho;* Gk., *topos*) with regard to "nothingness."[29] This is a question we are driven to by Nishida himself. For if the premise nothingness ⇆God is allowed, then we must also be concerned with nothing other than what Western thinkers have been concerned with—though admittedly without much success to judge from the state of faith in the world of today—in speaking of the "proof" for God.

The basic position undergirding *Zen no kenkyū* holds good with Nishida right through to his last philosophical essay on "The Logic of Locus and the Worldview of Religion." What is new vis-à-vis his starting point is the first half of the title, inasmuch as he comes to show how in the course of the years the search for a more logically deducible definition of experience has grown up out of originally more psychologically sounding deliberations on "pure experience." What is called the "logic of locus" plays the role of mediator here.

Toratarō Shimomura has paraphrased Nishida's understanding of locus:

"Locus" is neither objective existence nor subjective existence; since it is that *wherein* both worlds "are located," and since it is that *wherein all* existences—of course objective existence, but even subjective existence which can never be objectified—"are located," then "locus" is not existence, it is nothingness. This, however, is not nothingness in opposition to existence, i.e., *relative* nothingness, for since it is that *wherein all* existences appear as determinations (*Bestimmtes*) of it, it is *absolute nothingness.* All existences become self-determinations of this kind of absolute nothingness. Herein Nishida freed himself completely from subjectivism, and attained the most basic ultimate principle which combines perfectly that which is subjective with that which is objective.[30]

The problem of "locus" thus has to do with the possibility of a final unity of the one and the many, of object and subject, and later of immanence and transcendence, affirmation and negation, etc. Schinzinger describes it as the "unity of opposites." Nishida himself uses a term that is clearer in Japanese but more easily given to misunderstanding and problems in the translation: *"zettaimujunteki jikodōitsu"* ("absolutely contradictory self-identity"). Accordingly the logic of locus, as Ueda says, consists in the fact that locus defines itself as locus in the contradictory self-identity of the one and the many.[31] To put it in other words, while in objective logic things that contradict one another as such do not allow of identification, this logic has to do with discovering the place in which contradictory self-identity, or the self-identity of contradictories, is reached, i.e., in the language of Nicholas of Cusa, the *"coincidentia oppositorum."* It concerns the search for a place in which all opposites or contradictories[32] are transcended, "subsumed" (*aufgeho-*

ben), or—to use Nishida's own word—"lined" (*urazukeru*).[33] This locus is, if all that is present truly *is,* "nothingness."

This "nothingness", however, should not itself be misunderstood. For we have to do here not with a nothingness *relative* to all beings,[34] but with the absolute nothingness that embraces both beings and relative nothingness. This nothingness in turn is not simply another denial but at the same time an absolute affirmation, so that in the logic of locus the two paths "from the many to the one" and "from the one to the many" are also made into one.[35]

This "locus" over whose understanding Nishida labors in his philosophical reflections,[36] is the "locus of religious consciousness." As he remarks in one of the essays translated by Schinzinger, "The Intelligible World" ("*Eichiteki sekai*"):

> Insofar, however, as the intelligible Universal is "lined" with the universal of absolute nothingness, the "lost self" becomes visible, and there remains only the proceeding in the direction of noesis. In transcending in that direction the highest value of negation of values becomes visible: it is the religious value. The religious value, therefore, means absolute negation of the self. The religious ideal consists in becoming a being which denies itself. There is a seeing without a seeing one, and a hearing without a hearing one. This is salvation.[37]

In this locus of absolute nothingness all words fall away as well:

> But when it comes to transcending even that intellectual intuition, and when that which has its place in absolute nothingness is conceived, no more statement can be made with regard to this; it has completely transcended the standpoint of knowledge, and may perhaps be called "world of mystic intuition," unapproachable by word or thinking . . . As determination by the universal of absolute nothingness, it is a determination without mediation by concept.[38]

With the absolute denial of the self man begins then "to live in God." And this "living in God" is no longer to be described as the vis-à-vis of God and man. Here only the poet can speak:

> If one is really overwhelmed by the consciousness of absolute nothingness, there is neither "me" nor "God"; but just because there is absolute nothingness, the mountain is mountain and the water is water, and the being is as it is. The poet says:
> "From the cliff,
> Eight times ten thousand feet high,
> withdrawing your hand,
> Flames spring from the plough,

World burns.
Body becomes ashes and dirt,
  And resurrects.
The rice-rows
Are as ever,
And the rice-ears
Stand high."[39]

Schinzinger adds a clarification that he himself had apparently obtained from Nishida:

The master has given a problem for Zen meditation, and you are laboring to solve the problems of being, as the farmer over there, on top of the high cliff, is laboring to plough his field. You are hanging on the usual way of thinking like someone who is hanging on an infinitely high cliff, afraid of falling into the abyss. Withdraw your hand! And see: From the farmer's plough spring sparks—and you, while the experience of nothingness springs from your laboring thinking, find "satori," enlightenment. The universe has become nothing, and the ego has become nothing. But in the same spark of nothingness, you regain the world and yourself in wonderful self-identity. In the experience of nothingness, everything is as it is: the rice-rows are as ever, and the rice-ears stand high.[40]

In the final years of his life, the concrete historical world became noticeably a philosophical problem for Nishida. In this regard his final essay once more brings together the logic of locus and the worldview of religion in a definitive manner. The question of the one and the whole is sharpened when focused on the question of the relative and the absolute. But this has to be understood in light of the peculiarities of the Japanese language.[41] Quoting Isaiah 6:5, Nishida writes:

Thus when the relative confronts the absolute, the relative must die, it must come to nothing. Only through death, in inverse correspondence, can our self touch God and be bound to God. Objective logic may say: "If the relative dies and comes to nothing, does it not thereby cease to be anything that can be related to?" But death is not simply nothingness. The absolute, of course, goes beyond objects. But what simply goes beyond objects is not anything, is nothing other than simple nothingness. A God who does not create is a God without power, is no God at all.[42]

The absolute (Jap. *zettai*) is not only to be defined by the fact that in "freedom," i.e., in the locus "breaking beyond all objects" (*zettai*), it permeates everything that represents an object (*tai*). This locus itself must not be reaffirmed as a new "object." It *is* the absolute only by virtue of the fact that it is confronted with its negation or its nothingness. In other words, the absolute is what it is only in that everything is disavowed that hinders it from being what it is. Thus we find ourselves anew in the realm not merely of intellectual negation but of an existential letting go, an existential setting-free. This is already familiar to us from the apophatic traditions of both Buddhism and Christianity. Talk of absolute nothingness is apparently not possible for Nishida, however, without talk of God. He expressly brings together God and what we have been calling here the absolute:

> The pure absolute must be . . . identical with itself in absolute contradiction [*zettaimujunteki jikodōitsu*]. When we express God in logical terms, we can say no other.[43]

It is necessary to speak of God when we speak of religion. As we read at the beginning of the essay:

> Before we discuss religion, we must clarify what we mean by religion. And in order to clarify what we mean by religion, we must first clarify what we mean by religious sentiment. Without God there is no religion. God is the basic concept of religion. But just as color appears to the eye as color, and sound to the ear as sound, so does God appear to the self as a spiritual reality. God cannot simply be thought of intellectually. What can be thought of simply intellectually is not God.[44]

Thus in discussing religion we must also discuss God. Yet God is not an intellectual problem, but rather a given that reveals itself in the depths of the "heart and mind," where all talk is surpassed. In this regard we should recall the question already referred to in *Zen no kenkyū*.

Behind this question stands another already posed from earlier considerations of the substantiality and self-sufficiency of being. According to Ueda, Nishida's position is distinguished from that of Christianity in that Christianity deals with the relationship of *God* and *man,* and thus is based on God and takes God as its starting point; while Nishida makes the *relation* of God and man his foundation.[45] The difference seems only to be one of accent. Christianity stresses "God and man, man before God." Nishida on the other hand stresses the *relation* (the *"and"*) of the *"in"* (*"in* God," *"in* man"), the becoming one, the being one, and this in connection with the fundamental Buddhistic understanding of the one as *anātman, pratītyasamutpāda*[46] and *śūnyatā,* although these names are not expressly mentioned by him. In assigning objective logic and "locus" logic their respective places, he refers the former to Christianity and the latter to Buddhism. Nonetheless, he sees the realm of Christian mystical language as a possible means for drawing the two standpoints closer to one another.

At this point two remarks regarding the discussion at hand can be made. First, even if Nishida admits of a distinction between faith and rational thought, consequent upon his own line of reasoning the characteristic claims of Christianity, revelation, the meaning of the historical figure of Jesus, the crucified Christ and the like do not make sense to him.[47]

Secondly, one must take seriously Nishida's assertion that he does not wish for his understanding of absolute nothingness, or God, to be interpreted as a pantheism. In his last essay he speaks of "panentheism," but as to whether he himself, in his search for adequate modes of expression, was completely aware of the implications of this ambiguous concept remains an open question.[48]

At any rate, it can be said that in Nishida we have a nonchristian Japanese thinker who undertakes the attempt to carry over the Buddhist experience and its meaning into the realm of the Christian experience and its meaning, or at least to expose it to wider historical, cultural horizons. The problem this poses is an open-ended one for us. It is no longer simply a problem for his Japanese followers, but also for those to whom, in the words of Suzuki, he believed he had a mission to fulfill.

Part Two

KEIJI NISHITANI AND THE PHILOSOPHY OF EMPTINESS

5. Stimuli

The ten Oxherding Pictures of the Chinese Zen master Kuo-an Chi-yuan (Jap., Kakuan Shien), dating from the twelfth century, stand among the classic expressions of the way of Zen. H. Buchner, together with Kyoto University's Kōichi Tsujimura, one of the students of Nishitani, has provided a commentary to the text accompanying the series of pictures and rendered the whole into German under the title *Der Ochs und sein Hirte*[1]—a phrase which recalls Heidegger's "Hirt des Seins" (shepherd of being).[2] It is this version we shall adopt here to show how the main stations of the ox path can be taken as a direct parallel of the intellectual path that Nishitani himself has trod together with the ox and his herdsman.

It opens with the situation in which man finds himself: a situation of estrangement, of non-identity with himself. Put in Buddhist terms, it is the condition of suffering that is expressed concretely in every historical moment, above and beyond the endlessly repeating forms of human non-realization. Accordingly man must set out along the way in order to seek and to find the ox. The stages of this way distinguish discovering the ox's tracks, finding the ox itself, catching and taming the ox, so as later to return home with it. The way up onto the back of the tamed ox leads to a forgetting of the ox and, in the eighth and last stage, to that emptiness wherein neither ox nor shepherd matters any longer. Here there is only unspeakable openness and fullness, a unity and communication that is expressed pictorially by a great empty, clear and sunlike circle. In fact, the eighth picture is not the last. Even in the experience of emptiness itself man has not climbed out of the world. He is still in the world in taking hold of what lies before him by virtue of the power that lies hidden and walking into the marketplace of world history as one who sees with open, empty hands: "Without humbling himself to perform miracles or wonders, he suddenly makes the withered trees bloom."[3] Hence the way comes to its end not in worldlessness but in a new tie to the world, not in a timeless eternity but in an open historicity, not in the privation of ego and self but in selflessness and in helpful communication. The enlightenment of the way of Zen, too, ends in the way of the Bodhisattva.

The beginning, middle and end of the way—the starting point, the way into "emptiness" and the relation of emptiness and world history—are also the three great themes under which the philosophical deliberations of Nishitani can be come to grips with. Thus we shall use them to mark off the main stages of our treatment here. This will lead us first back to Nishitani's earlier writings and later to his great work *What is Religion?*, which he himself describes in a subtitle as the first volume of a collection of studies on religion. Very helpful for a deeper appreciation of Nishitani are works on the subject that have been published by those in his circle of friends and colleagues, to name only a few: Shin'ichi Hisamatsu (1889–1980), Masao Abe (1915–), Kōichi Tsujimura (1922–) and Shizuteru Ueda (1926–).

*   *   *

Keiji Nishitani was born in 1900 in the prefecture of Ishikawa in central Japan but has spent the greater part of his life in Kyoto. There he graduated in 1924 from the Imperial University, and in 1935 became Assistant Professor. In 1943 he was promoted to full Professor of Philosophy and held that chair until his retirement as Professor Emeritus in 1964. Since then he has taught in the Buddhist Ōtani University in Kyoto, and at the same time functioned as President of the "Eastern Buddhist Society" there, and directed the "International Institute for Japanese Studies" in Nishinomiya, a city which lies between Osaka and Kobe.

Nishitani has described in great detail the way he has followed, the authors who have stimulated him, the problems which have concerned him.[4] But equally as important to Nishitani's thought as his personal equation is his estimation of the contemporary scene. This means at once his own country as well as the wider world in the context of which Japan continues, with ever greater resolve, to define itself and its obligations.[5]

The Philosophical Starting Point

In an essay entitled "My Philosophical Starting Point" Nishitani writes of himself:

Before I began my philosophical training as a disciple of Nishida, I was most attracted by Nietzsche and Dostoyevski, Emerson and Carlyle, and also by the Bible and St. Francis of Assisi. Among things Japanese, I liked best Natsume Sōseki and books like the Buddhist talks by Hakuin and Takuan. Throughout all these multiple interests one fundamental concern was constantly at work, I think ... In the center of that whirlwind lurked doubt about the very existence of the self, something like the Buddhist "Great Doubt" or *daigi*. Thus I soon started paying attention to Zen.[6]

Among the authors he names, the representatives of German idealism come quite early, especially Schelling whose work on the essence of
human freedom Nishitani translated.[7] Special mention is also made of
Western mysticism, above all German mysticism, of the female mystics
of the Middle Ages, of Meister Eckhart and his student Jacob Boehme.

He composed a short history of mysticism and wrote a reply to Rudolf Otto's *Mysticism East and West* that he called *God and Absolute
Nothingness*.[8] Shortly before the Second World War Nishitani studied
for a short time in Freiburg under Heidegger. This contact proved to
play a significant role in his understanding of Nietzsche, in his interpretation of nihilism, and in his discussion of the relation of being and
nothingness.

Despite his eagerness to learn from the West, however, Nishitani
has remained anchored in his own tradition. He is a disciple of Nishida,
with whose philosophy he expressly engages himself again and again,[9]
and a successor of Hajime Tanabe (1885–1962) at the occasion of whose
death he delivered a memorial address.[10] The concerns which he had in-
herited from his predecessors he has taken firmly into hand. Already in
his first major work, a collection of papers that was published in 1940
under the title *The Philosophy of Fundamental Subjectivity*,[11] it becomes
clear how much Nishitani was concerned with playing a mediating role
between Japanese thought and the increasingly dominant forms of
thought in the world at large. Not to be overlooked in this regard is the
great weight he attaches to the interrelationship between religion, history and culture.[12]

Yet even when he is pushing science to its ultimate consequences in
positivism and is following nihilism to its roots, Nishitani nowhere
shows a single trace of that kind of outright critical view of religion that
looks on it as a mere epiphenomenon or as a superstructure to more basic socio-economic patterns. Faced with such critiques, Nishitani remains anchored, in his own way, in a fundamentally Buddhist
religiosity that gives every indication of standing equally firm in its
sympathies for the Christian line of thought.

Insofar as he has been interested in Christian theology since the
turn of the century, Nishitani has kept understandably to Protestant authors, and principally to the representatives of liberal and dialectical
theology, to Karl Barth, and later also to Rudolf Bultmann.[13] Interestingly enough, the history of German mysticism is also understood
largely through the eyes of Protestant theologians who, since the second
half of the nineteenth century, have given new life to research into Eckhart. While modern Catholic theology is not altogether unknown to
him, Nishitani nowhere expressly refers to it in his work. For its part,
too, Catholic theology has gone entirely too long in neglecting to pay attention to the concerns and statements of the Kyoto School.

This gives us, then, the main coordinates on which Nishitani's
thought can be located. As a representative of the Kyoto School he is

fully and completely rooted in his own past, an understanding of which has once more become a concern to not a few of his students as well. At the same time, he is seeking to come to grips with the present for the sake of Japan's future. But this can only be accomplished, to his way of thinking, through intellectual confrontation with the wider world, of which his country is but a part. For Nishitani, it is a question of a fundamental religious option that he sees our historical situation grounded in a realm beyond space and time, a realm which is proclaimed in the mystical experiences of all times and in the basic Buddhist standpoint of emptiness. Nishitani's intention is to direct our modern dilemma to a solution through that basic notion of emptiness. These dilemmas show up both where science and nihilism are recognized as two aspects of the present world, and also, more importantly, where the question of the essence of religion erupts, again and again, in the East and the West. Here Nishitani strives to steer a course between a false security on the one side, and a drifting about in meaningless nihilism on the other. He directs his efforts at an openness that reaches down to the very roots of human Dasein, and which answers the question that forms the title of his great work on the philosophy of religion, *What is Religion?*, with the key word "emptiness."

The Description of the Situation

In his lengthy review of *What is Religion?*, Masao Abe has compared the book to Schleiermacher's *On Religion: Speeches to Its Cultured Despisers.*[14] According to Abe, Schleiermacher was aiming at something, 150 years earlier and in an obviously different historical context, that is similar to what Nishitani is after, in the middle of the twentieth century. Faced with the currents of the Enlightenment and with a basic intellectualistic tendency that idealized the concrete individual and made it into a universal, Schleiermacher set himself the task of clarifying the essence of religion in the context of European Christian traditions. Nishitani, on the other hand, has set himself the task of clarifying the essence of religion in a contemporary world marked by the coming together of East and West. Further intensifying this situation, the cultured classes of today have, in Abe's phrase, been baptized in the waters of natural science, of Marxism and nihilism. By and large they have ceased to be "despisers" of religion and have come instead to greet it with total indifference and with the simple refusal to get involved with it. It is no longer a question of facing the tendencies of the Enlightenment, but with facing the standpoint of atheistic nihilism and of a modern scientific world that has become increasingly radical and domineering. It is a matter of historical fact that the sciences and nihilism, whatever language one uses to describe their forward march in the world of today, grew up as surrogate movements of Christianity. Hence concern with them of necessity involves a fundamental questioning and critique of Christianity as well. Yet even as Christianity threatens to become a questionable source for a solution to the paradoxes of modern developments, recourse remains open to the basic religiosity of Japan in which Buddhism represents a dominant force alongside the general pervasiveness of Shintoism.

Scientism

In describing the present situation, Nishitani always takes as a starting point reference to the meaning of the sciences:

> . . . The fundamental driving force behind the process of modernization is the development of science and scientific technique. I think we can say that science and scientific technique have permeated every phase of man's personal and social life and that this is the most important factor effecting the severance from tradition.[15]
>
> The problem of religion and science is the most basic one facing contemporary man.[16]
>
> One of the greatest and most fundamental problems all religions are now confronted with is their relation to science.[17]

The modern sciences touch on human life in a variety of ways. In a word they define human life insofar as the natural sciences claim a universal, indeed a cosmic character for their knowledge of nature and its regulation by laws.[18] Moreover, the laws of nature are seen to point to a self-regulation which allows nature to bring itself into being.[19] Nishitani repeatedly refers to this lawfulness and its worldview as "mechanistic."[20] This is not to be understood, of course, as a statement made in ignorance of recent advances that biology and physics have made to the theories of natural science since the time of the Enlightenment. Rather it is to be taken as an assertion that the modern worldview no longer leaves room for a teleological conception of the world in the sense in which such conceptions have circulated with Aristotelean thought in the West. Masao Abe in turn adopts Nishitani's own manner of speaking in answering objections to these claims:

> What is important here . . . is not necessarily "science" itself but the *scientific way of thinking* which thoroughly objectifies and analyzes everything including man's psyche and tries to reduce it to inorganic mechanism or lifeless law. However elaborate a theory of science may be, the very *nature* of the scientific way of thinking, it seems to me, does not change.[21]

Human life is more and more defined by science, therefore, as the phenomenon of man himself is increasingly viewed from and judged ac-

cording to a physical-chemical point of view.[22] Moreover, insofar as
man is taken as only one aspect of a world ruled by mechanical necessity, the world of nature itself is seen as insensitive to the fact of man:

> ... The natural world has come to bear more and more strongly
> the features of a world cold and dead, governed by laws of mechan-
> ical necessity, completely indifferent to the fact of man. To be sure,
> it is a world in which we are living, which is inseparably connected
> with our existence, but nevertheless a world in which we cannot
> live as "man," which excludes (and obliterates) our "human"
> mode of being. We can neither reject nor accept such a world. It is
> within such a paradoxical relation that the natural world has come
> to reveal itself to us.[23]

The domination of man through nature, however, leads to his de-
personalization:

> In this world man is not simply personal. He is simultaneously
> completely material and completely biological, controlled by indif-
> ferent natural laws. The natural laws dominate the existence of ev-
> erything, whether non-living, living or human. They dominate
> them with indifference ...[24]

In fact, both man and the powers of nature are more and more becoming pure functions of a powerful technological process. As a result,
nature is becoming denaturalized in the same way as man is dehumanized:

> ... To consider water, wind, or fire as waterpower, the power of
> wind or fire—to consider everything as physical power—this is a
> fundamentally different posture. This way of relating to a given
> "thing" is essentially different. In this case, every "this" is de-
> prived of its being by abstraction and finally reduced into atomic
> power or energy. If every thing is considered as a source of energy,
> then, for example, cattle and chickens become mere sources of ani-
> mal protein, and a human being becomes just a source of manpow-
> er. Thus also in everyday practical life, man comes to be
> considered according to his war potential, his labor power, his ca-
> pacity for political combat—always accounted as physical energy.
> From the theoretical viewpoint as well, in the case of the social sci-
> ences, man is thought of as nothing more than energy flowing
> within the social framework. Man is, at most, a mere mechanism,
> a cogwheel in the social machine. These are the problems which
> are involved in technology. Therefore, technology, as used here, is
> not only a problem relating to industry, but must be seen as a more
> comprehensive problem of both theory and practical life—the

problem of the way of "being and seeing" of man. In a word, at the basis of technological thought lies the "denaturalization" of nature and the "dehumanization" of humanity; and I think this is, in turn, closely related to the fundamental attitude of indifference toward things religious.[25]

The leading role that scientific thought in general and the natural sciences in particular have come to play for human existence poses at the same time a threat for the religious realm of man. Nishitani urges our attention to two main points in this regard.

First, man has come to see himself less and less as placed in a world that has been laid out according to a divine plan and made to run along the lines of that plan. The teleological image of the world has broken down. Nishitani mentions as a symbolic point in history the 1775 earthquake in Lisbon that gave rise to heated debate not only in that region but throughout all of Europe. While some saw in it a sign of divine punishment, Kant, along with others, argued that that very sort of interpretation was blasphemous because it was grounded in a false, human teleology.[26]

Secondly, when teleological thinking collapses, the fundamental understanding of the world according to which the relationship between man and God forms the axis and the non-human world as a whole is relegated to the periphery of this relationship is also threatened as a result:

> When, however, the world becomes an indifferent world, and as mentioned before, confronts man with the paradoxical relationship in which he can neither abandon it nor abide in it, there the world, instead of remaining peripheral with the God-man relation as its axis, cuts horizontally across the vertical God-man axis, and becomes independent, a sort of horizontal axis in itself. In its relation to the human mode of being, the world came to take on the form of a paradoxical contradiction in place of a teleological harmony. At the same time, in its relation to God, the world could no longer simply be thought of as ordered according to divine providence or divine will. The world's absolute impersonality now appears as something qualitatively different from both human "personality" and divine "personality." It comes to be something which severs the "personal" relation between God and man.[27]

And thereby the position of man is altered as well.

The Self-Discovery of Man
With regard to man himself, two opposing movements can be established as present throughout this process.

On the one side we have modernism, characterized by an "event" which Nishitani has spoken of as "subjective self-consciousness," as the awakening of the individual man to his subjective essence.[28] Man becomes conscious of his fundamental "human rights." He recognizes nature as the stuff of his own experience and experiments. At the same time, man, who is defined in the entire Western tradition as *animal rationale* by virtue of his possessing "logos" and who accordingly sees himself as close to God who is wholly "spirit," more and more comes to transfer to himself the role of this God.

Then there is the opposing movement. On the one hand it is introduced through the Darwinian theory of evolution and on the other it shows up as an about-face of the relation between man and nature. Darwin's idea came as a shock inasmuch as it led man to define himself no longer primarily as a participant in the world of spirit but rather as a particular development of the "animal" world. It was no longer that man was to be seen as derived from and conditioned by God; he was a product of matter. At the same time a noticeable reversal occurred in the relationship between the ruler and the ruled. Nature and its laws, which man had begun to dominate, became in ever stronger measure a factor that once again began to dominate man.

> The field [*ba*] in which man found himself when he had produced the machine and which has ever since come to the fore, intensifying its strength, was one in which two things—one of which is, on man's side, abstract intellect looking after scientific rationality, and the other is, on the side of nature, "denaturalized" nature, so to speak, which I have above described in terms of "purer than nature itself"—stood in correspondence to one another. But this same field is now gradually emerging as something which deprives man of his own human nature.[29]

The situation is still further intensified if one considers that man himself, precisely at the point that he seems to be directing matters, in fact ends up further deprived of the subjectivity he would like to confer on himself. For in directing and managing he makes use not only of things but of other men as well. The human *thou* becomes the human *it.* And when the Thou is lost, the I cannot be saved:

> ... When everything is reduced to power and energy, we might suppose that subjectivity remains in that man is in the position of using this power and controlling this energy. However, the truth is that this is not even the standpoint of subject. Because man in such a position takes not only every "thing," but also other human beings and himself as well, as something mechanically manipulatable and controllable, this is a position having nothing which comes to resist it as "other." That is, it has no substantial objects, finds out-

side itself no "being in itself," finds no being which confronts it, and finds nothing to which it can attach itself. Neither is this a position where a relationship is made with any being, not to speak of a relationship with a "thou." Here there is absolutely nothing which we could call a "thou." Everything is in the third person—an "it" (*Es*), which when reduced to power or energy, may even cease to be an *Es*. This is a standpoint where the "I" (*Ich*), man, has extraordinary power. Facing this standpoint, essentially, there is nothing to offer the slightest resistance. In principle, in a world where everything is reduced to and taken as power or energy, everything can be freely disposed of and manipulated at will. This is, in a sense, the standpoint of a subject which is pushed to its climax of development. But on the contrary, this very act leads to a point where the meaning of subjectivity is lost, and at the same time, man is dehumanized.[30]

The domination of man through the laws of nature forces him to a standpoint in which he behaves as if he were completely outside the regulation of the laws of nature. He stands then on the brink where nothingness opens up:

> Eventually, the place where the machine comes into being—the field in which, as I said before, the correspondence of abstract intellect demanding scientific rationality with denaturalized nature obtains—opens up *nihilum* [*kyomu*] at the bottom both of man who relies on that intellect and of the world of nature as well.
>
> It is now only in standing on this *nihilum* that man is able to find himself detached and completely free from the radical and thoroughgoing rule of the laws of nature.[31]

There are any number of attitudes that one may assume toward this nothingness, however. For some, it exists in a pervasive but covert manner in the superficiality of the flight from a conscious assessment of and adaptation to the current situation into an enthusiasm for sport and amusement. Others make a clear and conscious decision to accept nothingness as the ground of their own existence. Between these two poles lies a wide and variously shaded spectrum of attitudes towards nihilism.[32]

In the foreword to his book, *Nihilism*, Nishitani himself lays out three forms of nihilism: the tendencies linked to the names of Nietzsche and of Dostoyevsky, and that of Buddhism. Of the first two he claims that at the age of twenty they had made a strong impression on him. In later years the Buddhist standpoint of emptiness came more and more to influence the direction of his thought.[33] For all the warmth with which Nishitani speaks of Dostoyevsky, it becomes clear in the course of the book that he falls back almost entirely on Nietzsche and his intellectual predecessors and successors, and among these latter Heidegger in particular.[34] One reason for this may lie in the difference between the two that he mentions in the Foreword. Both thinkers were concerned with the history of a radical battle of subjectivity for the conquest of every authority alien to the subject, and at the same time, in the very battle for the sake of the ego, were concerned with battling with the ego. Both catch sight of nothingness. But while Dostoyevsky wrenches himself away from the edge of the abyss of meaningless nothingness so as to let himself fall into the arms of God, Nietzsche blocks this route off with his assertion that "God is dead." From him there remains then only the way to a new image of man transcending the old image, one in which, through the heroic acceptance of nothingness, the advent of the new man, the *übermensch,* is foreshadowed.[35] In the end Nishitani himself devotes the greater share of his attention not to the tendency of Dostoyevsky—which he further associates with Kierkegaard—but to that of Nietzsche whom he places alongside Sartre. And this because he sees the way of Nietzsche to be the more radical and more effective of the two in terms of the present, and since it is tied up with atheism.[36]

If it is true that modern atheism was initially the result of the three elements of materialism, scientific rationalism and the idea of progress, it is also the case that in the meantime it has come to be related to the perception of nothingness at the base of the world. For the realization of the radical subjectivity of man consists in the decision to be dependent on nothing and to ground existence on nothing:

> In the case of the awareness of nothingness in contemporary atheism, the *"nihilum"* in *"creatio ex nihilo"* becomes, by virtue of the fact that the existence of God is negated and nothingness is seen in the place of God, an abyss, and this abyss comes to be revealed at the foundations of the world and of oneself.
> ... This means that atheism has been subjectivized and *nihilum* has become the field of the so-called *ekstasis* of < man's > self-being, the dimension of transcendence opening up in the direction not of God but of *nihilum.*[37]

Nishitani ascribes to Nietzsche the first realization of this form of atheism:

> It is primarily in Nietzsche that atheism came to its truly thorough subjectivization, that nothingness came to possess a transcendental character by becoming the place of the *"ekstasis"* of self-existence, and that man's freedom and independence came to a thoroughgoing confrontation with his being < essentially > dependent on God.[38]

Nothingness and the "death of God" are one:

> That is, *nihilum,* which signifies the death of God, emerges from
> beneath the ground of the material, mechanical world and is real-
> ized by modern man as an abyss < in which he reaches the "ec-
> static" transcendence of his own self-being >. Only when a man
> has such an abyss opened at the base of his existence does his sub-
> jectivity become subjectivity in the word's true sense. He becomes
> aware of himself as truly free and independent.[39]

Thus does the question of the self-discovery of man end in a religious assertion, which in the final analysis subsumes "religion" as a "re-
ligio" (a being bound to) into a "being upheld in nothingness." When
Nietzsche speaks of himself as "Europe's first nihilist, and one who has
first experienced nihilism in himself to its limits—behind him, beneath
him, outside of him"; and when he announces "the advent of nihilism"
as "the history of the next two centuries," Nishitani listens in utter ear-
nestness.[40]

The Critique of Christendom

Both observations, the coming into dominion of science and the
process of the self-discovery of man, end up not only in the religious
question but in a critique of Christendom as well. The basis for this is
surely, though not exclusively, to be sought in Nietzsche's understanding of nihilism as the "devaluation of the highest values." "What is nihilism? That the highest values be devalued. There is no goal to be had.
There is no answer to the question 'Whither'? "[41] On the ground of his
own historical position Nietzsche's brand of nihilism embraces a fundamental critique of Christendom.

Nishitani is quite right in pointing out that the modern statement
of the problem in the Western world grew up in and remains in many
ways tied up with Christianity.[42] He goes still a step further to claim:

> In considering Eastern culture as a whole, the first problem com-
> mon throughout the Orient is that from within itself it could not
> give birth to science or technology, nor could it create what we call
> an "individual subjective self-consciousness,"—for example, the
> human posture upon which democracy is based.[43]

This assertion leads to new problems that are peculiar to the peoples of Asia. And the solution to the problems that result for the entire
world from the introduction of the Western mentality and Western
thought among them is not easy to come by either. For:

> On the one hand, modern science and technology, as well as mod-
> ern man-centeredness, were born in opposition to the classical

Greek spirit and thought (e.g., *Humanismus* and the standpoint of "science" in the philosophical sense) and the "spirit" of primitive Christianity (e.g., a personal relationship with God). But, on the other hand, in a sense, modern science, technology, and man-centeredness originated from and are rooted in Greek and Christian thought. I myself have great difficulty in trying to interpret this complicated relationship. At any rate, it seems to be something like a "stiff muscle" [*shikori*]. On the one hand, ancient and medieval Western tradition and the new standpoint in the modern age both seek to be set free from each other. Yet on the other hand, they are tied to each other in such a way that the more one exerts efforts to be set free from the other, the more the other resists that effort.[44]

In his treatment of Christianity, Nishitani of course never exhibits the harshness one finds in the critique of Nietzsche. Still, he does not see the solution for the modern statement of the problem to lie in the simple return to and reawakening to the original spirit of Christianity. It consists for him rather only in a return to the originality of original Christianity, in a going back to the origin behind original Christianity and the West.[45] And if one wants to reach this goal, recourse is available, according to Nishitani, through the aid of a completely foreign and alien form of culture or religion.

In a German-language contribution to the demythologizing debate set loose by Rudolf Bultmann, Nishitani tried to show through the example of the virgin birth (which he unfortunately confuses with the term, if not also with the doctrine of, the Immaculate Conception of Mary) how the dehistorization and demythologization of language of "immaculateness" can carry on into a realm where, in his view of the matter, it becomes meaningful to speak of an "original immaculateness" of mankind in general:[46]

This concerns a purity which lies in the original essence of man, prior to all differences, something of a purity of absolute "indifference." It has to do with an absolute purity discoverable in the essence of man's being in spite of all natural purity or impurity, in spite of all intellectual stain or stainlessness. However much man may lose his purity in body and spirit, he still remains in possession of that original *puritas*.

...The unconditionally immaculate and corporeal-spiritual being are thoroughly two and at the same time thoroughly one; they are thoroughly one and at the same time thoroughly two.[47]

In making this assertion Nishitani is employing, as we shall see more precisely later on, insights that accrued to him from the area of Buddhism. In fact he is of the view—thereby differentiating himself in the long run from Nietzsche's appreciation of Christianity—that with the help of Buddhist insights, the sort of elements that can be brought to light in Christianity are such as to offer it, too, the possibility of entering meaningfully into contemporary discussions of nihilism, and of permitting man to achieve the "breakthrough" to his true being and true self.[48]

In this connection he turns above all to the kenotic theology of the cross (Phil. 2), to Christian mysticism as found first in Galatians 2:20 and then later in St. Francis of Assisi, in the Rhine mystics, in Eckhart and Tauler, to the proclamations of the modern God-is-dead theology, and to the eschatological understanding of Christianity.[49] That Nishitani has not thereby been fair in every respect to Christian self-understanding is less important than the observation that the "breakthrough" to the essence of man apparently remains a fundamental possibility in Christianity for him even after the purifying bath in the waters of nihilism. And in our case this is likewise significant in that the question of God comes thence to be posed anew.

Japan

Finally, for Nishitani as a Japanese, the question of the role of Japan in today's world must come to bear on any attempted description of the contemporary scene:

> Modern Japanese are westernized and see things from the Occidental viewpoint. And yet it is the Occidental viewpoint held by the Japanese in Japan, and moreover the locus is in Japan.[50]

This peculiar combination of Asiatic-Eastern and Occidental-Western thought makes Japan "a kind of laboratory for an experiment in a future world culture."[51] The creation of a new Western-Eastern culture represents at once a need and an opportunity. Nishitani sees it as the raison d'être of contemporary Japan:

> ... One could say that Japan, faced with the need to absorb Western culture more deeply (a Western culture which up until now has been unaffected by Eastern culture) and in the midst of this process create a "new" Japanese culture, is placed in an essentially advantageous position. To make the most of this self-imposed task of creating a fusion of Eastern and Western cultures and of pioneering the way to the world culture of the future—herein, I believe, is to be found a raison d'être for the Japanese nation.[52]

While during the period prior to the Meji restoration Japan remained for a long time a closed, self-encapsulated country (Jap., *sa-*

koku), such can no longer be the case today. Nishitani propagates the image of an open Japan with a broader notion of space and time. This attitude shows up understandably in his own thinking as well.

On the one hand, Nishitani makes no secret of the fact that in his view the religious standpoint that he has in mind is at least fundamentally already present in Zen Buddhism:

> It seems to us . . . that this standpoint of a religion with the above demanded universal character has already been realized in advance, at least basically, in Buddhism, especially in Zen Buddhism, even though there are in Zen, in its traditions and actualities, various points to be amended, complemented, or perhaps radically reformed.[53]

Jan Van Bragt correctly refers to Nishitani's work, therefore, as a *"theologia fundamentalis* of Zen Buddhism."[54]

On the other hand, when Nishitani speaks of culture and religion, he cannot restrict himself to Japanese culture and religion if he intends to make a contribution to the understanding of religion in general. Hence in *What is Religion?*, too, he examines religion not because he is interested in using the tools of the scientific study of religion to make sense of phenomena of days gone by, but because he is concerned with investigating, from the point of view of the subject in the here and now, the "ground" that has released out of man that which we call religion.[55] Accordingly it is worth paying less attention to what was than to what *ought to* be, even if our view from the present into the future can never fully be cut off from our view from the present into the past. Nishitani wants to forge ahead in the here and now to the sources of reality, to probe behind all appearances of religiosity, a-religiosity and anti-religiosity. For this reason he is not concerned with a definite interpretation of a historically realized religion, nor with a definite confession of faith or a definite dogmatics.

He repeats the same thing in conceding that while he deliberately uses the primary language of Buddhism,[56] these terms are not to be taken as pertaining to a definite religion or to the teachings of a definite school. They are rather "borrowed," says Nishitani, so that he can say in the context of modern philosophy what he is able to say and would like to say from the standpoint of his own tradition. In this way Nishitani braces himself firmly in front of the difficult task of standing at one and the same time within and without his tradition.[57]

In so doing Nishitani embodies in himself the fate of his own country. He sees himself situated among the various fronts as a *"werdend gewordener* Buddhist" and at the same time a *"werdender (nicht gewor-*

dener) Christian" as he has described himself with a view to the fate of Tanabe:

> I do not feel satisfied with any religion as it stands, and I feel the limitations of philosophy also. So, after much hesitation, I made up my mind and have at present become a *werdender Buddhist* [a Buddhist in the making]. One of the main motives for that decision was—strange as it may sound—that I could not enter into the faith of present-day Christianity and was nevertheless not able to reject Christianity. As for Christianity, I cannot become anything more than a *werdender Christ* [a Christian in the making], in the same sense as Tanabe. For I cannot bring myself to consider Buddhism a false doctrine. When it comes to Buddhism, however, I can enter into Buddhism as a *werdend gewordener Buddhist* [a Buddhist in the making who has found his home in Buddhism] . . . and from that standpoint I can, at the same time, be a *werdender* (not *gewordener*) Christian. Insofar as I am a Buddhist, I cannot be a *gewordener Christ.* However, I do not consider Christianity a false, "outside" doctrine . . . From the standpoint of Buddhism I can do this . . . Christians are inclined to speak ill of such Buddhist "looseness," but I do not feel that way, and, in my opinion, people who feel that way cannot possibly come to a real understanding of Buddhism. Be this as it may, I am fully aware of the shortcomings of Buddhism and I understand the strong points of Christianity. Because of this, I am all the more convinced that I can, as a Buddhist, with the help of Buddhist dialectics and always from within Buddhism work for the solution of these difficulties.[58]

The picture is rounded out, then, by seeing how the two sides contribute to one another's realization. Nishitani is a Buddhist and continually involved in "becoming" even more so, as he himself admits. But he is likewise ready at all times to be let loose into what is "outside-of-himself"—just as his country, Japan, through all its efforts at a new identity within the advancing world culture, wishes to be and to remain. As for what the sustaining "ground" of this new identity of man and his world is to be, that must be rethought in view of the "emptiness" that bursts open in the yawning abyss of nothingness.

6. From Nihilistic Despair
to the Emptiness of "Open Hands"

For Nishitani all attempts to describe the present come to rest ultimately in nothingness. His entire thought revolves about this nothingness. This poses the question of how meaningful our reflections on nothing can be. For whatever one is reflecting and speaking about meaningfully cannot be that radical, absolute nothingness that shakes man and his world to their very foundations. But this is a question to which Nishitani devotes particular attention.

It comes as no surprise that a great number of words are to be found in Nishitani's Japanese which refer to nothingness. Yet in the end they all represent an attempt to avoid too hastily associating definite notions, which might only conceal its true meaning, with "nothingness" itself. In contrast to Japanese, Western languages turn out to be rather poor and helpless in the face of such tasks, and this is even more so the case with German which is not free to shift back and forth between words of German and Latin origin as English can.[1]

Some brief introductory mentions need to be made, therefore, of at least the most important Japanese words. From then on, wherever it seems important or helpful, we shall include the original Japanese words in brackets as a further aid to insight.

Japanese expressions for "nothingness" are composed of three basic words, all of which are "Chinese" readings of the respective character with which they are written. Mention of the *kun* (or "Japanese") readings will help to fill out the meaning:

> *mu* = nothing; nothingness
> > *kun* reading: *nai* = verbal form of negation
> *kyo* = empty
> > *kun* readings: (1) *munashii* = empty, vain, useless
> > (2) *kara* = empty, hollow
> *kū* = (basic meaning) opening, empty sky, horizon; breadth and emptiness; (derived meanings) emptiness, vacuum; spatial,

spiritual, or moral state of being empty; a translation of the Sanskrit *śūnyatā*

kun reading: *sora* = sky, the vault of heaven, air

From these three basic words come the following words and compounds:

mu = naught, nothing; simple and unqualified nothingness that can be taken in a relative sense as the negation of being and beings, or in an absolute sense[2]

kyomu = negativity, emptiness of meaning, nihilistic nothingness, nihility, nihil

kyomushugi or *nihirizumu* = nihilism [The latter is the Japanese equivalent of the English word rendered in the syllabic writing system.]

kūmu = the combination of emptiness and nothingness

kū = the vast and empty, to be empty, emptiness in the positive sense as radical openness; air, sky, heavens, space, void, emptiness, vacancy, vanity, vacuum, *śūnyatā*.

In this way we can see how the spectrum of meanings given to nothingness stretches from what is *unknown* because man has closed himself off from it and is therefore ignorant of it, to what is *unspeakable* and *unknowable,* in the face of which man is powerless, despair or trust in it as he might. At this end of the spectrum man can only endure if he lets himself go in order to find himself in selflessness. In fact, then, the spectrum reaches from the despair of nothingness to that emptiness in which man, having come to the end of the ox path, steps into the marketplace with open hands:

If one understands how to meet one's own self and yet to remain unknown to the self—
The gate to the palace will open wide.[3]

The starting point remains doubt and despair, or what Nishitani calls in the tradition of Zen Buddhism the "Great Doubt." This is not to be confused with metaphysical doubt, as whose prototype we may take the Cartesian doubt that drags down all beings of the world with it into its abyss even as it seeks to secure a final footing for the *"ego"* of the *"cogito, ergo sum."* The starting point of our exposition here will also be the "Great Doubt" seen as a form of existential engagement. From there we shall inquire into the relation of being and nothingness, of the I–Thou relationship and nothingness, in order finally to catch a glimpse of the radicalizing of nothingness in the "emptiness of open hands."

As for the fulfillment of the negative way, Nishitani himself says that it comes together with the positive way:

> In this ultimate point, the negative direction converges, so to speak, with the positive . . . [4]

The Great Doubt

The "Great Doubt" is released in many by the great negative realities of life, by the experience of nihilization and death.

> *Nihilum* [*kyomu*] means the absolute negativity as regards the being of the other various things and phenomena; death means the absolute negativity as regards life itself.[5]

In these experiences man comes face to face with the question of the meaning of his existence. For modern Western man the great symbolic figure of questioning and doubt is Descartes. If one carries his "*cogito, ergo sum*" over into the realm of religion, one can find in it, Nishitani suggests, a kind of "*cogito*" that aims at exploring the "*sum*" of man:

> Religion is therefore an existential exposure of the problematical which is contained in the usual mode of self-being. In this lies the unique import which religion, and religion alone, has. In this sense religion may also be called the path of the great and fundamental "I think," in order to search into and elucidate the "I am."[6]

But the doubt of Descartes is still not the "Great Doubt" that is alluded to more and more in Zen Buddhism after Hakuin. Nishitani expressly uses the Zen Buddhist word *daigi-genzen*, "the self-presence of the Great Doubt."[7] It is doubt that is to be called "great" for several reasons:

(1) because of its wide-reaching content, for it touches the fundamental uncertainty of man regarding human existence, both one's own as well as that of others, and all necessity that results therefrom;

(2) because of the special attitude that man must assume in the face of this fundamental necessity;[8]

(3) because of the radical way in which man therefore transcends even the distinction between doubter and doubted, between subject and object, and himself becomes the "Great Doubt":

> We say "great," because that Doubt does not concern only the isolated self of self-consciousness, but concerns this self together with the existence of everything else, and hence is not a consciousness,

but a real Doubt presenting itself to the self from the foundation of oneself and all things ... Through this manifestation of the "Doubt" in our self, our self really becomes the Doubt itself. It becomes itself the *realization* of the Great Doubt, which is in itself a *reality.* This is what is meant by the "self presence of the Great Doubt" [*daigi genzen*]. And in such a way, the uncertainty at the foundation of oneself and all things is really experienced and "bodily" realized by oneself. < This may be called *"dubito"* but not in the meaning of *ego dubito;* that is, it is not the "I" (as *ego*) doubting. In Buddhist terminology, it is doubt as *"samadhi"* ... >[9]

(4) because of the issuing of the "Great Doubt" into the "Great Death" in which the great reversal then takes place:

The Great Doubt emerges always as something that opens up the field of nothingness, which gives place to the turn-about of the Doubt itself. < For this very reason, too, it is the "great" Doubt. > And, as such, it is also called the Great Death. For example, the sayings: "Once (when occurs) the Great Death, then the Universe becomes new," and "Under the Great Death, there is the Great Enlightenment," refer to that turn-about. As in the case of Doubt, this Enlightenment is an enlightenment we attain, but at the same time it must be the "falling off" of our mode of existence in which the "I" is the agent. It comes to present itself as Reality from the foundation of the self-together-with-all-things.[10]

Here Nishitani's claims reach the same point that he himself, in an interpolation in the English text of the opening chapter of *What is Religion?*, refers to from the preaching of the eighteenth-century Zen master Takasui:

... Doubt deeply in a state of single-mindedness, looking neither before nor after, right nor left, becoming wholly like a dead man and becoming unaware even of your own person being there. When this method is practised more and more deeply, you will come to a state of being totally absent-minded and vacant. Even then, you must raise up the Great Doubt ... and must doubt further, being all the time like a dead man. And after that, when you are aware no more of your being wholly like a dead man, are no more conscious of your procedure of "Great Doubting" and become, yourself, through and through a Great Doubt-mass, there will come all of a sudden a moment when you come out into a transcendence called the Great Enlightenment, as if you woke up from a great dream, or as if you, being completely dead, suddenly revived.[11]

Hakuin had described his own way in similar fashion:

If a person is confronted with the Great Doubt, then in the four directions of heaven there is only wide, empty land, without birth and without death, like a plane of ice ten thousand miles in expanse, as if one sat in an emerald vase. Without there is bright coolness and white purity. As if devoid of all sense one forgets to rise when he is sitting, and forgets to sit down when he is standing. In his heart there remains no trace of passion or concept, only the word "nothingness," as if he stood in the wide dome of heaven. He has neither fear nor knowledge. If one progresses in this fashion without retrogression, he will suddenly experience something similar to the breaking of an ice cover or the collapse of a crystal tower. The joy is so great that it has not been seen or heard for forty years.[12]

When the Great Doubt in the Great Death becomes the Great Enlightenment, there appears again the image of open, free hands as well:

If you wish to attain the true Nonego you must release your hold over the abyss . . . What does it mean to release one's hold over the abyss? A man went astray and arrived at a spot which had never been trodden by the foot of man. Before him there yawned a bottomless chasm. His feet stood on the slippery moss of a rock and no secure foothold appeared around him. He could step neither forward nor backward. Only death awaited him. The vine which he grasped with his left hand and the tendril which he held with his right hand could offer him little help . . . Were he to release both hands at once, his dry bones would come to nought.
    . . . By pursuing a single *kōan* he [the Zen disciple] comes to a point where his mind is as if dead and his will as if extinguished. This state is like a wide void over a deep chasm and no hold remains for hand or foot. All thoughts vanish and in his bosom burns hot anxiety. But then suddenly it occurs that with the *kōan* both body and mind break. This is the instant when the hands are released over the abyss. In this sudden upsurge it is as if one drinks water and knows for oneself heat and cold. Great joy wells up. This is called rebirth (in the Pure Land). This is termed seeing into one's own nature . . . [13]

It becomes clear then that the "Great Doubt" is in fact only reached when it is seen to be a "declaration of bankruptcy of the Cartesian ego."[14] According to Nishitani, this is a position that not even Sartre in his atheistic existentialism had reached.[15] While Buddhism understands nothingness *(mu)* as *anātman (muga),*[16] Sartre's nothingness remains immanent to the ego in spite of its transcending tendency.

In this connection Nishitani makes a remark on Sartre's understanding of nothingness whose negative and repudiating tone throws some helpful light on his own understanding of nothingness:

> Although he considers it the foundation of the subject, it is still considered like a wall projected in the base of the ego, or like a spring-board on which the ego is standing. His nothingness is turned into a basic factor that shuts the ego up within itself.[17]

The result, as Nishitani himself states repeatedly in a positive way, should be that the "Great Doubt" frees man from his prison. It should not lock him up or close him in, but unlock and open up. In this concern of his for the liberation or opening up of man, or conversely with his enslavement and captivity, Nishitani enters into a critique of the philosophy of being and interpersonalism.

Being and Nothingness

The question of the relation of being and nothingness belongs not only to contemporary Western philosophy but also to the thinking of Nishitani and his colleagues. Nishitani himself, of course, presents a special case, as Abe has shown in his review of *What is Religion?*[18] In the discussion of this issue Nishitani takes his lead resolutely from Heidegger.

In his essay *What is Metaphysics?* Heidegger had already defined anxiety as the locus of the revelation of nothingness: "Anxiety reveals nothingness." [19] And of human Dasein he had this to say:

> *Da-sein* means a being-upheld in nothingness.
> Nothingness is neither an object nor a being at all. Nothingness neither comes forth by itself alone nor together with beings to which it adheres, so to speak. Nothingness is the making possible of the revelation of beings as what they are for human Dasein. Nothingness does not initially stand as a counter-notion to beings, but belongs to their very essence.
> The question of nothingness brings us—the very questioners—into question. It is a metaphysical question.[20]

While Nishitani agrees with Heidegger's approach as far as it goes, he cannot hide the fact that for him it does not go far enough. And this leads him to the following difficulty: on the one hand, the personal relationship that Nishitani had with Heidegger apparently forbids him an open critique. Accordingly, Heidegger is only mentioned occasionally, here and there. On the other hand, according to Abe's analysis of the work, as a whole it represents nonetheless a fundamental confrontation with Heidegger in that Nishitani has in mind to take a great stride beyond him.[21]

For this reason, the following procedure suggests itself to us: instead of going at once into the work of Nishitani to track down the nature of his confrontation with Heidegger, it seems advisable to begin by pursuing the problematic in Nishitani's circle—and thus at a greater personal remove from Heidegger—where the fuller complexities of the question can be gone into more thoroughly. In general this is the procedure of Abe, which we shall sketch first. In line with this, we turn then once again to the views of Nishitani himself.

Nothingness and the Relation between Being and Non-being

Abe has repeatedly undertaken the attempt to relate Western and Eastern categories to one another, and in so doing also to distinguish them from one another.[22] In a contribution presented at a philosophical congress in Varna, Bulgaria, in 1973, entitled "Non-being and *Mu*," he looked into the metaphysical nature of negativity in the East and the West.[23]

As the starting point for his deliberations he chose not Heidegger but Paul Tillich, principally because Tillich approaches the question through the "shock of non-being"[24] and is well aware of the struggles in the West to overcome this shock.

Here two fundamental theses need to be pointed out:

... Non-being is literally nothing except in relation to being. Being precedes non-being in ontological validity, as the word "non-being" itself indicates.[25]

And secondly:

The being of God is being-itself. The being of God cannot be understood as the existence of a being alongside others or above others.[26]

On the question of the relation of God to being, Tillich replies similarly to the effect that:

The only possible answer seems to be that God is being-itself, in the sense of the power of being or the power to conquer non-being.[27]

For Abe these theses represent the two basic tendencies of the West (Greek philosophy and Christianity) as they have fused together into a basic understanding that has defined Western intellectual history up to the present. But he then goes on to ask what the ontological grounds for the priority of being over non-being might be once it is granted that being includes both, itself and non-being. In his view, the all-encompassing must be neither being nor non-being.[28]

In his description of Western understanding, Abe can appeal as well to Tillich as to Heidegger, since each in his own way presents "nothingness as the counter-notion of real beings, i.e. as their negation," to use Heidegger's own words made in reference to "raw historical memory."[29]

For his part, Tillich portrays the Christian teaching of *creatio ex nihilo* as a repudiation of Platonism's me-ontic matter, so that the "*nihil*" out of which God created the world is presented not as relative nothingness μὴ ὸν but as absolute nothingness οὐκ ὸν.[30] God as essence pure and simple—"I Am the I-Am" (Ex. 3:14)—does not admit of being understood as a second principle in a dualistic world. Yet the initial question remains for Abe, and is indeed transformed into the deeper question of the priority of life over death, good over evil, etc. This in turn results in the view that man must overcome the opposition of being and not-being—which are not nouns but verbs in their most fundamental sense—in seeking to achieve as his goal being pure and simple, life pure and simple—"eternal life"—goodness pure and simple, etc.[31]

Abe illustrates these two basic tendencies in contrast to the Eastern mentality in the form of three diagrams:[32]

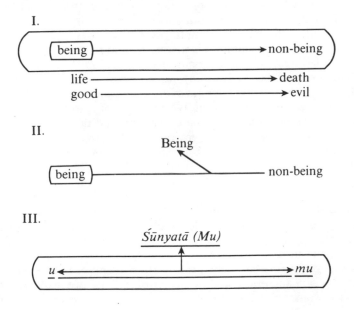

In clarifying this final diagram, Abe is able to have recourse both to Taoist and Buddhist traditions. In the *Tao te ching* of Lao-tzu, Ch. XL, he finds a literal contrast to the introductory thesis of Tillich:

> Turning back is how the way moves;
> Weakness is the means the way employs.
> The myriad creatures in the world are born from
> Something, and Something from Nothing.[33]

Similarly we read at the opening of the work:

> The way that can be spoken of
> Is not the constant way;
> The name that can be named
> Is not the constant name.
> The nameless was the beginning of heaven and earth;
> The named was the mother of the myriad creatures.[34]

In the Asiatic world one runs into, again and again in the course of history, the search for "a realization of thoroughgoing negation to reach the ultimate reality which is completely beyond beginning and end, existence and no-existence, something and nothingness."[35] Abe outlines this history in broad strokes by drawing attention to the denial of substantial *ātman* in the Buddhist doctrine of *anātman,* to the doctrine of the *pratītyasamutpāda,* which he renders as "dependent origination, relationality, relational origination or dependent co-arising," and finally to Nāgārjuna's doctrine of *śūnyatā* and his interpretation of the middle way that ends in the paradox: emptiness = fullness, fullness = emptiness.[36] We need only mention this in passing and refer the reader to the more detailed treatment of these notions provided in Part One.

The point for Abe is this: *śūnyatā* can never enjoy in any form the ontological priority that being does over "to be" and "not to be." In this connection *u* and *mu*—unlike the Western pair of opposites ὄν and μὴ ὄν, *ens* and *non-ens, être* and *non-être,* being and non-being, sein and *nichtsein*—mutually affirm and deny one another. In other words, *mu* is never a mere privation of *u,* but is inseparably bound up and coordinated with it.[37] In comparisons of the notion of being in the West with that of the East, one would do well to avoid too hastily equating that which the Japanese history of philosophy has up to the present day not equated but distinguished as *"u-mu"* on the one hand (covering Asiatic thought and its pairs of opposites such as the Sanskrit *sat asat* and *bhāva-abhava*) and *"yū-mu"* on the other (used to translate the Western pairs of opposites).[38]

Abe adds a final corrective to the third diagram that renders the reciprocity of *u* and *mu* as well as the transcendence of the dualism of *u* and *mu* in *kū* or emptiness, but at the same time establishes the line of a new dualism between *u-mu* on the one side and *kū* on the other. Actually the demand to renounce every attachment to emptiness for the sake of emptiness shows up repeatedly in the history of Mahāyāna Buddhism. The self-emptying of emptiness that allows *u-mu* to be what they really are, is what is spoken of as *myō-u*, "wondrous being," or in the longer formula as *shinkū myō-u*, "true emptiness, wondrous being." Abe clarifies this last step in the following diagram:[39]

IV.

u ⟶ mu

sūnyatā (mu)

The result for Abe is this:

> The Buddhist idea of emptiness can be properly realized not conceptually, but only holistically, subjectively, or existentially through the realization of one's own existence as a self-contradictory oneness of being and non-being, that is *u* and *mu*.[40]

By way of summary Abe offers five points for consideration:[41]

(1) If the idea of nothingness in Buddhism is given the central position, this is so because it is not a question of any relative form of nothingness but of absolute nothingness,[42] that "true emptiness" *(shinkū)* in which the "wondrous being" *(myō-u)* reveals itself.

(2) The realization of absolute nothingness is not to be seen as a gateway to the great hall of final reality, but is itself that great hall of final reality. For absolute nothingness is realized existentially when it is experienced in the return to relative being and non-being as they are, and no longer as a *tertium quid* beyond them.

(3) The idea of "wondrous being" is to be distinguished from the Western idea of being insofar as this latter is not non-dualistic and is seen as final reality possessing ontological priority over non-being.

(4) What distinguishes the basic attitudes of East and West is whether the realization of absolute nothingness is essential for the revelation of being as final reality, and whether relative being and non-being are taken as totally coordinated and reciprocal to one another.

(5) If being maintains ontological priority over non-being, then being pure and simple is the ultimate, the symbol of deliverance in which negativity is overcome through positivity. If, on the other hand, positivity *(u)* and negativity *(mu)* are co-ordinated and reciprocal, then the antinomial/contradictory tension of positivity and negativity must be

overcome. In that case, as Buddhism teaches, deliverance is realized in emptiness as emancipation from the existential antinomy. As a final step, however, the process of emptying must also take place in emptiness itself as well. Only then does the dynamic of emptiness-fullness become the symbol of deliverance.[43]

In conclusion, Abe mentions two areas in which he finds a fundamental tendency at work in the Western world like that of the East: in negative theology and Christian mysticism, and again in the philosophy of Nietzsche and Heidegger.[44] But in Heidegger the influence of mysticism and of Nietzsche come together and, in Abe's view, this makes him the one person in Western history to take more seriously the question of nothingness and to probe most deeply into it. Thus the circle closes, and we return to the point at which Nishitani's work can be called a fundamental confrontation with Heidegger.

But this is also important to note: both orientations, the theological as well as the philosophical, seem to Abe each in its own arena to be unorthodox. The question that we must later answer for ourselves is whether this assessment of the situation is a valid one.

Neither Object-Substance nor Subject

The question of being and nothingness begins in Nishitani with the assertion that in the history of Western thought being or existence has been treated for the most part with the categories of substance or subject:

> Whether inanimate or animate thing, human being or even God, when one takes something as a being-in-itself, its beingness is considered usually as substance. The concept of substance indicates in something that which makes it be itself, that which makes it preserve its self-identity in spite of the incessant changes that occur in its more or less "accidental" properties. We must say, however, that we come to the concept of substance regarding something only because we view it from the outset as an "object," < or (from the opposite side) as a thing posited in front of, viewed from and represented by the subject. > [45]

For both substance or object, as well as the personal self or subject, remain unknown, unspeakable in their ground and origin:

> Each and every thing, no matter how familiar and acquainted it may be to the self, is originally a thing unknown in that basic sense. The self as a subject also in regard to its origin, that is, in its "beingness" as such, is something unnamed that refuses to be determined in any way. It is what I meant when, speaking of the "Great Doubt," I said that the self becomes a realization of the Doubt.[46]

And this in turn poses the question:

But can we conceive of a mode of being that is neither subjective nor substantial?[47]

The question arises for the following reasons:

The concept of substance as well as that of subject is established after all on the field of ᵕubject-object duality; the former is concerned with the "object" and presupposes the "subject," and it is the same with the latter, *mutatis mutandis.* This field of duality is broken through by *nihilum* [*kyomu*] in which, as I said above, things and the self are brought back to their ground; where, however, the concepts of substance and subject must lose their ground that is no other than the subject-object duality itself. Thus, in the field of *nihilum,* the being of things as well as of the self becomes thoroughly questionable by being transported to a region beyond the reach of "logical" thinking. It follows as a necessary consequence that with the further turning away from *nihilum,* that is within emptiness [*kū*], the mode of being of things as well as of the self can be neither subjective nor substantial. The mode of being of things when they are truly on their own home-ground in their ultimate being-in-themselves [*jitai*], or in their selfness wholly beyond all modes of being in which they are reflected upon the subject-object relation, cannot be substantial, much less subjective. Equally, the mode of being of the self, when it is ultimately on its own home-ground and in its true selfness, cannot be subjective, much less substantial.[48]

In this lengthy quotation we find Nishitani's basic thesis with regard to being. His philosophical deliberations lead, as the English text shows more clearly than the original Japanese, into a realm that surpasses logical thought. His way of treating the question of being leads through the experience of negativity—"nothingness" *(kyomu)*—into unspeakable and unobjectifiable emptiness *(kū).* It becomes, therefore, a religious question in which the call for a ground ends in the groundlessness wherein man must repudiate every form of attachment.

There is no need to follow this line of thought through the details of its full philosophical exposition.[49] But to avoid misunderstanding it as pure, unrelated speculation, we should take note of its relationship with Eckhart, Heidegger and Buddhism, as Abe has already pointed out.

Already early on Nishitani has observed the connection between God and absolute nothingness in Eckhart's distinction between God and godhead.[50] "God's ground" *(gotes grunt)* or "God's godhead" *(gotes gotheit),* however, do not mean God the Father but rather "the ground of the father" *(grunt des vaters),* "the primacy and ground of fatherliness" *(die êrstekeit und den grunt der vaterlicheit),* "the ground of divine essence" *(grunt götlîches wesens),* "the ground of being" *(grunt des wesens).*[51] Nishitani himself remarks briefly:

> Godhead means God being in Himself . . . This essence of God, which transcends every mode of being or every aspect, cannot be expressed except by absolute nothingness.[52]

His disciple Ueda quotes in his book on Eckhart:

> *"Got ist ein wesen, ez ist niht wâr: er ist ein überswebende wesen und ein überwesende nihtheit."* [God is an essent that is not a someone: he is an essent that hovers above, a super-essential nothing.]
> God is nothingness. Not that he is without being; rather he is neither this nor that, nor anything that man can predicate of him— he is a being above all being. He is a modeless being.[53]

Coupled with the threefold interpretation of darkness in Eckhart's exposition of John 1:5,9 is the threefold understanding of nothingness that results for him:

(1) nothingness as *"privatio,"* as the nothingness of the creature in distinction from God who is pure *esse;*

(2) the nothingness of God as his superiority over man and all creatures;

(3) the nothingness of God in itself above and beyond any opposition between God and creature, God and man: "it is neither being nor nothingness"; "it admits of nothing more positive than itself."[54]

Nishitani then goes on to indicate a threefold uniqueness to Eckhart's approach:

> First, the "essence" of God is thought to be found only where the personal "God" which stands in confrontation to created beings is transcended.
> Second, the "essence" of God or "Godhead" is discovered as absolute nothingness, which presents itself to us moreover as the place of our absolute death-*sive*-life [Jap., *sive* = *soku*].
> Third, in the "Godhead" alone is it possible for man to be truly himself, and only in the openness of absolute nothingness is the consummation of man's freedom and independence (man's subjectivity) to be found.[55]

In this way Nishitani aligns Eckhart's thought with the understanding of nothingness in the world of Buddhism to which he himself assigns the greatest degree of radicalness. In contrast to Eckhart's idea, which we shall have occasion later to probe still further in speaking more directly to the question of the relationship between God and man,

Nishitani can find in Nietzsche's nihilism only the achievement of a relative "absolute nothingness."[56] It is otherwise with Heidegger.

Being and Nothingness—"The Same"

For Heidegger the question of being is from the very outset intimately related with the other question: "How do things stand with nothingness?"[57] "It discloses itself as belonging to the being of beings."[58] The question is, for Heidegger, a metaphysical one:

> From the standpoint of metaphysics (i.e., of the question of being in the form: What is it to be?) the first thing to be uncovered is the hidden essence of being, its negation as a pure and simple not-being, as a nothingness. But nothingness, as the not-ness of beings, is the strongest opponent of pure *nihilum*. Nothingness is never nothing; even less is it a something in the sense of an object. It is being itself, to whose truth man is converted when he has overcome himself as subject, and that means when he conceives of beings no longer as objects.[59]

Writing in a Festschrift dedicated to E. Jünger, Heidegger uses "S~~ein~~", a convention that Abe, in his essay on Nishitani, would like to correlate with the Japanese "*kū*".[60]

> The crossing-out only temporarily acts as a check against the almost eradicable habit of conceiving "being" as an object that is self-subsistent and only approaches man now and again. As a result of this idea it looks as if man were excluded from "being." Nonetheless, not only is he not excluded—that is to say, not only is he included in "being"—but "being's" inclusion of the essence of man is dependent on its giving up the semblance of a for-itself, and for that reason its essence is also something other than what the notion of a totality which embraces the subject-object relationship would like to admit. . . .
> Like b~~ein~~g, nothingness should also be so written and conceived. That means that the thinking nature of man belongs to nothingness, and not only as an added extra . . . [61]

Recalling his essay *What is Metaphysics?*, Heidegger goes on:

> This nothingness which is not a being and which all the same is, is not a *nihilum*. It belongs to what is present. Being and nothingness do not exist alongside one another. One uses the other in an affinity whose wealth of essence we have hardly begun to comprehend . . . Being "exists" as little as nothingness "exists." But both "are."[62]

And yet again:

Only *because* the question, "What is metaphysics?," from the outset ponders the surpassing of, the transcendence, the *being* of beings, can it think of the nothingness of beings, of *that* nothingness which is of like origin and one with being.[63]

Statements of this sort which could be multiplied make it easy to understand how Nishitani must feel bound to Heidegger in his thought. Where being and nothingness become "the same," the distance from the formula of co-ordination and reciprocity stemming from Mahāyāna thought, *soku = sive/quā*, does not seem so great:

< Viewed in the context of Mahāyāna thought, the primary principle of which is to transcend all duality emerging from logical analysis, > the phrase "being *sive* nothingness" implies the demand that, in order to realize truly its meaning, one should place himself initially on the basis of this *sive* and see from there being as being and nothingness as nothingness. Of course, in our daily life we live in a situation in which being is viewed solely as being, a situation shackled by being. Once such a standpoint is broken through and negated, *nihilum* [Jap., *kyomu*] arises. The standpoint of *nihilum* is, in its turn, a standpoint of viewing nothingness [*mu*] solely as nothingness, a standpoint which is shackled by nothingness; it is a position to be negated in its turn. It is then that emptiness [*kū*], as a standpoint of absolute non-attachment free of this twofold attachment, makes its appearance.[64]

The co-ordination and reciprocity that appears in the famous formula *"shiki soku zekū kū soku zeshiki"*—"form and color, where all is emptiness; emptiness where all is form and color"—a formula that Heidegger is also familiar with,[65] is found in Nishitani in a variety of forms. Among them belong the formulas already cited, *"u soku mu,"* "being *sive* nothingness," "live *sive* death," "affirmation *sive* negation," and the converse of each.

For Nishitani it is clear that where the being of beings is disclosed in the "Nichtung des Nichts," Heidegger has reached a point where everything that is, is assigned its authentic reality:

The field of *nihilum* [*kyomu*] is thus the field where the subject becomes more authentically subjective, and at the same time things reveal themselves more in reality.[66]

Nonetheless, Nishitani raises gentle doubts as to whether Heidegger, in speaking of the "upholding of Dasein in nothingness"[67] or of the "abyss of nothingness,"[68] might not still disclose traces of an idea of nothingness that is not free of the tendency to objectification:

> Rather, when standing on self-being we come into contact with *nihilum* [*kyomu*] opening up at its ground, *nihilum* comes to appear, in fact, as an abyss into which, as Heidegger points out, our self-being is held, suspended out. But the point here is that the *nihilum* in this case is always a *nihilum*-for-us, that is, a *nihilum* encountered by us, we ourselves standing on the side of "being." From this it follows that the *nihilum* is seen outside "being" < of all things as well as of ourselves > (outside beingness, so to speak), as something which is nothingness [*mu*], as an entity absolutely other than beingness. It is the same with the common view that simply sets nothing against being as its mere negation.[69]

In so doing, Heidegger takes a step backward, for Nishitani, in the direction of the traditional essential notion of nothingness. Whether the suspicion so advanced, which also led Abe to the remark cited earlier that Nishitani may have taken a giant step beyond Heidegger, be valid or not is a question we shall lay to one side of our considerations here. Indeed, Abe himself finally comes to qualify his own remarks to the effect that in his view one could perhaps also say that Nishitani has only drawn out the inevitable consequences of Heidegger's notion of "being" or the "achievement" of "being."[70] More important is that we have a clear idea of what Nishitani himself means. And that is that he is concerned with letting go of every form of attachment, but that he considers this possible only where the negativity of the process of letting go is also radically effected, both intellectually and existentially. To appreciate this, the standpoint of nothingness [*kyomu*] needs more clearly to be contrasted with that of emptiness [*kū*].

Before returning to the radical process of letting go in the light of this distinction, however, some attention should first be given to that particular relation-to-being wherein man is viewed not in relationship to an objective world of things, but in relationship to other subjects.

I-Thou and Nothingness

Among the fundamental questions that preoccupy Nishitani's attention is that of man's being human. For Western man, this involves the further question of man's being a person. Moreover, insofar as being a person says something unconditionally positive about man, and since nothing that is positive can be lacking in God but must rather be realized in a form surpassing all other possibility, the same is to be claimed for God's being a person.

The question of the primacy of positivity over negativity returns here with renewed force. At the same time, the question of man's being human has come to a critical point today inasmuch as man himself is being dragged into the undertow of technology and, like a cog in the vast, faceless technological process of our times, is losing his own inimitable face:

> At the basis of technological thought lies the "denaturalization" of nature and the "dehumanization" of humanity . . . If the being of all things (e.g., water) is grasped as power or energy in a form such that their being is destroyed from within, then the "weight" of the "is-ness" of things is nowhere to be found. With regard to a human being, the dimension out of which a "thou" confronts an "I" is completely erased.[71]

As a result, every possibility for an I-Thou relationship is endangered, along with everything that enables man, in the language of Francis of Assisi, to enter into a brother-sister, I-Thou relationship with all created things,[72] and the fundamental I-Thou relationship between God and man.

"Person" and Nothingness

The second chapter of Nishitani's *What is Religion?* bears the title "The Personal and the Impersonal in Religion." At the start of its concluding section he asserts:

> There is no doubt that the idea of man as a personal being is the highest idea of man which has thus far appeared. The same may be said as regards the idea of God as personal being. Since subjectivity with its self-consciousness came to the fore in modern times, the idea of man as a personal being became practically self-evident. But is the way of thinking about "person" which has been generally prevalent up to now really the only possible way to think about "person"?[73]

Be that as it may, the concept of person that Nishitani has in mind is only to be inferred from the critique that he offers, which proceeds along the lines of the claim that the concept of person originated out of a view which sees the person as central, much the same as the self and ego in modern times have developed out of a self-centered or egocentric perspective:

> In the way of thinking up to now, "person" has been viewed from the standpoint of person itself. It has been a person-centered idea of person. As had already been pointed out, in an ontologically more basic sense, even the self was viewed in the modern period from the self-centered perspective of the self, and was grasped, in

Descartes, for example, from the viewpoint of *ego cogito*. It is the same with person. Since ego or person [*jiga toka jinkaku toka iu mono*] involves by its very nature its own inward self-reflection, and can exist as ego or person only in that way, it is only natural that this way of self-comprehension from within should come about.[74]

This "egocentric" view of one's own ego leads to the result that man gets caught in a kind of self-fettering or narcissism:

The self-immanence, in the perspective of which man catches his ego or his own personality, necessarily signifies a sort of confinement, in which his self-being is caught; a confinement where lingers inevitably the mode of man's being captured in and by himself, or even of his self-captivation, so-called narcissism.[75]

In this connection Nishitani has recourse to the etymological attempt to explain "person" from "persona" (mask). This presents him with another opportunity for referring to the nothingness behind the mask:

Person is an appearance with nothing behind it which might make an appearance. Behind person there is nothing at all; that is, behind it lies absolute nothingness.
    While this absolute nothingness is wholly other to his person and means the absolute negation of the person, it is not some*thing* different from the person. Absolute nothingness is that which, becoming one with that "being" called person, brings into being that person. Accordingly, the previously used expressions, "there *is* absolute nothingness," and "it *is* behind," are, in fact, inaccurate. Nothingness is not a thing which *is* nothingness . . . Rather, there not being èven any nothingness is true nothingness, absolute nothingness.[76]

There is no need here to hide the fact that Nishitani does not expressly take into account either of the two great Western traditions regarding the person. Nowhere does he expressly mention the classical definition of Boethius, *"persona est naturae rationalis individua substantia,"*[77] although it was this idea that remained effective from the *"incommunicabilis subsistentia"* of Aquinas[78] and his successors up until modern times, humanism and the Enlightenment, and that enabled for the first time the understanding of person as "the core of spiritual individuality in self-consciousness."[79] Nor, in going into the interpersonality of the I-Thou relationship, does he speak of the history of the competing notion of person that sees person much less in terms of individuality than as a relation—a notion that is particularly evident in the doctrine of the Trinity. This latter tradition reaches from Augustine and Richard of St. Victor through Jacobi, Hegel and Feuerbach, to Buber, Ebner, Haecker and Guardini, and most recently is found also in the theology of Barth, Pannenberg, Ott, Ratzinger, Mühlen and many others.[80] A quotation from Ratzinger's *Introduction to Christianity* may serve here, in anticipation of our conclusions, as an indication of how a deepening of the dialogue between Christianity and Buddhism, between a Christian-inspired philosophy and a Buddhist-inspired philosophy, is possible on an essentially wider base:

> For St. John, "Son" means being-from-another; he uses the word thus to define the being of this man as a being from another and towards others, as a being who is altogether opened at both ends and leaves no room reserved strictly to the pure ego. If it is so plain that the being of Jesus as the Christ is a completely "open" being, that this being is pure relationality (not substantiality) and as such is pure unity, a being from and towards which at no time clings to itself and in no place stands by itself, it is likewise plain that what can thus be said of Christ fundamentally becomes . . . at the same time the interpretation of Christian existence. Being a Christian means for St. John being like the Son, becoming a son, and so not standing by oneself or remaining within oneself, but living in a wholly open fashion in the "from" and "towards" . . . [81]

Somewhat later he adds the remark that the "Trinitarian doctrine passes over into a statement about existence." At least here we find a point of contact with what Nishitani has to say:

> Absolute nothingness, in which even that which "is" nothingness is negated, is not nothingness merely thought but nothingness which can only be lived . . . The shift of man as person from person-centered self-apprehension to self-opening as the realization of absolute nothingness . . . ought to be an existential turn-about, a kind of conversion, within man himself. . . .
> The true nothingness is a living nothingness, and a living nothingness can only be self-attested.[82]

There is essential agreement at least on the point that, both in a definition of person as pure relationality as well as in absolute nothingness "behind" the person, (a) there is present a radical openness in the sense of a liberation from every form of self-imprisonment and self-fettering; (b) openness is not a purely intellectual conception but in the last analysis is only realized existentially; and (c) in both viewpoints the way of viewing a person as centered on or related to the self is overcome.

The Interpersonal

Even if Nishitani does not expressly consider the idea "person = relation," he does pursue the I-Thou relationship. In an essay entitled "On the I-Thou Relation in Zen Buddhism," he starts with the well-known example of the *Hekiganroku* (Ch., *Pi-yen-lu*):

Kyōzan (Ejaku) asked Sanshō (Enen): "What is your name?" Sanshō replied, "My name is Ejaku." "Ejaku!" said Kyōzan, "that's me!" "Well then," replied Sanshō, "my name is Enen." Kyōzan roared with laughter.[83]

On the basis of this example Nishitani illustrates Zen Buddhism's attempt to solve the problematic of the everyday encounter of I and Thou. Two facts form his starting point:

The first is that the *I* as well as the *Thou* are absolutes in their respective subjectivities. The second is that the I and the Thou directly through their relation upon one another are, on the other hand, absolutely relative.[84]

Nishitani finds the absoluteness of subjectivity and its universal validity at work in the state, in practical reason, and in God. The I-Thou relation—or, we might also say, brotherhood—can only work imperfectly in Nishitani's view so long as equality and freedom are not fully realized. This is the case with subordination to a universal law, be it of the state, of practical reason or of God. There are two reasons for this.

First, every individual, although it possesses an unexchangeable subjectivity, is in some way also subordinated to the universal, and in this regard is equal to all other individuals and can therefore be represented by any other individual. Secondly, the subordination of an individual to a universal cannot absorb the freedom of the individual without remainder. This means that the representation of one individual through another is not completely possible.

Hence there is no real encounter between man and man in interhuman relationships where a universal is included and where freedom and equality must accompany only in incomplete form. Nishitani looks for a possible equality in which the absolute negation of the individual and his freedom is at the same time its absolute affirmation, and this absolute affirmation in turn is at the same time its absolute denial. To this end, he calls upon the standpoint of *soku,* as he finds it realized in the area of "absolute nothingness" as *"śūnyatā."* In grounding this idea, the critique of the philosophy of being comes once again to the fore:

A universal that would posit itself in a relation to the individual, and thus become a universal that *is*—be it as state, practical reason, God, etc.—would in any case mediate, each according to its own law, between individual and individual, and through this bring them to unity. Within this unity through law the universal manifests itself as *being,* as something with self-identity, as "substance." State, reason, and God are "beings," or "substance"; there the relation between man and man itself is substantial. The individual, therefore, loses half of itself in the relation. Here it cannot be an absolute individual completely absolved from all relations, simply standing independently as a whole. On the other side, the universal, to a certain extent, is inherent within individuals, and brings forth from within them their relation to each other. In its immanency it cannot completely transcend the individual and cannot, as it were, deprive him of his roots.[85]

The answer given by the story of the exchange of names cited at the beginning represents for Nishitani the solution of the dilemma resulting from the fact that I and Thou are absolutely absolute and at the same time absolutely relative. And indeed "naming" has been of undeniable significance through the course of the history of religion as well as philosophy. In a commentary on the initial question "What is your name?" the interchangeability of name and essence, of name and being becomes apparent: "He robs at one time the name and the being." Nishitani adds:

To ask someone for his name is also to take his being to yourself as well.[86]

And making use of the same example he elaborates further:

When asked his name, Sanshō answered "Ejaku," but Ejaku was the name of the questioner, Kyōzan. In his answer Sanshō in effect takes Kyōzan's absolute nature—Kyōzan, who is Kyōzan himself, and who will not allow any Thou to stand opposite him; Kyōzan, who would take all others to himself—as it is, for his own. He simultaneously seizes all Kyōzan's actions and true existence from behind, going around hostile defenses and running up the banner of his own self in the rear. In so doing he pulls the floor from under Kyōzan's feet.[87]

What is more important, however, is that the subjective relation between man and man is no longer the I-Thou relation in the universal sense of the term:

The *I* is the *Thou,* the *Thou* is the *I.* It is the same from Kyōzan's standpoint. In short, the *I* is not merely an ordinary *I;* it is the *I* (Sanshō) that is at the same time *Thou* (Kyōzan). The *Thou* is no simple *Thou;* it is the *Thou* that is simultaneously *I.* Hence the *I* and the *Thou* blend completely into one another.[88]

At this point there arises an objection:

Here one might think of absolute non-differentiation, absolute sameness, or absolute oneness. In Western thought it has been expressed as Oneness (for example, by Plotinus), or as Absolute Identity (for example, by Schelling). Here no more relation exists, and there is nothing that can lead to one. There is neither self nor other, thus there is no person and no personal relation.[89]

Nishitani rejects the objection. The genuine I-Thou relation consists for him much more in the fact that this I and this Thou are not only an I and a Thou. I *am* Thou, and Thou *art* I—the absolute indistinguishability belongs to both and is precisely that which connects the one to the other and thereby relativizes it:

I can be I and Thou can be Thou as absolute individuals because each of them is grounded on the absolute identity in which I am Thou and Thou art I, and every form of relation and relativity is superseded. Here, I *am* with you being in no way discriminated from you, and you *are* with me equally undiscriminated from me.[90]

In the concrete context of the example, this means:

Where the other is at the center of the individual and where the existence of each one is "other-centric," absolute harmony reigns. This might be called "Love," in the religious sense. I say in a religious sense because it is a case of "void" [emptiness] or *"muga"* (non-self) that has severed absolutely the self and other from the self and other in the relative sense. Thus, absolute opposition is at the same time absolute harmony. Both are the same.[91]

This last remark makes it plain once again that for Nishitani the question of the I-Thou relationship is no purely metaphysical-ontological question, but necessarily passes over into a religious problematic. The question of the not-I or "egolessness" is always bound up with the question of what we refer to, with all its difficult to translate nuances, as "selflessness." The question of interpersonality is like that of the relation of personality and apersonality—at one and the same time a question of the realization of true love.

God and Man
The relationship of God and man represents for Nishitani another

special kind of I-Thou relationship. A number of steps and deliberations can be singled out from his argument.

(1) Even as person, God is overtly understood—and here not without clear allusion to Heidegger—to be something standing before and over against man as an object, be it an object of faith or an object of mystical union. Compare the following statements of Heidegger, Nishitani and Abe:

> "Being" is not God and not the ground of the world. Being is wider than all beings and yet nearer to man than any being, be it a field, an animal, a work of art or a machine, be it an angel or God. Being is the closest of all. Yet the closeness remains furthest from man. For man clings primarily, again and again, only to beings. [Heidegger][92]

> Even the so-called *unio mystica,* which in the tradition of mysticism had been regarded as the final stage of perfection in mystical experience and which had been assumed to be the unification with God *(Deo unitum esse),* still presupposes God's Being as the object to be united with. There still lies hidden in the background the duality of subject and object. [Nishitani][93]

> The Ground of our existence is nothingness, *śūnyatā,* because it can never be objectified. This *śūnyatā* is deep enough to encompass even God, the "object" of mystical union as well as the object of faith. For *śūnyatā* is not the nothingness from which God created everything but the nothingness from which God Himself emerged. *Śūnyatā* is the very ground of the self and thereby the ground of everything to which we are related. [Abe][94]

(2) From this point of view the search for a God-man relationship is understood as one in which love is realized in such a way that selflessness *(muga)* or, in the word of Nishitani inspired by Heidegger, "ekstasis," can be affirmed of God as well as of man:

> *Ekstasis* consists in the direction from self to the "ground" of self, from God to the ground of God; that is, from being to nothingness. Negation-*sive*-affirmation consists in the direction from nothingness to being.[95]

(3) Nishitani finds openings for a corresponding understanding of God in Christianity in (a) mystical theology, as for instance in that of Eckhart with his doctrine of the "godhead" of God and the birth of God in the soul:

> The soul reaches absolute nothingness which is the essence of God. It reaches the place where there is not a single thing, what Eckhart calls the "desert" of Godhead.

While this is the place where the soul is completely deprived of its selfness [*gasei*], it is, nevertheless, the final ground of the soul, its bottomless ground, so to speak; only when the soul returns here can it truly be itself. At the same time, it is the place where God is in Himself: it is the ground of God. . . .

Here one can no longer speak even of unification or union. Eckhart stressed that this does not mean to be unified with God *(Deo unitum esse),* but to be One with God *(unum esse cum Deo).*[96]

(b) in the doctrine of kenosis based on the second chapter of the Letter of Paul to the Philippians in which Nishitani would prefer to see not only the self-emptying of Christ but that of God himself as well:

> The origin of His [i.e. Christ's] "making himself empty" *(ekkenō-sis)* is in God. It is God's love which is willing to forgive even the sinner who has gone against him. This forgiving-love is the expression of the "perfection" of God who embraces equally the good and the evil. Therefore it may be said that also within God Himself is included the meaning of "having made himself empty" . . . If the case of the Son is called *ekkenōsis,* the case of the Father is *kenōsis.* In Buddhist terminology it is < anātman or> *muga,* <*that is, non-ego or selflessness.* >[97]

(c) in the challenge of the Sermon on the Mount to love one's enemies because God himself lets the sun shine on the just and sinner alike in undifferentiated love (Matt. 6:43–48).

(4) Nishitani finally speaks of an impersonally personal—or a personally impersonal—relationship between God and man. When we encounter God, we meet nothingness as an iron wall that separates everything absolutely from God in the sense of the *creatio ex nihilo,* and yet at the same time, in belief and trust, as the omnipresence of God that mediates all Dasein and all life:

> To encounter this nothingness [*kyomu*] must be, so to speak, to encounter God as an iron wall. It means an encounter upon the absolute negativity in God, the absolute negativity manifested in the fact that God is *not* what was created, and what was created can *not* be God. At the same time, the fact that all things exist as they are in actuality, means, seen from the standpoint of a believer, that he encounters in them God's power of creation, which gives them existence and preserves them, in spite of nothingness. . . . God is omnipresent as the absolute "No," as well as the absolute "Yes" to the created existence.[98]

It is to be attributed to the influence of Protestant theology that the accentuation of the transcendence of God as "wholly other" is taken as the "more orthodox" view, in contrast to which the doctrine of the immanence of God almost seems to give off the odor of "unorthodoxy." But this latter corresponds better with Nishitani's stated intentions, for in immanence negativity and positivity meet again:

> An absolutely transcendent God is, as such, absolutely immanent. That a certain thing was created from nothing means that this "nothing" is "immanent" in the very being of that thing—more "immanent" than the being of that thing is "immanent" in that being itself. This is the meaning of what we just called "absolutely immanent." This is immanence in the form of absolute negativity, for the being of what was created < is grounded upon *nothing* [*mu*] and, seen fundamentally, > is nothing. It is, at the same time, immanence in the form of absolute positivity; for the nothingness of what was created is < the ground of > *being.* And so, the omnipresence can be said to contain for man the moment of the turnabout from absolute negativity to absolute positivity, < from being absolutely negated to being absolutely affirmed. > To entrust one's self to this moment, to ride on it, as it were, in order to die to self and live in God, constitutes faith. The appearance of Christ, too, can be considered to be the corporeal manifestation of what was just called the moment of turn-about for man, which is contained in God Himself.[99]

In this consideration Nishitani comes to speak then of love streaming forth from the breath of God, the Holy Spirit. In the existential realization of a love defined by the omnipresent God and his Spirit, the personal God-man relationship takes on what we called above an impersonally personal or personally impersonal character.[100] Or perhaps the expression that Nishitani adopted later is easier to understand: "transpersonal."[101]

(5) In the light of modern dialogue-theology—for instance, of Emil Brunner who himself visited Kyoto as guest professor and whose book *Truth as Encounter*[102] Nishitani cites—Nishitani clarifies yet again that the "*nihil*" of *creatio ex nihilo* can only mean a relative nothingness.[103] But for reasons of premises stated earlier, he is concerned rather with absolute nothingness, and this means an idea of God radicalized as far as God himself, similar to what we find in Eckhart's talk of the "godhead" of God:

> Godhead is where God is not God within God Himself. This may seem to contradict what I said before about godhead being that place where God is in Himself. But in fact these two statements say the same thing. God is God in and by Himself in the absolute nothingness in which God is not God Himself. This is no other than to think of *ekstasis* as applying to the existence of God also.[104]

At this point, a further list of remarks may be appended as part of our ongoing critical appraisal:

(1) One misses in Nishitani a fundamental confrontation with the ancient church, with regard to the patristic traditions[105] as well as the Catholic theology of the Middle Ages. In consequence of this, he pays equally insufficient attention to the orthodox tradition of negative theology—as, for instance, it was still taken as a matter of course among the theologians of the high Middle Ages—as he does to analogical thought, which is all the more important given the context of his particular concerns. He is apparently unaware of the proposal of the Fourth Lateran Council in 1215 to imbed every positive statement about God in an all-embracing negative horizon:

No similarity can be noted between creator and creature without taking note of the greater dissimilarity between them.[106]

This lack of attention to the orthodox Christian tradition, combined with an awareness of the suspicions and criticisms that have attended the thought of Eckhart, bring it about that the Christian doctrine of God is not viewed by Nishitani without prejudice.[107]

(2) One of Nishitani's fundamental concerns is the struggle with the *ekstasis* or the *ekkenōsis/kenōsis* of God. No doubt Philippians 2 offers a statement central to this theme. But the fact that he hardly notices that the incarnation of God in Jesus of Nazareth is spoken of in Christendom as an historical event, i.e., as an occurrence that not only interprets our world history but actually affects it, and is acknowledged as such in the Christian confession of faith, is far from satisfactory. Here Abe is quite correct in stating that Nishitani seems to treat the question of God in a manner that almost totally leaves out of account the figure of Jesus Christ.[108] Yet precisely what the doctrine of the incarnation of God and the death of Christ on the cross speak of is the most radical "self-alienation of the God who remains with himself, and thereby radically unchanged":[109]

The Absolute, or more correctly, he who is the absolute, has, in the pure freedom of his infinite and abiding unrelatedness, the possibility of himself becoming that other thing, the finite; God, in and by the fact that he empties *himself* gives away *himself,* poses the other as his own reality . . . The basic element, according to our faith, is the *self*-emptying, the coming to be, the κένωσις and γένεσις of God himself, who can come to be by *becoming* another thing, derivative, in the act of constituting it, without having to change in his own proper reality which is the unoriginated origin. By the fact that he remains in his infinite fullness while he empties himself—because, being love, that is, the will to fill the void [*Leere* = emptiness], he has that wherewith to fill all—the ensuing other is his own proper reality. He brings about that which is distinct from himself, in the act of retaining it as his own, and vice versa, because he truly wills to retain the other as his own, He constitutes it in its genuine reality. God himself goes out of himself, God in his quality of the fullness which gives away itself.[110]

(3) The same may be said of Nishitani's consideration of God and godhead. He is correct in the view that the *ekstasis* of God, his love of all and everything, before it is bestowed freely on creatures, must affect God himself in his own essence. Indeed, this expresses precisely the Christian doctrine of the Trinity. The frequently cited thesis of Karl Rahner remarks similarly:

The Trinity of the economy of salvation *is* the immanent Trinity and vice versa.[111]

In this thesis we see a particular form of the *"soku"* formula. Nonetheless, this has not yet been given full consideration by Nishitani. There might be some point to asking here how the relation of singular and plural, of the one and the many, is to be assessed with regard to its initial origin and ground in the light of the doctrine of the Middle Way. Both the uniqueness of the God-man Jesus Christ and the unity-in-trinity of God have yet to receive adequate reflection from this angle.

Nothingness and Emptiness

In any event, the various reflections brought up for consideration all lead for Nishitani, each in its own way, into the realm of nothingness or emptiness. Undoubtedly, he often uses nothingness—and above all, absolute nothingness—and emptiness as synonymous. But there are differences to be established in the encounter with nothingness, as well as in the process of nothingness. Nishitani himself has somewhat systematically summarized the standpoint of "emptiness" and the approaches to it.[112]

His *point de départ* is the "this-sidedness" of our everyday life. It is characterized as a condition of captivity and of the attachment of the self to itself. The process of reaching beyond the this-sidedness of man's self-captivity allows of several alternatives that Nishitani expresses in terms of degree of angle.

90° up from the earth towards heaven: while the world of Platonic ideas is a world beyond, standing over against the perceptual world, it is not a world beyond when seen from the standpoint of *śūnyatā* wherein "heaven" and "earth" stand on the same level.

90° from heaven down to earth: The world beyond of God reveals itself from heaven down to earth. Nishitani parallels this "common representation of Christianity" as he calls it with the Platonic arrangement, noting only one difference:

> The only difference is that in Plato the direction from earth to heaven (the direction of *eros*) predominates, while in Christianity it is, conversely, from heaven to earth (the direction of *agape*).[113]

This schematization never once reaches the level of appreciation of Christianity that Nishitani exhibits in other sections of his work.

90° from the earth downwards: the abyss of nihilistic nothingness is no beyond in the strict sense of the word. For the depth of the earth still belongs to the sphere of the earth.

180°: this standpoint of emptiness, in its strict sense, involves no angle of turning, but rather an openness that realizes the absolute yonder-side in the absolute this-sidedness of the world:

> Here what I mean by emptiness is < absolute openness > in the sense that, while presenting itself as the field in which the yonder-side in the direction of heaven as well as the beyond in the direction of the depths of the earth can both be established and representatively conceived, it is in itself sheerly unable to be represented in any way whatsoever and so is always < present as > the absolute this-side.[114]

360°: the standpoint of emptiness is only really realized, however, when emptiness is "emptied" of itself:

> The field wherein emptiness is emptied to become true emptiness is none other than the place where each and every thing appears in its own reality, in its true suchness. It is the field wherein the zero degree means at once three hundred and sixty degrees. Therefore in spite of, or rather because of it being essentially absolute this-side, it can also be absolute yonder-side . . . In short, it means the place of man's death *sive* life and life *sive* death, man here being taken as a whole, < including his body and mind, his rational and personal modes of being. >[115]

With this Nishitani reaches the place that, in the tenth station of the ox path referred to earlier, is called "entering the marketplace with open hands." Nishitani himself does not refer to this image here, but ties the standpoint of "empty emptiness" to the Buddhist locus of radical deliverance and to Eckhart's *Abgeschiedenheit* (detachment).[116] As the locus of *"soku/sive"* it is then also the "middle" in which radical negation becomes radical affirmation since everything that is, is what it is.[117] What is radical *"Nichtung"* (a passing into nothingness) is likewise radical *"Ichtung"* (a passing into being).[118] Absolute emptiness and absolute fullness are one. *Saṃsāra* is *nirvāṇa*.

At this point we may ask in the light of one final look at emptiness: How does it go with the relation of emptiness and world, emptiness and history, emptiness and everything that makes up the surface of our human life? It is to this question that we turn in the following chapter.

7. Emptiness and the Appreciation of World, History and Man

The ox path ends with three poems of praise describing the tenth station:

With bare chest and feet he enters the market.
His face is smeared with earth, his head covered with ashes.
A huge laugh streams over his cheeks.
Without humbling himself to perform miracles or wonders, he suddenly makes the withered trees bloom.

In a friendly manner this fellow comes from a foreign race.
From time to time his face clearly shows the traits of the horse or the donkey.
If he flashes the iron staff as quickly as the wind—
Amply and wide suddenly open doors and gates.

Straight into the face the iron staff springs out of his sleeve.
Sometimes he speaks Hunnish, sometimes Chinese, with a great laugh on his cheeks.
If one understands how to meet one's own self and yet to remain unknown to the self—
The gate to the palace will open wide.[1]

The Japanese Zen master Ōtsu calls the man who walks back into the marketplace with open hands a "holy fool":

"His face is smeared with earth, his head covered with ashes." Thus he wanders around from morning till night in the town, in other words like a fool in the dusty world. He freely throws himself into the painful, heaving sea of timeless reincarnation and liberates those who are sunk in it.[2]

93

And when he "suddenly makes the withered trees bloom" this means "leaping out of the great 'no' into the great 'yes'."[3] The words of this "holy fool" are like an "iron staff" striking:

> "Sometimes he speaks Hunnish, sometimes Chinese," means that he sometimes says, "Nothing" and sometimes "Being." He might teach that "heart is Buddha," or again "not heart and not Buddha." In spite of that, what he says is always clear and unmistakable. The phrase "with a great laugh on his cheeks" contains something indescribable that cannot be put into words.[4]

Thereby the enlightened reaches a kind of "emptiness become empty" in which he shares himself selflessly and sympathetically. Thus knowledge (Skt., *jñāna*) becomes compassion (Skt., *karuṇā*):

> The enlightened one clearly sees how he has been submerged in delusion and suffering from time immemorial. The enlightened one, being emancipated from attachment to "I" and "others," now fully realizes the truth of non-self *(anātman)*, that is, the truth of the equality of "I" and "others." The moment he realizes that he has been immersed in delusion and suffering, he equally realizes that all sentient beings have been and are now immersed in delusion and suffering. Then an aspiration arises in him to break up the delusion and suffering . . . that captivates all sentient beings . . . The principle, "*śūnyatā* is also to be emptied," thus develops as the practice of *mahākaruṇā* (great compassion); preaching, instructing and emptying all sentient beings of . . . suffering. This is, then, the *karuṇā* aspect of the principle.[5]

Nishitani, too, in referring to the standpoint of emptiness, repeatedly speaks of the great affirmation:

> On that field of emptiness, each thing comes into its own and reveals itself in a self-affirmation, each in its own possibility and *virtus* [Jap., *toku*] of being, each in its own shape. The conversion to and entrance into that field means, for us men, the fundamental affirmation of the being of all things < of the world >, and at the same time, of our own existence. The field of emptiness is nothing but the field of the great affirmation.[6]

But the great affirmation, even if it is to be maintained continually in the form of the negation-as-affirmation, must hold good in one's attitude toward or appreciation of world, history and man. Here too the *karuṇā* aspect must finally come forward. Abe praises Nishitani's work for its meticulous and fundamental research into and clarification of the relation of history, or historicity (Jap., *rekishisei*) to the standpoint of emptiness, a matter which has gone a long time without hardly being discussed in a fundamental manner.⁷ In fact the final chapters expressly thematize the relationship of time and history to emptiness. The headings "Emptiness and Time" and "Emptiness and History" call to mind in a way Heidegger's phrase "Being and Time." Since world and time always mean the concrete world and concrete time, in using these words Nishitani gives us to understand that as a modern Japanese Buddhist he cannot avoid the question of the meaning of today's world and the present time. This raises two questions.

First, we must ask how world, history and man are to be presented, for Nishitani, against the horizons of emptiness. This question is all the more significant in that it coincides with the fundamental question for Buddhism of a positive attitude to the world and a positive relation of man to concrete man and to concrete creation in concrete conditions of need, destitution and despair.

This raises the further question, whether in fact Nishitani has arrived at the point of fully "subsuming" [*aufheben*] positivity into his formulation of "positivity *sive* negativity, negativity *sive* positivity." On the one hand negativity should no more be the last word than should positivity if the middle position is to be preserved. On the other hand, this neither/nor should not end up looking like another pure negation either. Rather it must reveal itself as an openness—the Japanese word *kū* signifies the breath of the heavens—for something that can no longer be named, which is only to be achieved in letting go, in the loss of the self.

This leads us to give some consideration to the view voiced by Ueda that in contemporary Japan the Buddhist non-discrimination seems "to have turned into a destructive non-discrimination":

> In place of the original non-discrimination which, in practical life, means a safeguard for man's being in nature, a destructive non-discrimination is gaining ground, through which nature threatens to be taken advantage of with highly technological means for the sake of immediate human goals, and thereby to be destroyed. And all along this is taken not to be the destruction of nature but its organization for the modern world. . . .
>
> The original non-discriminating is inverted from a selfless non-discrimination of the self from the other into a non-discriminating which selfishly no longer differentiates the other from the self.⁸

It may be said here of "emptiness" that it is to be known by its fruits (cf. Matt. 12:33). Should Buddhism offer no final word as an answer, it must nevertheless allow the word to remain in the form of a critical, discriminating, probing question. For it is only the question that is concerned with a new openness and which sets man loose from those situations where he might prefer to take up a false position.

World, History and Man

We all live, whether as believers or non-believers, as religious or non-religious, in the world. We share its history and live in it as men who make use of our intelligence in order to live humanly.

Critique of Buddhism

The critical questioning of Buddhism as to whether or not it takes this concrete world seriously enough is widespread. Abe has illuminated the problem from several angles. He levels the criticism that "Non-thinking" has all too often become a "not thinking":

> Precisely because of its standpoint of Non-thinking, Zen has in fact not fully realized the positive and creative aspects of thinking and their significance which have been especially developed in the West. Logic and scientific cognition based on substantive objective thinking, and moral principles and ethical realization based on subjective practical thinking, have been very conspicuous in the West. In contrast to this, some of these things have been vague or lacking in the world of Zen. Because Zen (at least Zen up until today) has thus not fully realized the positive and creative aspects of human thinking, its position of Non-thinking always harbors the danger of degenerating into mere not-thinking. In actual fact, Zen has frequently degenerated into this position. That Zen today lacks the clue to cope with the problems of modern science, as well as individual, social, and international ethical questions, etc., may be thought partly to be based on this.[9]

Abe recognizes that Buddhism does not finally answer the question of the grounding of man's ethical responsibility and of his social and historical behavior, and that the distinction between non-discriminating wisdom and discriminating intellect does not suffice to clear up the issue:

> Buddhism must face the following difficult problem: how can it account for man as "person" distinguished from "nature," with his freedom and hence his possibility to do evil? Where can Buddhism find the basis of ethical responsibility and man's social and historic action? Buddhism is certainly concerned with human values, with the problems of right and wrong, truth and falsehood, good and evil, etc. However, when Buddhism grapples with the problem of good and evil, it is not treated as an ethical problem pure and simple, but rather as the problem of the discriminative mind which is considered the basis of the good-and-evil distinction. Accordingly, it teaches that the true way to realize the non-discriminating Wisdom, which is Wisdom, which is at the same time *mahākaruṇā*

(The Great Mercy), is to do away with the *avidyā* (fundamental ignorance). Therefore, although Buddhism is concerned with ethical problems, it does not always struggle with them seriously enough as *ethical problems* . . .

Where man's personality and responsibility with regard to individual and social life, and history are concerned, the following question must be asked: how can an individual person . . . deal with the social and historical conditions which can not be directly derived from the *ground* of his own individual existence? For man's social life and history are not simply made up of an aggregate of individual persons. Through the centuries Christianity has seriously struggled with this problem. Its personalism and its clear distinction between God and man give Christianity an advantage in this respect. It has offered its own solution of the problem in the ethic of good-Samaritanism derived from divine love and a view of history based on eschatology. Up to the present, it seems that Buddhism has not wrestled with this problem successfully. Only rarely has Buddhism even raised a basic question about it. The time has come for it to ask whether and how the problems of ethics and history can be solved from the standpoint of *jinen,* which is entirely non-dichotomic. In order to be able to answer this basic question, Buddhism must break through its traditional patterns of thought and rethink the whole matter from the depth of its genuine spirit.[10]

Abe himself is of the view that a positive attitude to the modern world with its science and technology is possible from the standpoint of non-discriminating wisdom, although this possibility has not as yet been actualized:

Buddhist Realization of *śūnyatā* or Non-discriminating Wisdom can, in principle, embrace my discriminative knowledge, including autonomous pure reason, by its very nature of voidness. Non-discriminating Wisdom which is another term for *śūnyatā,* is not a counterpart to discriminative knowledge, but rather a Wisdom which stands beyond all discursive or discriminatory mental constructions and thereby is liberated from the very opposition between discriminative and non-discriminative knowledge. Thus it can give a place to scientific rationality or autonomous pure reason within itself. However, this can be said only *in principle* or *in terms of possibility.* For, throughout its long history, Buddhist Realization of Non-discriminating Wisdom, until the recent time of East-West encounter, has never been confronted with the autonomous pure reason on the basis of which Western modern science has been able to be founded as "science." So it is a future task for Buddhism to *actualize* the possibility of embracing scientific rationality in terms of Non-discriminating Wisdom.[11]

This in turn poses the question whether Nishitani, in his work, has achieved any degree of actualizing this possibility. As a matter of fact, he is aware of the weaknesses of Buddhism when it comes to matters of historical consciousness. Yet he chooses himself not to pursue the reasons for this. Instead, he has in mind to take up the challenge of the West in the hopes of making a contribution from the standpoint of "emptiness." Thus he remarks in his conclusion to a lengthy discussion of Dōgen and his maxim *"shinjindatsuraku"* (the dropped-off body-mind)[12] as the locus in which the original countenance *(honrai no menmokugenzen)* of things appears:

> The problem concerns the historicity of "time." No matter how the standpoint of the dropped-off body-mind may be evaluated, human history is a world of men whose body-mind has not fallen away and who are wandering all the time in illusion, ignorant of the right way. Though man may be saved through religion, is that not only a concern of the individual? We must conclude that human societies in history go their own way regardless of whether the individuals are saved or not. Especially the Buddhist idea of "emptiness," is it not super-historical and hence non-historical? We know indeed the general conception of Buddhism tends to affirm this question. It is an incontrovertible fact that a consciousness of history in the sense it now seems to have taken has scarcely developed from within Buddhism. It would be quite natural to expect during the long development of Mahāyāna Buddhism that the problem of history would have been called in question from the standpoint of saṃsára-*sive*-nirvāṇa, especially in the discussion about Bodhisattvahood. But this expectation was not to be fulfilled. What was the reason for that? It is surely an issue of importance for us today to return to the past to study the causes for this. But here I cannot embark upon such a task. I will instead take up another problem: namely, the question of whether the several basic viewpoints of history which have to the present appeared on the scene in the West do, in fact, exhaust all possible ways of viewing history, or whether the aforesaid standpoint of "emptiness" can contribute anything new.[13]

This preliminary decision of Nishitani's leaves us two possibilities. Either we follow the line of thought he proposes and take up a critical confrontation with the Western concepts of history, and finally come to the critical contribution which Buddhism can offer to the question. Or else we inquire directly into the appreciation of world, history, and man that Nishitani has developed from a Buddhist background, and thereby perhaps arrive at the possibility of mutual correctives for East and West.

Both approaches have their strengths and weaknesses. The first seems topical in that it thematizes more clearly a way of thought that is coming to be more meaningful in modern Japan as well. The only question is whether reflection on Buddhism as a reaction to a concrete situation will allow its basic orientation to achieve the full impact that it might. The second approach is more consistent with the way we have proceeded up until now in that it takes up the standpoint of "empty emptiness" directly and follows it through to the end. But here it remains to be shown whether the way of "empty emptiness" can deliver what it promises. In any case, we should like to give it the preference here, all the more so as Nishitani, in spite of his own mode of proceeding, has in fact given us statements on the matter that can point the way for us.

Buddhism as the Religion of the Absolute This-side

Nishitani himself has given clear expression to the dynamic of the movement back and forth between turning away from the world and turning toward the world when he says of Buddhism:

> Of course, even in Buddhism, which expounds the standpoint of emptiness, a transcendence to the yonder-side, or "other-shore," is spoken of. But in this case the transcendence is realized as a disclosure of a horizon which may be called absolute this-side in the sense that it has transcended the opposition between yonder-side and this-side. The essential characteristic of Buddhism can be said to consist in its being the religion of the absolute this-side.[14]

The movement back and forth with regard to the world comes out clearest in talk of *śūnyatā* and *tathatā*, *kū* and *shinnyo*, "emptiness" and "truth/thusness," and in the coming to be of *tathāgata* from *tathatā*. In the light of Nāgārjuna, Susumu Yamaguchi has distinguished three aspects of *śūnyatā:* (1) "emptiness" as the true nature of all beings; (2) the continuous self-effecting of emptiness as emptiness; and (3) the emptying out of emptiness as praxis of the Great Compassion. And in describing them the selfless figure of the Buddha likewise appears:

> The truth of *pratītyasamutpāda*, interdependence and non-self-existence of all existent beings, is designated as *śūnyatā* or "emptiness," in the sense that any hypostasizing apprehension of "I" and "mind" turns out to be empty in the awakening to this truth. It is further denoted as *tathatā* or "suchness," in the sense that all existent beings are seen as they really are. The one who has realized *śūnyatā* or *tathatā* is called "Buddha," the enlightened one.[15]

The life of the Buddha does not end under the bodhi tree, but finds its essential characteristic in dedication to mankind. He becomes *Tathāgata* (Jap., *nyorai*). The word may be described according to its derivation from *tathā-gata* or *tathā-āgata* as follows: "he who has reached *tathatā*" or "he who comes from *tathatā*" (that is to say, he who comes into the world in order to make the way to *tathatā* accessible to others as well).[16] The double aspect of coming and going also becomes important in the doctrine of the Pure Land (Jap. *jōdo*), principally as it was developed in the amidistic *jōdo* schools:

> The teachings, from the part of the Buddha, mean something which he, as *Tathāgata,* turns over to sentient beings. From our part, the teachings mean something turned over to us by *Tathāgata* which enables us to go to the realm of *tathatā.* In the Pure Land doctrine, the former aspect is called the "returning aspect," in the sense that the seeker for the ultimate truth now "returns" to the world of his fellow beings carrying with him the teachings to awaken and save them; the latter aspect is called the "going aspect" in the sense that we are enabled to "go" by the teachings. Underlying both aspects we see the natural, necessary flowing out of *tathatā.*[17]

In a comment added to the English translation of the second chapter of his book, Nishitani links the process of "coming and going in the thusness of the thus" as it is and as it becomes evident in the breakthrough of emptiness, with the "three-body doctrine" (Skt., *trikāya*) of Mahāyāna Buddhism.[18] In this way emptiness, compassion and selflessness come together in concern for all living things. The text itself shows to what extent the thought of Nishitani is deliberately tied up with the dynamic of Mahāyāna thought. However, it is obvious that here, too, this coming and going does not come very clearly into play as the activity of the Bodhisattva:

> *Śūnyatā* is the original nature of Eternal Buddha, of Buddha as Buddha eternally is *in actu.* It is an unchanging state of perfection of Eternal Buddha, which at all times is found already fulfilled, always in the modus of "present perfect," so to speak. In traditional Buddhist terminology, *śūnyatā* is the Dharma of Buddha, the most original and authentic way of Buddha-being. And as such, it is simultaneously the ground of the *saṃbhoga-kāya* (the "reward-body"), that is, of the way of Buddha-being in its self-manifestation as the compassionate *Tathāgata* (Thus-Come). This compassion is a compassion grounded in "emptiness." It is the so-called Great Compassion. "Emptiness" takes on here the character and meaning of *anātman* or *muga,* of non-ego or selflessness. Moreover, this Emptiness identical with the Great Compassion is the ground of the *nirmāna-kāya* (the "transformation-body") of the Buddha, that is, of the way of Buddha-being in its manifestation in the form of man as the *Tathāgata* Shakamuni. Buddha, being originally "empty" and "formless," takes the form of the Thus-Come, whether the

simple form of Buddha as in the *Saṃbhoga*-body or the double form of man-Buddha, and thus is revealed. This means essentially an *ekkenōsis* (making oneself empty) though it seems at first glance to be the contrary. The transition from being "formless" to being in form means selflessness and compassion, as in the case of a school-master playing with his children. In any case, all through the basic thought of Buddhology, especially in the Mahāyāna, the concepts of emptiness, compassion and selflessness are seen to be inseparably connected. The Buddhistic way of living as well as the way of thinking are permeated with *kenōsis* and *ekkenōsis*. *Tathā-gata* is thought to mean "Thus-Gone" as well as "Thus-Come." The reason is easy to understand, as being manifest is here insepa-rable from being hidden, being formless from being in form, empti-ness from compassion. Rather, taking form means a self-determination and self-determination means negation (or self-nega-tion). Compassion means a self-negation, that is, "making oneself empty," which is a manifestation of the original "Emptiness." Thus-Come means always Thus-Gone.[19]

Two remarks need to be made with regard to the process of the "emptying out of emptiness." First, a distinction must be drawn be-tween the situation in which man, unenlightened and ignorant, lives in the world of suffering or "wanders,"[20] and the situation of enlighten-ment. This *distinction* is rarely given full stress in deference to the great concern accorded "non-discrimination" and to the overcoming of the dualistic subject-object tension. But the question is whether this distinc-tion does not need to be maintained also with regard to the standpoint of emptiness, as an end to be achieved or as already achieved, as a not-yet and a no-more.

Secondly, as soon as emptiness is experienced, this emptiness actu-ally stresses its non-discrimination from the world "as it is." Emptiness therefore entails no new locus beyond the world, but is realized in this world. This realization is then likewise a radical, selfless compassion for everything and everyone.

This dichotomy of discrimination and non-discrimination is de-scribed by Ueda as having to do with "a dimensional encounter of non-discriminating discrimination and discriminating non-discrimination."[21] At first sight the phrase is a confusing one, but becomes more illuminat-ing when one recognizes its connections with the *soku* relationship.

At this point we are led to inquire into the actual state of the world "as it is."

World as "Nature"

When one speaks of the world, one must also speak of it as "na-ture." This is in fact the case with Nishitani's circle of associates. On the other hand, let it be stated from the outset, "world" in our day and age can no longer anywhere on earth simply be identified with "nature." The world is no more what it once was in its origin "from nature," but is a world shaped and changed by man. The "natural world" has come more and more to be a "historical world." And technology threatens continually to become a "nature of a second order."[22]

Against this question the question needs to be asked what it means to say that in emptiness everything comes to light "as it is." The concept of nature met with in Japan has various facets that need first to be singled out. First of all we may observe that the Japanese writing system allows two readings for "nature": *shizen* and *jinen.* Abe clarifies the two words in this way:

> *Shizen* is generally used as the Japanese equivalent to "nature" in English as used in the phrases "the laws of nature," "nature worship," "natural science." *Jinen* in Buddhism, on the other hand, is not nature objectively observable by man as if he were standing outside of nature. In the Orient, nature is not understood as something opposed to man but as something of which man is a part, and with which man is in harmony. Instead of utilizing nature in his own interest, man in the Orient wants to be one with nature. *Jinen* in the Buddhistic sense represents this Oriental attitude informed and deepened through the realization of the stubborness of the human ego, and through the discovery of the way of emancipation from it. Literally, *ji* means "naturally," "of itself," "by itself," "spontaneously," "for oneself," while *nen* means "being so," "being such," or "being as it is."

In similar fashion Nishitani also emphasizes that in this view of nature, what matters is that one understands "nature" neither substantially *(jittaiteki)* nor subjectively *(shutaiteki),* but in the sense of a being that is what it is *(jitaiteki)* of its own accord:

> The meaning of the word "nature" is said to be *onozukara-shikari*—being so of itself. Nature (or *"jinen"*), being so of itself, being what it is of itself—these mean that something like water, for instance, realizes itself in a given place as water, the being of which is of-itself. This water is of-itself as water. Thus, first of all, this means that no power from outside forced it to be what it is. Or, we can say that is is what it is of its own accord. This "of its own accord" *(hitorideni)* corresponds to the meaning of the Chinese character *"ji"* of *jiko* (self), or the *"shi"* of *shizen* (nature). This character has both the meaning of "of-itself" *(onozukara)* and "for-itself" *(mizukara).* Water presents itself as water "of itself." Both of these notions in one is what we call *hitorideni.*[24]

In describing this *"ji"* Nishitani excludes both the meaning of the force of nature as well as that of volitional freedom. Nishitani answers the question of how, on such a view, the particular can still remain itself/himself in a positive sense by claiming that every particular is "simply" itself, in contrast to Western thought where the distinction of essence and existence destroys this "simplicity":

> When we perceive substance or subject in this latter way, then we inevitably divide the existence of an individual thing from its essence. We grasp the being of a thing twofold. As opposed to this, on the Eastern view of "nature," the being of a thing is simply onefold—*einfach* in German, and *hitoe* in Japanese. Each individual is "onefoldly" its own self.[25]

Similarly, every particular exists in a kind of mutual interpenetration with other particulars, such that the divisions which substantial or subjective being create can fall away. In illustrating these mutual relationships, Nishitani brings us up against some further basic concepts that are significant for the understanding of his attitude to the world:

> In nature with no "framework" of being such as substance or subject, while A is A itself and B is B itself (A=A, B=B), yet at the same time, A and B penetrate each other. This is what we call *"ji-tafuni"* (self and others are not two). A and B are not fixed; they are *yūzūmuge*, interpenetrating and reciprocal—A=B, or rather A⇄B. Neither A nor B has a "framework of being." In Buddhist terms, both A and B are *mujishō*, selfless, *mujishōkū*, selfless nothingness. A is A itself and B is B itself, and yet A B is *funi*, "not two." This is, in formal logic, a contradiction. In "natural being," however, this is not a contradiction but two sides of the same coin. This is because being is being without a "framework of being." I think perhaps the Buddhist *shikisokuzekū-kūsokuzeshiki* (Matter is Void-Void is Matter) points to this way of being. This is being "of-itself" and "for-itself" as well—that is, being of-its-own-accord, being what-it-is-of-itself.[26]

These remarks provide a neat summary of what Nishitani has detailed in his book with regard to the "standpoint of emptiness." The substantiality of an essence shows up, paradoxically, at the very point where it is lost:

> Being is only being if it is one with emptiness. It is only on the field of emptiness that beings are on their own homeground, that they are truly as they are, < abiding in their own selfness >. One may say that the thing appears again as substantial, < but this substantiality does not consist in its logical self-identity, but only paradoxi-

cally, > in its self-identity with emptiness. It is an absolutely unsubstantial substantiality. If one wants to use the language of reason, the concepts of our intellectual thinking (to which substance belongs), one has to express the thing-itself as we did. That is to say, it is essentially inexpressible in words.[27]

The same holds true in the case of man. Man is only man where the field of absolute formlessness is opened up:

The "what" of a thing is a real "what" only there where it is absolutely no "what" whatsoever. The form of a thing is truly form only at one with absolute formlessness. For example, the form "human being" of "this is a human being" originates where it sheds all forms. Within every human being there is opened up a field of absolute formlessness, a field of non-determinability as "human being" or some other "what." The fact that man reveals himself as man from such a field constitutes precisely the most original meaning of his existence as man.[28]

That which seems continually to defy expression in words since it is only acquired in its actual execution, Nishitani illustrates through the image of a circumference-less circle that can have its center everywhere. If one takes this to illustrate the unity of all things, then the One can not be treated as a fixed description, as a center defined by its circumference:

There is, so to speak, a circumference-less center, a center which is a center only, a center on the field of emptiness. We could express this also by saying that on the field of emptiness the center is everywhere. Each "thing," in its selfness, manifests the mode of being the center of all things. Each and every thing, becoming the center of all things, becomes one absolute center. This is the absolute uniqueness of things, their Reality.[29]

The gathering together into a unity of all things is "the world":

"All are one" signifies the "world" as the unifying order < or system > of all things. The real feature of that world must be such as I just explained. In the above, the non-objective in-itself mode of being of things whereby each is on its own home-ground, has been called the "middle." In its mode of being as "middle," the tiniest thing, insofar as it "is," is one absolute center, and is posited in the center of all things. This is its "being," its reality. And the "world" is nothing other than the gathering of such "beings." It is the "all are one" of all that is in that mode of being. The world wherein we actually live and which we actually see is precisely that "All."[30]

At this point Nishitani asks himself how such a collection of "absolute centers" can avoid leading to a total anarchy and chaos. He finds the answer in the peculiar interrelation that obtains among all things in the world referred to earlier. Nishitani describes it in Japanese as *"egoteki kankei,"* a word that caused considerable difficulty for Van Bragt in trying to come up with an English equivalent. With due precaution he rendered it as "circuminsessional," seeking thereby to make use of a concept drawn from the doctrine of the Trinity to describe inter-Trinitarian relationships, and which is variously referred to as *"circuminsessio," circumincessio"* and *"perichoresis."*[31] He justifies his translation in this way:

> I have translated this as "circuminsessional" because the relationship described here seems to imply such a degree of reciprocity that nothing in Western culture can approximate it, except this term used to describe the relationship between the divine Persons in the Trinity. I do not suggest that the Japanese word and the English word are exact equivalents.[32]

The need for precaution with such translations is obvious. At the same time, it helps advance the cause of dialogue and encounter. For on the one hand, experience tells us that as a rule in such cases participants from the Buddhist side feel inclined not to identify too hastily with the conceptual translation but rather to stand firm, indeed as firm as possible, on the differences between Christianity and Buddhism despite their commitment to the notion of "non-discrimination." On the other hand, Asiatic thought likewise experiences a great deal of difficulty in finding the words for what needs to be said. We may recall here Nishitani's expressed claim that we have to do here with a realm which in essence repudiates all verbal expression.[33] It is little wonder, then, that he is better at saying what he does not mean than at saying what he does.

Reciprocal interpenetration—the "circuminsessional relationship" *(egoteki kankei)* brings it about in every case that the self in its autonomy also subjugates itself to all others selflessly.[34] In this way, there comes to light a "power" (Jap., *chikara*) that gathers everything that is together into a reciprocal relationship.[35] This same reciprocal interpenetration obtains between different periods of time, between time and place, and even between this world and other actual or possible existent worlds.[36]

Yet even when the one no longer gets in the way of the other (Jap., *jijumuge*) nor the non-particular in the way of the particular *(rijimuge),*[37] the question of this time and this place, of the before and the after, of the historical moment, the historical situation and the historical deed, and of the role of man in the course of the world still remains. What does it mean for the world that not just anybody but I come to enlightenment, or can I go my own way uninterested and indifferent to enlightenment or non-enlightenment?

The Role of Man in the "World"

We have already spoken of man in another context in discussing the I-Thou relationship and nothingness (Ch. 6). There it was essentially a question of how man can survive as man in the locus of nothingness. Nishitani has come to a solution regarding the I-Thou relationship that we may now describe belatedly as a realization of a "circuminsessional relationship" *(egoteki kankei).*

It remains for us now to take up directly the question of the humanity of man in relation to all other worldly being and to inquire into what role man plays as man in the world. One's first spontaneous reaction might be that there is no special role in the world to be finally assigned to man. The anthropocentrism found in the West—Abe, like Nishitani, adopts the unhappy English neologism "homocentricism"—[38] is treated with mistrust. Even in the "man-centeredness" of traditional thought Nishitani sees a special danger for our times.[39] He criticizes religion for being too much oriented toward man up until now:

> Generally speaking, religions hitherto have shown too much the character of being oriented toward man. Even when "God" or "gods" have been thought about, they have been conceived in such a way that their concern has been exclusively directed to the affairs of a certain nation or of mankind at large. Conversely, man has understood his own relationship to "God" or "gods" solely in connection with his own demands and purposes. Consequently, even when man has tried to understand himself in a religious way, his viewpoint has been oriented toward himself.[40]

In contrast, the natural sciences no longer treat things in coordination with man. Indeed, they dehumanize man and reduce him to the mechanisms of nature:

> The image of the universe it [modern science] views is totally exempt from the character of an environment for man and is not in any sense man-oriented . . .
> However, it must be said that modern science, while bringing about brilliant results in its inquiry into the natural world, has been unable to come in contact with the essence of man and has exposed itself as an inadequate way to approach the investigation of man himself . . . The consequence has been that a confusion has arisen

and still prevails today, a confusion in which those sciences so often mistake man himself to be a mechanism.[41]

The solution to human misery does not lie, for Nishitani, in man's reinforcing his self-affirmation, but in recognizing that he belongs to an encompassing realm that is no longer merely human. Nishitani describes this realm with the term "being-in-the-world" which he borrows from the second chapter of Heidegger's *Being and Time,* and goes on to interpret this "being-in-the world" in the sense of the Buddhist term *"shujōteki":*

> At the extremity of human existence the essence of human being is no longer merely "human." It rather shows the character of "sentient being" [*shujōteki*] in the sense that it includes in itself all other forms of existence.[42]

The word *"shujō"* (*"teki"* is an adjectival ending added to the substantive) is deliberately untranslated at first. In its origins it goes back to the Sanskrit word *"sattva"* which played an important role above all in the philosophy of the *Sāṃkhya.* There it stood for one of the three attributes (Skt., *guṇa*) of basic matter. Konow translates the word as "being-being" and elaborates thus:

> The first and most excellent of the *guṇa* is *sattva,* being-being, which corresponds to the *sat* or being of the *Vedānta. Sattva* is the truth in matter and meets us in light and lightness, in purity, good fortune, cheer and happiness, in virtue, self-mastery, peace of mind, well-wishing and friendliness.[43]

Dōgen provides the immediate context from which Nishitani derives his understanding of *shujō.*[44] It is precisely in reference to him that Nishitani is indeed able to shift *shujō* closer to "being-in-the-world" at all, and to bring together in it the living and the non-living alike.[45] In its strict sense, *shujō* signifies initially only the total realm of the living in this world, that is of *saṃsāra,* the succession of life and death:

> The term *shujō, sattva* in Sanskrit, means all the living, i.e., living beings which are in *saṃsāra,* the round of birth-and-death. Buddhist texts show that the term *shujō* is interpreted in one of two ways: in its narrow sense it refers to "human beings" and in its broad sense, "living beings."[46]

If one seeks a common dimension that binds man to the full range of beings, the fact is that through life and death he shares in common with all beings the nature of coming to be and passing away:

This common dimension may be said to be *shōmetsusei, utpādni-rodha*, the generation-extinction nature. Man's "birth-and-death" *(shōji)* is a human form of "generation-and-extinction" that is common to all living beings. Although the problem of birth-and-death is regarded in Buddhism as the most fundamental problem for human existence, Buddhism does not necessarily approach this as a "birth-death" problem on a "human" dimension, but as a "generation-extinction" problem on a dimension of "living beings."[47]

Moreover this partaking in all beings must embrace the living and the non-living alike. Just as birth and death belong to the dimension of generation and extinction, so also does each in turn belong to the dimension of appearing and disappearing:

The dimension of all beings is no longer that of generation-extinction, but that of appearance-disappearance *(kimetsu)* or being-non-being *(u-mu)*. The "living" dimension, though trans-homocentric, has a life-centered nature that excludes non-living beings. The "being" dimension, however, embraces everything in the universe, by transcending even the wider-than-human "life-centered" horizon. Accordingly the "being" dimension is truly boundless, free from any sort of centrism, and deepest precisely in its dehomocentric nature.[48]

Thus does the process of "dehomocentrism" come to its end. What was said earlier with regard to the world as a whole shows up here again in Dōgen:

To attain the Buddha nature, one must transcend one's egocentrism, homocentrism, and living being-centrism, and thereby ground his existence in the most fundamental plane, that is, in the "being" dimension, which is the dimension of Dōgen's *shitsuu*, i.e., "all beings."[49]

Abe calls this dimension of Dōgen a "thoroughly cosmological dimension."[50] It would still have to be shown how this "cosmological" thought, freed of every egocentricism, anthropocentrism and biocentrism would stand up to a view of man that sees man as a microcosmos. Similarly, in this regard the usual Western interpretation of *samsāra* (Jap. *rinne*) as a "transmigration of the soul" or a "rebirth" would have to come up for reconsideration. But we must refrain from such questions here.[51]

Instead we must inquire further into the meaning of man in general, and of the individual man in particular, within the framework of the cosmological dimension. In a symposium devoted to Abe's thought on

"Buddhism and Christianity as a Problem of Today" I posed the following question:

> Has *man* as man and the *finitude* of man in its positive aspect ever been taken seriously into consideration by Buddhist scholars? The extension of *shujō* (sentient beings) to man, animals and even to everything, as it is found in Dōgen, makes this doubtful.[52]

After treating the thesis of the overcoming of the homocentricism of man, Abe expressly asserted, in terms clearer than Nishitani:

> The non-homocentric nature of Buddhism and its idea of *jinen*, however, do not imply, as is often mistakenly suggested, any denial of the significance of individualized human existence.[53]

The meaning of human existence lies precisely in that man is the being in which, by reason of his self-consciousness, the "fact" of the transitoriness of all being becomes a "problem" to be solved:

> Since only man who has self-consciousness can realize the nature of generation-extinction as such, this becomes for man a "problem" to be solved rather than a "fact." When a "fact" becomes a "problem" the possibility of solving the problem is also present, i.e., the possibility to be liberated from transmigration. Because of this peculiarity of man, Buddhism emphasizes the need for him to practice Buddhist discipline to attain enlightenment while he, though transmigrating endlessly through other forms of life, exists *as a man.*[54]

Just as *saṃsāra* becomes a problem in man, it follows then that *nirvāṇa* becomes the solution to the problem in man. But that takes place not in mankind "as a whole" but in individual human existence:

> The realization of transmigration is a personal realization for one's self (ego), not for human existence in general. Apart from one's self-realization there can be no "problem" of birth-and-death, generation-and-extinction. Only through one's self-realization one can attain *nirvāṇa* by solving the problem of generation-extinction, i.e., the problem of *saṃsāra.*[55]

In other words, the particular individual ego must at times die in order to become aware of the fullness of reality as it is:

> Buddhist salvation is thus nothing other than awakening to Reality through the death of ego, i.e. the existential realization of the tran-

siency common to all things in the universe, seeing the universe really *as it is*. In this realization one is liberated from undue attachment to things and ego-self, humanity and the world, and is then able to live and work creatively in the world.[56]

The realization of reality as it is represents at the same time an epistemic procedure that Nishitani calls "knowledge of no-knowledge." For although at this point also a special role falls to everything "objective" vis-à-vis the "subject," the realization of reality must not be located on a plane of objective, reflecting knowledge. Rather it takes place on a "field" that lies beyond:

> This is a place where the standpoint of consciousness, discursive (discriminating) intellect and intuitive intellect, is broken through: a place beyond the domain of the standpoint of the subject that knows things objectively and knows itself as an object or thing called the self.
>   This not-knowing is the self as an absolutely non-objective self-in-itself [*jitai toshite no jiko*]. And the self-awareness which originates in that not-knowing is a kind of "knowledge of no-knowledge."[57]

Whenever the ego threatens to raise up its head, it is put back in its place. One continually faces the fear that a false attachment to the ego will find its way back in again through a little back door. Thus the battle over non-duality and non-substantiality, over the conquest of the tension between subject and object, practice and enlightenment, act and potency, means and end, *saṃsāra* and *nirvāṇa*.[58] In the light of Rinzai's understanding of the person (Jap., *nin*), Suzuki has given expression to the fundamental difference between Western and Eastern concerns with being human:

> There is a sentence in the Zen records: "A mind-wheel never has turned; the moment it does, it invariably turns into two." Grasp the point prior to this "turning into two"—that is what I call Person. They speak of the union of man with God, but what we must grasp is that in which God and man have not yet assumed their places. The two situations, therefore, are substantially different. Rinzai's Person has nothing to do with the humanistic thought people so often talk about today. The fundamental difference lies in this: while the one aims at what comes after division, the other aims at what is prior to division. Our problem is how to grasp this undivided something.[59]

Yet in all defensive argumentation aimed at preserving the fundamental insight of Buddhism, it must not be overlooked that precisely in and through this insight a superior place is accorded to man. Should not then the question of the responsibility of man for "what comes after division" also be pursued with still greater courage?

History as the Locus of Samsāra and Nirvāna

In connection with the *Statements of Lin-chi* (Jap., *Rinzairoku*), Suzuki finds the realization of the true man (Jap., *nin*) in the struggle for what comes before all division. Conscious that even the smallest movement is already accompanied by division, Lin-chi (Jap., Rinzai) is nevertheless concerned with communicating the incommunicable:

> The very moment something begins to move even the slightest bit, it runs into two. So the question is how to grasp what is prior to this movement. When we refer to something prior to even the arising of this concern, it appears to make no sense at all. And yet this is in fact the ultimate reality. What is interesting is this ability to communicate the incommunicable. The whole of the *Sayings of Rinzai* is also nothing but a communication of what transcends ordinary communication.[60]

This communication of the incommunicable, however, takes place in time and history. And the danger endures that in the succession of yesterday-today-tomorrow, of past-present-future, the claim of plurality may again come to light and that the promotion of non-duality may return to question. Nishitani offers an answer to the effect that the true self stands in its "selfness" in the "time outside of time":

> The in-itself-ness < (selfness) > of the self—insofar as the self is "being self," is "being"—lies radically in *time*, or rather, is bottomlessly in time. At the same time, on the field of emptiness—insofar as the being of the self is being only at one with emptiness, insofar as the self is "not being self"—the self is, in every instant of time, < wholly > outside of time. In that sense I have said above that everyone's self is originally anterior to world and things.[61]

The understanding of time itself is thus brought into characteristic relief. For "being-in-time" also means life in *samsāra,* in the cycle from birth to death. And then, in that case, a "living and dying" of this cycle itself takes place from the standpoint of emptiness:

> We live and die in time. "To be in time" means to be constantly inside the birth-death cycle. But it is not true that we are merely in time, inside the birth-death cycle. In the home-ground of ourselves, we are not simply drifting around in birth-death; we live and die birth-death. We do not simply live in time; we live time. In every moment of time, we are making time be time, we are bringing time

to its fullness. That is the meaning of what I said before: being bot-tomlessly in time.[62]

The ambiguity of time—the cycle of coming to be and passing away and the conquest of the cycle, self-assertion and self-enclosure and endless disclosure in selflessness—all this comes to light fully in the standpoint of emptiness. For it makes time the locus of fundamental change, of "conversion" and "rethinking."[63]

All time is revealed in every now, and in like manner the mutual penetration and absolute relativity of all times become clear. Moreover, every time is "this time," i.e., an opportunity, a "kairos" in which reali-ty is what it is or, as the Zen phrase puts it: "Every day a good day."[64]

Nishitani himself has expressed this ambiguity as well as the mean-ingfulness of every moment in time in clear terms:

On the field of emptiness, all times enter into each moment. In this circuminsessional interpenetration of "Time," or in Time itself, which only originates as such in interpenetration, namely, in the absolute relativity of Time on the field of emptiness, all times are phantom-like, and all "being" of things in Time is equally phan-tom-like.

Nevertheless, on the field of emptiness, each time is this time or that time in its "as-such" reality as it actually is. Or, it may be stated that, because in the field of emptiness each time is bottom-lessly "Time," all times enter into each time. And, only as a bot-tomless thing wherein all times can enter, each time actually comes into being as this or that time as it really is. Like-reality and like-phantom have to be at one. The essence of "Time" lies precisely therein.[65]

Viewed from another angle, history can be called the unending realm stretching from the past into the future of the "three worlds" in which *"karma"* (Jap., *gō*), by virtue of a demythologized and reinter-preted understanding of the doctrine of rebirth (*saṃsāra,* Jap., *rinne*),[66] is revealed as a burden. So viewed, history is a burden insofar as man feels continually pushed to accomplish, one way or another, something "new":

In the term *"karma"* is expressed the awareness of an existence wherein "being" and "time" constitute for us an infinite burden, and, at the same time, the awareness of the essence of time.

In short, in "ever-new newness" two sides are simultaneously included: the side of creation, freedom and infinite possibility, and the side of infinite burden and inescapable necessity. This "new-ness" is essentially ambiguous; which means that time is essentially ambiguous.[67]

In order to deal with this historical burden, Nishitani had already quite early on turned his attention to Western interpretations of history as well, including Christian eschatological doctrine, the theories of history of the Enlightenment, and Nietzsche's "will to power."[68] What disturbs him about all of these interpretations is their common tendency to lay the emphasis on will, and this is true of the theocentric standpoints as well as the anthropocentric and egocentric ones, and of course also in the "will to power."

The overcoming of all these "centricisms" occurs, for Nishitani, with the substitution of the locus of emptiness for the locus of *karma*.[69] The preference that the locus of emptiness is accorded in favor of all other interpretations of history consists in that it is the place of *anātman* (Jap., *muga*), of the "falling away of body and soul" (Jap., *shinjin-datsuraku*) in Dōgen's phrase. Thereby *anātman*, selflessness, is unveiled as the true self on the basis of the doctrine of the middle way expressed in "*soku.*" For from the standpoint of emptiness

non-ego [*muga*] cannot simply mean that the self is non-ego; it has to mean at the same time that non-ego is self. In other words, the self should come to self-awareness as the achievement [*shōki*] of a point where the self is absolute negation of the self. It cannot only be that the self is not "self" (is non-ego), but has to be that the self is self because it is not self.[70]

When it comes to the realization of this self⇄non-self, an exchange of centers results as well. Self-centering becomes other-centering, other-centering becomes self-centering;[71] and the previously mentioned standpoint of the "*jitafuni*" (self and other are not two)[72] is achieved.[73] Further, "time," perceived as "kairos" becomes one in its three forms of foreground/preliminary (Jap., *ke*), emptiness *(kū)* and middle *(chū),* wherein the "middle" becomes the full "realization of reality" in "*soku.*"[74]

With this Nishitani reaches the point where he can bring into the discussion the full gravity of time and indeed of every particular moment and point in time. This gravity of time is as familiar to Christianity as it is to the way of the Bodhisattva:

On this "Bodhisattva Path," every historical "time"-point which penetrates into the field of emptiness, is to be an infinitely grave and solemn time. In Christianity, the most solemn moments are, no doubt, the moment that God created the world, the moment that Adam committed his sin, the moments of Christ's birth and resurrection, and the moment of the end of the world when the trumpets will sound and Christ will come again. Or, one may say perhaps that the moment wherein the self is brought to conversion

is the solemn moment that truly realizes the solemity of these moments.

From the viewpoint of the Bodhisattva Path, every single moment of infinite time has the solemn gravity that these privileged
moments possess in Christianity.[75]

Finally, Nishitani gives a concrete illustration of the posture of the
Bodhisattva in his love of all creatures, but does not refer to one of the
historical figures of Buddhism. Instead he directs our view to Francis of
Assisi in whose attitude toward life he recognizes the same thing that he
himself, from the standpoint of emptiness or absolute openness,[76] had
seen at work in the *"da"* of *Da-sein."*[77] Maurus Heinrichs, who has
translated excerpts from this concluding section of the book into German,[78] makes a strong point of emphasizing what, in his view, is lacking
in Nishitani's interpretation of St. Francis: the theological-Christologi-
cal background to Francis's attitude. Whether, as he suggests, the
"breakthrough" of man in his authenticity and the "break in" of over-
flowing divine grace must really be set in opposition to one another[79] is
another question that needs more careful looking at. It should have to
be demonstrated that the opening up into absolute openness through
selflessness that Nishitani adjures is really to be identified in the end
with human autocracy, and also that this selflessness does not cry out
itself to be completed. And such demonstrations are not easily come by.
Could not after all his choice of Francis, with his love for all things, embracing them as brother and sister, as an example itself be a sign of Buddhist selflessness willing to recognize its own true self in the "other,"
the Christian?

Open Questions

Inasmuch as the Mahāyāna way of speaking from which Nishitani's thought draws its life is not accessible through the kind of statements that would have us name it as pantheism, monism or nihilism, we
must for that very reason look to its strong points instead. As may already be clear, its chief strength lies in its renunciation of every last
trace of self-affirmation and self-sufficiency in the sense of a final and
radical self-emptying-out and self-opening-up, as well as in its presump-
tion of the renewed danger of reestablishing the self implied in all attempts to ground this renunciation positively.

Renunciation, however, is a matter both of language and of behavior. When language itself threatens to create a new "position" through
its negations, it must, to remain true to its radicality, "subsume" these
statements into speechlessness. Renunciation can then only be a matter
of pure and speechless activity. That this letting go into speechlessness
does not entail a letting go into a renunciation emptied of all meaning
but is rather a letting go into unspeakable freedom, is also a matter of

experience. And this, in turn, provided it is not lost, can only be shared when men with the same experience come together in speechless communication. Nishitani illustrates this experience of speechless communication through the example of two people in love:

> Let us leave God and man out of the picture . . . and take two people who love one another as husband and wife. They sit together in the same room. Each goes about his own business. They say nothing to one another. They don't need to. Only from time to time do they look at one another. They understand one another completely—without a word.[80]

Presupposing the experience of wordless communication, recourse to the realm where it is not the experience of wordless communication but of worded communication that is had becomes all the more necessary. Nishitani says in this connection:

> The usual forms of communications through gesture, word, the expression of emotion and the like always remain somewhat half and incomplete. If they wish to be brought to completeness, they must forever pass beyond themselves and return to that mode of communication which is really no longer communication.[81]

If the formula "affirmation-*sive*-negation, negation-*sive*-affirmation" is still to retain its validity, the locus of "gesture, word, the expression of emotion and the like" must be fully acknowledged as the point at which wordless communication is embodied. And then the question becomes: has Nishitani really taken seriously this my speech, this my body, this my kairos in the sense of my historical situation in space and time in which my true ego acts in egolessness? Some thought must be given here to the fact that when Nishitani enumerates the "grace and solemn moments" of Christianity he mentions especially the moments of the birth and resurrection of Jesus but omits the moment which is all decisive for Christian belief, the death of Jesus. When human existence is seen as "living and at the same time dying" and hence, as Abe says, *"Our living-dying existence itself is death,"*[82] the Christian can refer back to the words of St. Paul, "I face death every day" (I Cor. 15:31). And yet, for the friends and colleagues surrounding him today, the question of the significance of that special moment in which Nishitani himself dies, in the everyday meaning of that word, remains open.

The concern over falling into new forms of dualism forbids the overt distinction between a "before" and an "after" to death. But it cannot be forbidden to distinguish between man with and man without enlightenment, between a "before" and "after" to enlightenment. Being consistent with the repudiation of all distinction would prohibit all dialogue and would have to end in the challenge to muteness or, more precisely, in muteness itself, as in the case of Vimalakīrti.[83] Yet for all the admiration of the silent figure in Buddhism itself since the time of the Buddha, we invariably encounter the image of new words being born from silence. Here it may remain open to question whether these words are definite statements or only catalysts, noting only that there are at least those negative limiting statements that serve to keep the middle way open and make it recognizable as such. In this sense there may indeed be many "forms of communication through gesture, words, the expression of emotion and the like" that are "half and incomplete." They are, however, themselves also "whole and complete" to the extent that they make room for "wholeness and completeness."

From Ueda we learned of the distinction between "original non-discrimination" and "destructive non-discrimination"; and from Abe, that between "non-thinking" and "not thinking."[84] Hints of this sort deserve in fact to be worked out thoroughly in the light of the Buddhist starting point. Discrimination is most obviously necessary when it is meaningful and indeed necessary to distinguish one's own standpoint from that of the other participant in the dialogue. But are meaningful discussions on "meaningful and indeed necessary distinctions" possible when good and evil are viewed as a "problem of the discriminating mind" so that the overcoming of good and evil consist in being liberated from the discriminating mind?

> Zen grasped the problem of good and evil not as a problem of free will, but as that of the *discriminating mind* which distinguishes the two dimensions of good and evil. Zen advocated that we must awaken to No-mind itself which transcends all discrimination . . .
>
> In Zen, therefore, the problem of good and evil is of course a real one, but it is grasped, not as a problem of the moral will and its laws, but as one of discriminating mind, and, in the last analysis, of objective substantive thinking which establishes the duality. Together with and in the same way as is the problem of life and death, the problem of good and evil is transcended in Non-thinking which is liberated from discriminating mind itself.[85]

For his part, Abe has issued the call for further details on the question of the relation of "is" to "ought."[86] At this point we should like also to make a request for more courage vis-à-vis concrete "reality as it is." It is an expression that can hardly be employed without a certain ambiguity. And yet in fundamental Buddhist thought, it is clear that it refers to the reality of things as they are experienced on the ground of experiential selflessness:

> That this staff is this staff is a fact which factualizes itself in such a way as to involve there, at the same time, the deliverance of the self. There, the fact manifests itself in its original factuality.[87]

The view of things as they are, however, also brings to light that other provocative trait that does not come fully to bear in Nishitani's work in spite of his appeal to the path of the Bodhisattva. Namely, much in this world is as it is without being what it is in its originally intended sense. It is the difference between what *is* and what *should* be or what *could* be. Here the question arises whether things as they are do not call for more than a simple knowledge of things as they are. It strikes us that "things as they are" is mostly described through examples from nature, of mountains and rivers, of birds and flowers, sun and moon. But for the man of today, "things as they are" are machines, electricity and atomic power, artificial products and manipulation, as well as hunger and war, infrequent peace, social injustice, political uncertainty, pollution. In this world in need of change, the gospel of selflessness has no doubt an appeal of its own. But can selflessness leave others in the marketplace of the world alone? In what does compassion for a tortured creation, for man and all living things in the world, consist? Where is salvation to be found?

This kind of question may sound obvious and superficial. Nonetheless, the philosophy of emptiness, particularly in the sense of the oft-cited *"soku"* formula, is responsible for providing answers. There is a correlation between the gravity with which the surface of things is taken and the gravity with which their depths are plumbed. If this philosophy is to be a workable one for the marketplace of the world, then the answers must come forth with corresponding greater clarity.

Part Three

STEPPING STONES FOR DIALOGUE

8. Mystical Experience
and Philosophical Reflection

Our presentation of Nishitani's philosophy of emptiness ended in a series of open questions. Providing them with answers is no doubt important both for those who do the questioning as for those who are being questioned. On the other hand, the presentation challenges us to take a stance, or at least to enter into discussion on this kind of philosophy as a whole. The only question is whether all of us—the participants in the dialogue from Kyoto on the one side, and Christian participants from the West both Protestant and (in my own case) Catholic on the other side—are sufficiently prepared for this kind of discussion.

In order truly to be foundational a dialogue cannot be made to conform to a plan. Its results cannot be deliberately programmed in advance, but should themselves properly issue as "results." Dialogue is thus seen as an experience to which both sides submit themselves selflessly, that is to say not with the intention of coming out victorious but simply of allowing the truth to come to light as it is. For such dialogue to take place, all the participants must indeed be able to listen. Barriers that threaten to impede full and mutual understanding are, as far as possible, to be left to one side. Whether this has been the case all along may rightly be called into question.

Looking at the Occidental-Western world, an openness to and sympathy for what is foreign, and more particularly for Asiatic thought as well, is no doubt on the increase. On the other hand, it is not without good reason that thinkers like Katsumi Takizawa, whom Nishida had sent to Karl Barth and who returned to Japan with an inner conviction of the "God-with-us," have complained:

I have . . . sadly all too often observed how most Christians among us, and this includes not only foreign missionaries but indigenous believers as well, completely miss the essence of Buddhism. In discussions with them I often had the feeling as if I were a poor child misunderstood by grown-ups who could not explain himself to their scoldings but yet knew all along that in reality things were not as they thought.[1]

What Takizawa says of the Christians of his own country holds true all the more so for Western Christianity.

Looking at Japan, the first thing one runs up against is the problem of language. The fact should not escape our attention that often enough it is to the Japanese that falls not only the task of translating non-Japanese texts into their mother tongue, but also that of rendering their own texts into foreign languages. This shows only too clearly how far removed we still are from a cultural "exchange" in the sense of a *reciprocal* give-and-take; for such double-translating is rather an "exchange" of asking-and-taking. And that leads in turn to the fatal result that certain points of Christian doctrine, even if they are falsely or imprecisely rendered, are taken over by Japanese intellectuals without dispute and uncritically:

> As a matter of fact, Japanese scholars know more about Western thought and Christianity than the average Western scholar knows about Eastern thought in general and Japanese thought and Buddhism in particular. However, this fact could lead to the fatal result that the concrete understanding of Christianity and Western thought common among non-Christian Japanese scholars is hardly ever questioned and, therefore, finally handed down from one generation to the next in a somewhat dogmatic manner.[2]

Van Bragt sees three tendencies responsible for this: (1) the tendency to judge Christianity by the writings of modern Western philosophers without drawing distinctions among philosophy, theology and the fundamental experience of faith; (2) the tendency to view Christianity onesidedly from particular Protestant authors, and to view Christian mysticism primarily from the standpoint of Eckhart; and (3) the tendency to disregard the Roman-Catholic tradition of Christianity.[3]

This situation, which is unsatisfactory from both sides, explains why we have restricted the aim of this final section from the start. We cannot be concerned with hazarding definitive judgments but must content ourselves rather with laying down a few stepping stones for dialogue—not all that needs to be laid down and perhaps not even the most important ones. In any event, we shall draw upon the aid of Catholic tradition and its theology to meet this aim, and shall concentrate on three topics.

First we must consider the fact that philosophy, as it is pursued by Nishitani following in the footsteps of Nishida, seeks to lead into the realm of "knowing unknowing"[4] wherein words and thoughts are no longer available.[5] What N. A. Nikam has to say of Indian philosophy and explains as valid for its contemporary forms as well, holds true, *mutatis mutandis,* also for this form of Japanese philosophy:

> In Indian thought philosophy is not primarily "thinking" *about* reality but rather an experience *of* reality, and as such a verified and verifiable experience.[6]

The resultant problem area is the relationship of language to unspeakable limit situations, of philosophical reflection to mystical experience. The long history of the relationship between cataphatic and apophatic theology deserves attention in this regard.

Secondly, insofar as theology manifests itself as "talk about God," our inquiry must direct itself to this "God" of theology. At this point the philosophy of emptiness poses anew the question of the relation of being and nothingness, of being, nothingness and reality, of being and nothingness, reality and God. But the locus of the experience of nothingness and of the experience of God is man. Hence the relationship between God and man, God and world, comes once more into play. And we are led further to ask how seriously the question of God has been taken in the philosophy of emptiness up to the present.

Finally, not without good reason Masao Abe has stressed in his review of Nishitani's work that the problem of personality ought to have been treated not only as a problem of the relationship of "nothingness and emptiness," but also of the relationship of "sin and emptiness" or of "belief and emptiness." Hence his complaint, referred to earlier,[7] that Nishitani almost completely abstains from reference to Jesus Christ in his treatment of the God question. In fact, the question would have to be faced here to what extent the fundamental doctrines of Christian belief in the widely disparate traditions of Christianity were taken cognizance of in the philosophy of emptiness, and that moreover precisely as they are in fact confessed by communities of faith. Moreover, interest in Christian mysticism[8] must take seriously the historical starting point of the Christian faith-experience, the figure of Jesus of Nazareth.

Perhaps it is the fear of falling back, in the end, into a dualism that explains why the manifold distinctions that first made possible the way of *ortho*doxy as a way that defined itself by "negation" in steering clear of the extremes set up to the left and the right pass by unnoticed; and why the basic mysteries of the incarnation of God, of the one and triune God, and of "God in the world" and "the world in God" as they were revealed in Jesus of Nazareth barely show up at all. In view of the logic of *"soku-hi," "sive-non"* through which identity-through-negation is realized in the Kyoto School, one wonders whether this insight might not also be extended, to be consequential, also in the direction of fundamental Christian doctrines and experiences. When reflection on *"soku"* clearly excludes unequivocal identity, and therefore leaves the way opened for a qualified identity, perhaps entirely new and unexpected possibilities are finally brought to light.

The sense of these concluding considerations, in any case, can only be one of opening up dialogue and keeping it open, not bringing it to term. The danger of premature closure for a dialogue that has scarcely begun is a real one for both sides: for Christianity when it promotes submission even where radical self-surrender and selflessness are still in the process of continual realization; and for Buddhism when it continues, in the end, to distort the process of radical selflessness and self-opening through false limitations. For both sides, the only point of radical encounter is the point of the radical letting go of the self.

*   *   *

All reflection, including the philosophical when it is properly undertaken, is grounded in experience. Now according to Gadamer, the notion of experience belongs among the most unclear of notions that we possess, above all since it has been seriously deprived of its historicity in the realm of the modern natural sciences. But experience, in its authentic sense, is not something repeatable but unexpected and unrepeatable:

> The same thing cannot become again a new experience for us; only some other unexpected thing can provide someone who has experience with a new one. Thus the experiencing consciousness has reversed its direction, i.e., it has turned back on itself. The experiencer has become aware of his experience, he is "experienced." He has acquired a new horizon within which something can become an experience for him.[9]

The fulfillment of experience, accordingly, does not consist in comprehensive knowledge but in the openness to new experience:

> The dialectic of experience has its own fulfillment not in definitive knowledge, but in that openness to experience that is encouraged by experience itself.[10]

In the end, experience is a learning through suffering: "the knowledge of the limitations of humanity, of the absoluteness of the barrier that sets him off from the divine."[11] It is a "religious insight":

> Real experience is that in which man becomes aware of his finiteness. In it are discovered the limits of the power and the self-knowledge of his planning reason. It proves to be an illusion that everything can be reversed, that there is always time for everything and that everything somehow returns. The person who is involved and acts in history continually experiences, rather, that nothing re-

turns. "To recognize what is" does not mean to recognize what is just at this moment there, but to have insight into the limitations within which the future is still open to expectation and planning or, even more fundamentally, that all the expectation and planning of finite beings is finite and limited. Thus true experience is that of one's own historicality.[12]

Nishitani's thought also leads to the limits of—and indeed would like to drive still further ahead into the reaches of "knowing unknowing" *(muchi no chi)*—where the intellect ceases to know and the "natural light" of things as they are shines beyond the duality of seer and seen:

Such knowledge of things-in-themselves (which is knowledge of no-knowledge) means nothing other than that we, in truly returning to our own home-ground, return to the home-ground of things which realize themselves in the world. It is realization (comprehension) as return and entrance into the home-ground where things < originate and > come to appearance in their true < (and "likely") > reality. Return and entrance into the point where "things" non-objectively realize themselves and posit themselves (into their *position* or their *samadhi*-being) is, for the self, immediately equivalent to the self's return and entrance into its own home-ground. This is knowledge of no-knowledge.

In a word, it is the non-objective knowing of the non-objective thing itself. This knowing, therefore, does not rely on the faculty of reason . . . Reason has traditionally been called "the natural light," but the true "natural light" is not reason . . .

The "natural light" within us is, more basically, the light of things themselves, coming to us from all things. The light that illumines us from our own home-ground and originally brings us to self-awareness, is nothing other than the non-objective in-itself "being" of things which obtains on the field where they realize themselves from their own home-ground.[13]

When Nishitani looks for analogies to his concerns in the Western world, he finds them, as had Nishida and Suzuki, in the realm of mysticism and above all in the Rhine mysticism centering about Meister Eckhart.[14] In this same regard, Dumoulin has spoken of the Zen experience as a natural mysticism contrasting with the experience of Christian mysticism.[15] Similarly, Enomia-Lassalle has repeatedly likened Zen to the experiences of Christian mysticism.[16] D. T. Suzuki, although himself having published a book on *Mysticism Christian and Buddhist: The Eastern and Western Way* in 1957, later came to take a critical view of such comparisons. In a book review of Dumoulin's *A History of Zen Buddhism* he writes:

> I cannot go further without remarking on the major contention of this book, which is that Zen is a form of mysticism. Unfortunately, some years ago, I too used the term in connection with Zen. I have long since regretted it, as I find it now highly misleading in elucidating Zen thought. Let it suffice to say here that Zen has nothing "mystical" about it or in it. It is most plain, clear as the daylight, all out in the open with nothing hidden, dark, obscure, secret or mystifying in it.[17]

Elsewhere, in a discussion with Ueda, he again takes occasion to contrast mysticism with the "clarity" of Zen:

> Mysticism takes it as something hidden, mysterious. That is the defect in mysticism. In truth it is something apparent in full grandeur, something presenting itself in all clarity right before us. It is unveiled, totally unbared.[18]

Accordingly, before inquiring into the role of language in relation to experience and reflection, and treating it more directly in light of the irrepeatability and unexpectability of experience, of the knowledge of no knowledge and direct mystical experiencing, a few remarks on the understanding of mysticism would seem to be in order. The clarification of what is meant by the term "mysticism" will ultimately also affect the question of whether Meister Eckhart is to be spoken of as a mystic or not.

Remarks on the Subject of Mysticism

The chief difficulty we encounter here is that the question of criteria for judging mystical experience is often settled in advance of the attempt to describe such experiences. Asked in what true mysticism consists, Karl Rahner replied in a letter to K. P. Fischer:

> I mean only (most modestly and hesitatingly) that the first and original experience of the Spirit of which I seek to speak is also the innermost core of what one may call mysticism. Hence, since what I mean by the experience of the Spirit is a faith-experience in its authentic and original sense, mysticism (in the usual sense of the word) is not a higher "stage" above normal faith but a definite kind of this faith-experience, one which belongs "as such," in itself, to natural psychology and to man's natural potentials for "medita-

tion," concentration, the emptying of the mind, etc. If this "kind" of graced experience of the Spirit as such is explained as "natural" it is not thereby devalued. In fact someone can find God in His most immediate sharing of Himself in selflessly giving his soup to a poor man and going hungry himself. This very natural sort of helping one's neighbor can "in itself" be very natural and yet be the concrete process in which and through whose mediation the most radical acceptance of the sharing of the Spirit and experience of the Spirit which signifies salvation and eternity takes place. Thus the phenomena of meditation, of modelessness [*Weiselosigkeit*], of stillness, silence, emptiness, of the absolute loss of self, etc. can be ways in which and in whose midst the experience of God's silence and unspeakable sharing of Himself is more radically and "purely" accepted: in a radical freedom that gathers man completely together.[19]

Rahner's attempt to answer the question of "authentic mysticism" leads to the question of the relationship between "natural" and "supernatural" mysticism, between mysticism as a phenomenon that can be grasped and described psychologically and the theological interpretations of the meaning of expressly Christian and non-Christian experience, between mysticism as original experience and the study of mysticism as reflected talk within a definite system of language and thought which aims at that "first and original experience of the Spirit." Rahner describes this original experience in the idiom of a Catholic theologian. It would have to be seen how far a non-Christian, translating into his own idiom, would be able to endorse it. In any case, the theoretically simple division into "natural" and "supernatural" mysticism is not of much practical use. Hans Urs von Balthasar makes a similar remark:

The fundamental availability of divine grace to everyone—wherein the visible realm of the churchly is transcended—allows no judgment concerning when, within a stirring of "natural mysticism," for instance that of a Hindu or a Sufi, the sphere of the living God is experientially come into touch with and when not. Indeed one may agree with Jacques Maritain that in "transcendental meditation" man could reach the point of discerning the very substance of his own soul; but no one can hinder the living God from making himself known in this same vision if he feels like it. Something of the kind must have happened to Carl Albrecht when he found the way to the Catholic Church on the basis of such an experience.[20]

Albrecht, who has gone into the phenomenon of mysticism not as a theologian but as a psychologist and medical doctor, has, in his two foundational volumes, *The Psychology of Mystical Consciousness* and *Mystical Knowing,* rendered a great service to contemporary Western thought in bringing the phenomenon of mysticism a step nearer to empirical research.[21]

In his view mysticism, in its narrow sense, is "the advent of an encompassing into meditative consciousness"; and in its wider, less scientifically strict sense, "both the advent of an encompassing into meditative consciousness as well as the ecstatic lived experience of an encompassing."[22] For him meditation is

a condition of consciousness that is fully integrated, ordered simply and without divisions, clearer than clear [*überklarer*], and emptied, wherein the stream of experience is slowed down, wherein the basic mood is one of quiet and the gaze inwards is the only function assigned to an as yet only passively experiencing ego.[23]

The "encompassing" he sees as a "quality of lived experience."[24] Applied to the "advent" into consciousness, it is experienced psychologically in meditation

as if it were purely and simply an ultimately unknown being coming from an alien sphere—a being to whose complete oneness everything that has been experienced, past, present and future, has some unrecognizable connection.[25]

Albrecht pursues the psychological treatment of mysticism through a phenomenological-gnoseological investigation. In it the "mystical relationship" heretofore described through psychological structures is seen to be a "phenomenal ultimate," that is, a phenomenal form that has so far resisted all "reductive, analytical and deductive tendencies of thought."[26] Yet it must be "accepted as a given, even though it cannot be rationalized."[27]

Insofar as philosophical thinking is provoked through phenomenal ultimates, it follows that "characterizing the mystical relationship as a phenomenal ultimate is, in effect, to surrender it to philosophy as one of its themes."[28]

In a discussion of Heidegger's hermeneutics of Dasein, Albrecht sees quiet as man's *Grundbefindlichkeit* (the fundamental self-situatedness of Dasein) on the same level as anxiety:

Quiet as "Grundbefindlichkeit," in contrast to anxiety, is not a structural moment in the disclosure of Dasein. Quiet has no disclos-

ing function. There is no why and wherefore of quiet. *Quiet is not situational [befindliches] understanding.* The ontological structural moment of quiet cannot therefore constitute the disclosure of Dasein, but what may be glimpsed through its phenomenal state is something other, something essentially different—namely, *the structural moment of an openness of Dasein.* Anxiety is a self-situating *[Sich-befinden]* in disclosure. *Quiet is a self-situating in openness.* The state of being open of being-in-itself is the condition for the possibility of receptivity. Set within the horizon of beings within the world, Dasein is disclosed in the anxiety of being-in-the-world as such. But displayed against the horizon of beings in the world, being-in-itself as quiet *is* neither a disclosure of being-in-the-world nor a disclosure of being-in-itself. It is *openness pure and simple and indeed openness as the possibility of receptivity.*[29]

To characterize the existential nature of mysticism, Albrecht finally ventures the term *Offenstand* ("keeping open").[30]

What Albrecht has deliberately kept free of theological considerations[31] August Brunner has brought to theological reflection. But before interpreting Albrecht's notion of *Offenstand* in the final sections of his work, he also pursues the phenomenon as it may be approached from the statements of the mystics. In so doing he wraps up the phenomenon of mysticism in a string of phrases, not all of which are to be taken with the same degree of seriousness:

elimination of the outer world, looking inwards, surmounting the world, advent of a transpsychic "Other," strengthening of intellectual perception, elimination of psychosomatic conditions, formlessness, novel experience of subjective being, deactualizing reflection, conceptionlessness, simplicity of vision, wordlessness, subsumption of discursive thought, super-clarity—stillness—presence, subsumption of sense qualities, mystical "unknowing," oneness of self-actualizing intellect, impression of passivity, reactivizing, elevation of being human, "spiritual feeling."[32]

We may indeed ask here whether Suzuki's late polemics against the mystical interpretation of the Zen experience is not to be seen as an intermezzo based on misunderstandings, and whether it is not time for a new phase of the discussion of "mysticism Christian and Buddhist" to begin. More recent interest in mysticism, and not only with its history, has already brought to light such a number of new aspects that a psychological, phenomenological, gnoseological comparison of experience in East and West, and thus also the experiences lying at the basis of the philosophy of emptiness, would already be worthy of consideration.

The Possibilities and Limitations of Language

The problematic particular to the comparison of mystical experiences lies in the area of linguistic articulation. Now it is a well known fact that Zen Buddhism shows a marked and firm reserve where linguistic formulation is concerned. Suzuki has substantiated this in his own graphic way:

> The one trouble we have with language whereby we are frequently misled to commit a gross error, especially when we encounter metaphysical questions, is that our language does not exactly and truthfully represent what it is supposed to represent. Language is a product of intellection and intellection is what our intellect adds to, or, it may be better to say, subtracts from, reality. Reality is not in language as it is in itself. To understand reality one must grasp it in one's own hands, or, better, be it. Otherwise, as Buddhists aptly illustrate, we shall be taking the finger for the moon; the finger is the pointer and not the moon itself. In the same way, money is a convenient medium which we exchange for real substance. When a crisis comes we let the money go and hold on to the bread. Language is money and the finger. We must keep our brains from being muddled.[33]

Western man is not readily satisfied with such a skeptical, pessimistic attitude toward language. This is true even when this attitude is substantiated positively by a fascination with actual experience of the total unity of all things, or negatively by the underlying anxiety of risking the loss of this experience through the admission of further distinctions, or of losing it altogether.

When all is said and done, talk is unavoidable among men. Nishitani's student, Shizuteru Ueda, has sensed this keenly. In the concluding remarks of his book on Eckhart he observes expressly:

> In Eckhart preaching is the authentic occurrence of the word and its very religious existence, while in Zen Buddhism "Question-and-Answer" (in Japanese the characteristic Zen dialogue is called *mondō*) is the authentic locus of the word and the very stuff of Zen ... A comparison of the different forms of the word-event would be particularly important here: on the one side, preaching in Meister Eckhart; on the other, *mondō* in Zen. The basic questions allied to such a structural comparison of the word-event would need to be set aside for later investigation.[34]

In a more recent book, *Zen Buddhism,* Ueda devotes two of the longer chapters to this question, "Zen and the Word," and "Dialogue and Zen *Mondō.*" In the first of these he treats the word as "original word" resting on the ground of the "non-word."[35] Word in this sense refers to "utterance," "expression"; or, in the oft used terms of Zen, *katsu, kachin, gacha* and the like, it refers rather to a stammering, incomprehensible statement of an inexpressible experience that in turn leads to negative words becoming the basic words of Zen.[36]

At this point we need to ask whether the more recent experiences of charismatic and pentecostal groups, which are also on the increase within the Catholic Church, and of the reawakened interest in glossalalia could not serve as a bridge for understanding here. Spontaneous experiences and utterances of this kind were in fact forced into sectarian quarters for centuries after St. Paul had delivered the keynote for intelligibility and moderation:

> I thank God that I have a greater gift of tongues than all of you, but when I am in the presence of the community I would rather say five words that mean something than ten thousand words in a tongue (I Cor. 14:19).[37]

While the meaningfulness of the language of *kōan* and *mondō* needs to be taught to the Occidental world,[38] the use of "intelligible" language as a means of interpersonal communication needs to come up for rethinking in the Japanese world. Ueda's chapter on "Dialogue and Zen *Mondō*" shows how this raises the question of the relation of the "one" and the "many" negotiated through *soku* (Jap., *ichisokuta, tasokuichi*).[39] In Ueda's presentation, dialogue turns out to be seen as an application and explication of the I-Thou encounter, as Nishitani had interpreted it in another context but without such clear links to language.[40] In fact, Ueda has explicit recourse to the conversation from the *Hekiganroku* between Kyōzan and Sanshō that Nishitani cites, and sees the exchange of names as terminating in a laughter that says as much as there is to be said, and which in any case is a very typical form of Zen "utterance."[41]

In this sense, therefore, the ultimate form of dialogue is the play of question and answer *(mondō)* that takes place between master and disciple, between the enlightened and the one seeking enlightenment. The course of such a dialogue initiated by the master consists in an immediate back-and-forth exchange with no time for rational analysis, and hence reveals the disciple's stage of progress by means of the answer he gives. Dialogues of this sort can only succeed between men who have awakened to "personhood" (Jap., *nin*) in enlightenment, i.e., to the "selfless self," since only in enlightenment does the breakthrough to the "ground" really occur.[42]

Thus in Ueda, both language and conversation are given consideration. At the same time, the general trend of his line of thought shows that this consideration of conversation encounters man right in his overt realm of experience even as it seeks to initiate him into the realm of transrational communication that Western man understands only with difficulty and has little access to. But, to use Buddhist terms, the significance of language in the world of *saṃsāra* has by and large not been thought out. But insofar as linguistic communication, in the sense of the Bodhisattva ideal as well, continually takes place between the enlightened and the unenlightened, between the enlightened and those seeking enlightenment; and insofar as the mediation of healing (or salvation) affects those in need of healing through sympathetic, helpful consideration, to that extent language must be taken as a way of expressing the need for healing and a way of offering healing consolation. In this regard, the tenth station of the ox path deserves further attention in the future.

In Christianity this same problematic is ultimately bound up with the question of witnessing to the faith and proclaiming the faith and preaching. With an eye to Eckhart, Ueda has correctly pointed to preaching as a word-event and a phenomenon of religious existence.[43] A. M. Haas has carried this thought further and pointed out that it is a fundamental teaching in the Dominican order to pass on to others what one has seen in contemplation, *"contemplata aliis tradere."*[44] Looked at from the other side, preaching does not so much render service to the reproduction of others' experiences as it lends guidance to the experience of the self. It should be "mystagogic."

In this connection Eckhart's way of speaking can help us to pay attention to something that needs to be seen by the Western world in a new way as a basic postulate: in order to become worthy in the Zen-Buddhist sense of *mondō*, the man of the West must first be retrained in the area of the breakdown of language. But this can only take place initially in linguistic form:

> The subversive achievement of Eckhart's preaching is the mediation from a God erected with words to a "Godhead" which is experienced as a limit to categorical speech. Eckhart's insistence on the absolute necessity of preaching reaffirms his case against comprehending this transcendence as something which is acquired and possessed. Again and again "God" must be spoken of in order that the realm of the silent experience of the "Godhead" be able to open up. The experience of the "Godhead" is not possible if "God" cannot first "become" and "un-become" in the speech of man. Only a becoming God can un-become to a Godhead of which then nothing further can be said. The destruction of God is tied to his construction in language. Experience which refers itself to the Godhead and defines itself then as divine self-understanding, hangs on to the linguistic process wherein "God" un-becomes apophatically and then the "Godhead" emerges in its unity as the limit of what can be said.[45]

The so-called "crisis of religious language"[46] in the West consists not least of all in the fact that religious language has largely lost its mystagogic character in favor of the ontological-dogmatic assertion as a form of expression. Analysis of Eckhart's preaching shows that its language aims, functionally, at the mystical *unio* of God and man.[47] In this *unio* man breaks through every ontological certitude about the self in experiencing himself as he is. The creature experiences

> fully his dependence on being in abandoning his nothingness to the Godhead; the apparently negative process is turned into pure positivity when the creature finally recovers his archetypal fullness of being as God in God.[48]

What Haas asserts of Eckhart, Jacques Maritain claims, in a corresponding manner, for John of the Cross whom he takes as "the great Doctor of this supreme incommunicable wisdom."[49] If one compares his language to that of the Scholastics, significant differences become apparent. For what the language of John of the Cross

> purports to express is sensible experience itself, and what experience! Philosophical language proposes to speak of reality without touching it, mystical language seeks to divine reality as if by touching it without seeing it.[50]

The most decisive element of all is the fact that mystical language is the servant of praxis. The lack of attention to the various levels of discourse often leads to catastrophic results:

> I am not saying that it is impossible to pass from one to the other. I am not saying that the formulas of a mystical writer, or of a practical doctor, are not big with speculative values and, from this point of view, cannot be judged ontologically true or false. The intellect goes from one conceptual vocabulary to another, as it goes from Latin to Chinese or to Arabic. But it cannot apply the syntax of one to the other, it cannot judge the ontological value of a mystical formula or of a practically practical statement except by taking into account the modifications which they must undergo in being translated to the ontological level.[51]

In the realization that the outer limits of the possibilities of language must also once again be mediated linguistically, one comes to stammering; one's speech is of "emptiness"[52] and of "silence."[53]

John of the Cross also speaks of emptiness in the sense of a radical "self-surrender" that leads to the stage where it can be said:

"Since I have taken up my abode in nothing, I find that nothing is wanting to me."[54]

In this connection Maritain fends off false interpretations. If the carrying out of self-surrender seems to create an opposition between "nature and grace," and to be bound up with a "disdain for the creaturely," it has not been properly understood. As a linguistic form "disdain" is at bottom nothing other than a form of expression for a most radical letting go. Indeed one could show that

> some formulas of the mystics, which are absolutely rash if understood theologically, assume their true meaning when it is acknowledged that love has its own autonomous mode of expression.[55]

If the Occidental world must pay rather more attention to the surpassing of the limits of language in unspeakable experience, the Oriental world must at this point be made more aware of the danger inherent in its way of thinking. Ueda has sensed this in recognizing the confusion of "original non-discrimination" and "destructive non-discrimination."[56] The Catholic philosopher Richard Spaemann, taking his lead from Wittgenstein, has referred to the same sort of danger with regard to mystical self-surrender. He is stern in his demand here for a constant recollection of the "way" which leads to the immediacy of unspeakable experience:

> But is it not possible that . . . the self-abnegation of mysticism could lead to total conformity? What in its result distinguishes the mystical experience of God as the total negation of all religious concepts from the banal reduction of man to his biological and need-dependent nature? What characterizes wordless prayer from that madness that . . . looks like idiocy? A parable might clarify the question: a painter reduces a purely figurative painting through a series of increasingly abstract concepts until he reaches the point at which he is once again standing in front of a white canvas. Is the last state of the canvas any different from the first? Not to the observer, who sees only the result. But for the painter, definitely— provided he bears in mind the process through which it all happened. Similarly, if mystical immediacy is not to become merely a return to nature it must not lose sight of its formative development, the process that gave rise to it . . . Unless this way was ever kept in mind and made present the goal relapsed back into its beginnings and the "dark night" of the mystic became instead a night of confusion in which one thing could not be distinguished from another. But by remaining mystically distanced while at the same time never losing touch with the process that formed it, religion could endure in a world that is the child of the scientific enlightenment

without becoming encapsulated by it and without having to define itself in that world's categories.[57]

Cataphatic and Apophatic Theology

In making the transition to the question of the experience of God, we are led first to point yet again to the necessary relationship between cataphatic-positive theology and apophatic-negative theology. Whoever seeks to guide us into the realm of "knowing unknowing" (Nishitani)[58] or of "the knowledge of non-knowing" (Maritain),[59] must do so initially through the mediation of language. Their guidance occurs through the recognition of appearances as "inauthentic," as what is not really real, and in the distancing of oneself therefrom (the *via remotionis*) in order to proceed from the experience of "authentic reality" back again to the world of appearances. What is to be said of this world, then, is to be said from the point of view of its final validity through negation. According to Maritain, two groups of texts in Aquinas on the *via negationis* may be set forth.[60]

A first series of texts are related to the process of knowledge and the formulation of theses. For instance, *In Boeth. de Trin.,* q.2, a.2 ad 2:

> The fact that we know what God is not provides a place in divine science for knowledge of what he is; for just as one thing is distinguished from another by virtue of what it is, so is it also so distinguished by virtue of what it is not.

And in the *Summa contra gentiles,* I c.14:

> Now, in considering the divine substance, we should especially make use of the method of remotion [*via remotionis*]. For, by its immensity, the divine substance surpasses every form that our intellect reaches. Thus we are unable to apprehend it by knowing *what it is.* Yet we are able to have some knowledge of it by knowing *what it is not.* Furthermore, we approach nearer to a knowledge of God according as through our intellect we are able to remove more and more things from Him. For we know each thing more perfectly the more fully we see its differences from other things; for each thing has within itself its own being, distinct from all other things.[61]

In this case, we are still involved in the formulation of theses

> (though the propositions be negative, as may happen in any science); it is not yet to have left cataphatic theology, to have passed on to a higher kind of wisdom, so long as these truths are known only and not experienced, so long as they are only spoken of, not lived.[62]

A second series of texts is related to "the knowledge of non-knowing considered as constituting the highest kind of wisdom, in other words, to apophatic theology insofar as it signifies an order of knowledge superior to that of cataphatic theology."[63] In this case apophatic theology is identical with mystical theology. For instance, we find the following in *I Sent.*, dist. 8, q.1, a.1 ad 4:

> When we approach God by the *via remotionis* we begin by denying him all corporeality; next, we go on to deny in him anything intellectual—such as goodness or wisdom to the extent that these are found among creatures. And then there remains in our minds only the fact that he exists and nothing more, so that a certain confusion comes to surround him. But we reach the end only when even this very fact of being, to the extent that it can be applied to creatures, is also removed. And then he comes to rest in a kind of shadow of unknowing in which, insofar as it is a stage along our way, we are most closely joined to God, as Dionysius says. This is the darkness in which God is said to dwell.

In this case then:

> Apophatic theology makes sense only because it is more than cataphatic theology (as to the mode of knowing). It does not duplicate it, it ought not to be substituted for it. It is borne on its shoulders; it knows the same things better. It is negative, not because it simply denies what the other affirms, but because it attains [its aim] better than by affirmation and negation, that is to say better than by communicable propositions because it experiences by way of non-knowing, the reality that the other affirms and will never be able to affirm sufficiently.[64]

Apophatic theology thus does not end up in pure agnosticism and negativism provided that language be seen as a positive opening up and keeping open of the knowledge and experience of the "non-." In opposition to Neoplatonism and its successors, Maritain calls our attention to the error of Neoplatonic apophasis in pretending "to be a mysticism, and to remain at the same time a metaphysics; to raise itself dialectically to ecstasy." Over against this Maritain claims that mystical contemplation is "essentially supernatural."[65] The same consideration might well be brought to bear on the circles of the Kyoto philosophy of emptiness. For precisely because it speaks and argues, it must question itself—and let itself be questioned—on its appreciation of language. Then, too, the question of how selfless speech itself is through all of this comes to the fore. Taken properly, talk about the "supernatural" refers to that realm of "speechless speech" in which man is speechless from wonder and at the same time blessed with the good fortune of being able to see himself opened up and liberated even as language is closed off to him.

Josef Pieper has described this experience as "unquenchable light,"[66] a light that time and again brings to naught the claims of systematizing thought to self-containment, and yet at the same time does not set man loose into a chaotic problematic but makes possible a higher intellectual order. But the decisive element here is to have had the experience of this "unquenchable light" at all in the first place.

If one is looking for a catch phrase within new Catholic theology to express this challenge, Karl Rahner's "negative anthropology" might be of some help:

> Is theology . . . anything more than an *anthropologia negativa,* i.e., the experience that man continually loses track of himself in the uncomprehended and intractable mystery?[67]

These words can also serve to express the ties between positivity and negativity in such a way that in the end an anthropocentricism, or way of being human, becomes visible that is characterized by its letting go of, or its "letting be swept away" of the concrete fulfillment of Dasein and the concrete understanding of Dasein for man:

> . . . since in fact humanism is not the affirmation of an abstract formal idea of "man" but the affirmation of a particular, concrete, familiar, beloved and cherished mode of historical existence, Christian theism, by contrast, is the very denial of such a humanism as an *absolute* quantity. Naturally this does not mean that it forbids a humanism of this kind. On the contrary, a genuine negation as an act can only take place with reference to a concrete affirmation. One can only negate by positing something, not by refraining from doing so under the misconception that one can achieve a pure negation. In this way every man necessarily carries out *his own* humanism, i.e., his concrete understanding and actualization of existence. But it is precisely the latter which comes under criticism when man, in being a theist, lets it be swept away into the intractable, nameless mystery of God.

> This Christianity does not erect a particular *concrete* humanism but denies it an *absolute* value; Christianity accepts the experience of its own humanism as one which remains constantly questionable.[68]

9. God and Emptiness

The "uncomprehended and intractable mystery" of which Rahner speaks is God. When Christian theology comes into play and when Christian mysticism is understood in its proper sense, we cannot escape inquiry into the "God" of theology and of mystical experience. And insofar as the Kyoto School has, in the case of all of its representatives, been steadfast in its confrontation with Christianity, the God question necessarily arises for them as well. For this issue to become a subject of deeper dialogue, a number of observations issuing from circles in which Nishitani's understanding of God is influential need to be brought to the attention of the Christian side. And on the other side, considerations brought to bear by Catholic theology may aid a better understanding in the Kyoto School of the relationship between the experience of God and the doctrine of God.

Observations on the God Question
from Nishitani's Circle

Without going into the entire area of the "God question" as it is treated in the Kyoto School,[1] two tendencies visible in the circles of Nishitani's philosophy may be taken note of.

In the first place, God and emptiness are sometimes seen as intimately connected. This is not the case when dogmatics comes into question, however, but when the mystics, through their utterances, are brought into the picture. Again and again, to the end of his life, Nishida identified God and absolute nothingness when considering the mystics, but this identification was less a verbal one bound to the word "God" than it was an existential one that led into the realm of the unspeakable and hence also, into the neutral realm of the "godhead":

The true God is not the usual idea of God, but rather *die Gottheit* such as spoken of by the mystics in the West. The true God is the "emptiness" of the *Prajñāpāramitā Sūtra.*[2]

Although the charge of "pantheism" is repeatedly made against this way of speaking, the possibility of a confusion of levels of discourse, such as referred to earlier, also comes up for question. In any event, we ought not too lightly pass over the serious rejection that Nishida, Nishitani, Abe and others aim at what they call "pantheism." If from Nishida to Nishitani Eckhart has remained the point of contact where it might be possible to see, or at least to surmise, what they have in mind, the question would have to be asked, conversely, whether that "nothingness" which opens itself up at the "ground" of God and man is not indeed that same "Uncomprehended and Intractable" that shows itself when man radically lets go of himself and allows his self to fall into the Other.

We find the startling remark in Nishida's writings:

A *Deus absconditus* cannot be said to be the absolute God.[3]

In one sense, the phrase makes sense when one sees from its context that it is directed primarily against dialectical theology and its radical notion of a transcendent God. In that case Nishida's words serve above all to reconfirm the criticism leveled against him of a certain lack of understanding of a theology that is concerned with disassociating the final, original ground of man and all things from man himself and allowing the original ground to be what it is: freedom, grace and love.

Apart from this lack of understanding, however, the phrase shows, conversely, that the inner presence of an abyss or "original ground" is the main thing being sought beyond all outer appearances. Indeed, from a Christian standpoint one might even be able to find in Nishida's words an intuition of the absoluteness of the absolute God that is arrived at when God himself, in creative freedom, posits an other to himself, and in incarnational freedom himself becomes that other. Great concern for the proper understanding of emptiness is shown also in the effort to drive back, beyond the duality of creator and creation, to the undivided original ground of God, and this as, ultimately, part of the ongoing tendency towards an existential understanding of *tathatā*, to the being of things as they are.

W. L. King, one of the Western thinkers most familiar with the Kyoto scene, has rightly drawn our attention to this last point:

It would seem that in conversation with the West about Ultimate Reality, at least the words Suchness or Thatness should be more frequently used than Nothingness. And perhaps indeed the term "Nothingness" is altogether an unfortunate one to indicate the Buddhist Empty-because-Full Reality called Suchness.[4]

With regard to the understanding of the self, King has shown that the formulations of the West are conceptually stronger, while those of the East, on the contrary, are existentially stronger:

A basic clarification might be found in the fact that the Christian-Western view of selfhood has been predominatly *conceptual* and the Buddhist-Eastern *existential*.[5]

This comparison cannot be said to be completely valid, however. Much more attention needs to be given, as has been shown, to levels of discourse within the language of Christianity. Precisely in talk of God, it often happens that what seems to be conceptual needs to be understood existentially. This makes attention to the second Kyoto tendency all the more important.

If God and emptiness are treated as intimately connected, then, we find also and quite frequently, in the second place, the opposite assertion that God and emptiness are not the same and are not to be confused with one another.

The reasons for these reservations regarding the understanding of God come down basically to two: (1) the interpretation of God as a "substance" that is presented as something objective and objectifiable; and (2) the opposition in duality which comes to light in the relation of creator to creation, or of God to man, and the objectifiability of the two opposites which, therefore, remains possible in the relationship between subject and subject as well.

In this connection Masao Abe remarks:

Identity as an ontological principle of absolute *Mu* is neither identity as the sheer negation of individuality nor identity in oneness as the ultimate, *substantial,* ground such as God, *esse ipsum, substantia* (Spinoza) or Indifference (Schelling)—just as equality in *Nirvāṇa* is neither equality as the mere negation of differentiation nor equality in oneness as the ultimate, *substantial,* ground. Identity as an ontological principle of Nirvana is, accordingly, not identity with oneness which is substantial, but, identity with absolute Nothingness.[6]

And yet again:

The Ground of our existence is nothingness, *Śūnyatā,* because it can never be objectified. This *Śūnyatā* is deep enough to encompass even God, the "object" of mystical union as well as the object of faith. For *Śūnyatā* is not the nothingness from which God created everything, but the nothingness from which God himself emerged.[7]

These considerations are then carried over to Christian mysticism:

In Pseudo-Dionysius, identification or *union* with God is for man to enter the Godhead by getting rid of what is man—a process called *theosis,* i.e., deification. This position of Pseudo-Dionysius became the basis of subsequent Christian mysticism. It may not be wrong to say that for him, the Godhead in which one is united is the "Emptiness" of the indefinable One. The words "nothing, nothing, nothing" fill the pages of *The Dark Night of the Soul,* written by St. John of the Cross. For him nothingness meant "sweeping away of images and thoughts of God to meet Him in the darkness and obscurity of pure faith which is above all concepts."

Despite the great similarity between Zen and Christian mysticism we should not overlook an essential difference between them. In the above quoted passage, Pseudo-Dionysius calls that which is beyond all affirmation and all negation by the term "Him." Many Christian mystics call God "Thou." In Zen, however, what is beyond all affirmation and all negation—that is, Ultimate Reality—should not be "Him" or "Thou" but "Self" or one's "True Self." I am not concerned here with verbal expressions, but the reality behind the words. If Ultimate Reality, while being taken as Nothingness or Emptiness, should be called "Him" or "Thou," it is, from the Zen point of view, no longer ultimate.[8]

Objections of the sort that we have brought to the discussion here by using the formulations of Masao Abe find widespread support from a number of quarters. Hisamatsu, in illustrating the characteristic attributes of Oriental nothingness, finds negative statements on God equally insufficient,[9] as does Nishitani in whose writings there is no want of corresponding statements.[10]

At this point the dialogue would have to be guided through the tangle of complexities involved in the development of the concepts of "substance," "subject," "object," and "person" in order to discover to what extent the dissent is real and appropriate. We could as well be led to a clearing along another route, and to this end I should like now to recall a phrase of Nishitani's that has been accorded entirely too little attention in the discussion: "impersonally personal or personally impersonal relationship."

Taken in the context in which the phrase occurs, two things strike us about this formula: (1) it concerns an existential kind of encounter of man with God's transcendence and omnipresence wherein words become inadequate; and (2) there results a proximity to theological language regarding the Holy Spirit.

Nishitani's text reads:

When we encounter His [God's] transcendence and omnipresence in . . . an existential way . . . that encounter can be termed a personal relationship between God and man. But it must be in a very different sense from what is usually meant by "personal." If we speak in the usual sense in which the relationship between God and the "soul," or the "spiritual" relationship and so forth are called "personal," the above relationship must be said to have rather an impersonal character. But it is not impersonal simply in the usual sense of being the opposite of the personal . . . When we meet with God's omnipresence existentially as the absolute negativity to the being of all created things, when it presents itself as an iron wall that prevents us from all further movement, forwards or backwards, it is not impersonal in the usual sense of the word. Rather, here appears a totally different point of view with regard to "personal" and also with regard to "impersonal." This should be considered, so to speak, as an im-"personally" personal relationship, or as a "personally" impersonal relationship. *Persona* in its original meaning is probably close to what we are speaking of now. In Christianity, what is called the Holy Spirit possesses such characteristics. At the same time that it is thought of as one *persona* in the Trinity of "personal" God, it is no other than God's Love itself, the breath of God; a sort of impersonal person or personal imperson, as it were. But if such a point of view be once introduced, not only the Holy Spirit, but also God Himself with this Spirit, and man himself in his "spiritual" relationship with God, can be seen in the same light.[11]

This text merits attention above all because it is one of the few places in which Nishitani has achieved clarity in his use of "*soku*" in the relationship between the "personal" and the "impersonal," and in which he employs the notion of the "emptying out" of emptiness. Were this reciprocal reversibility of the terms "personal" and "impersonal" maintained in the sense of "personal-*sive*-impersonal, impersonal-*sive*-personal" a good bit of the suspicion that the impersonal—or, more generally, negation—is the dominant notion in Zen Buddhism would be laid to rest. For the original countenance of "emptiness" indeed first becomes visible at the point that man is brought to that basic attitude that delivers him from *every* attachment of a positive or a negative sort. Only when this basic attitude is realized can everything disclose itself as it is—*tathatā,* thusness, truth.

The objection needs to be raised here against Abe and Hisamatsu, as Takizawa and Yagi have done, that in their preoccupation with preserving the single original ground or the experience of total unity, neither of them arrives ultimately at that posture of "letting go" that shines through again and again in Nishida and Nishitani. For his part, Yagi, who comes to the discussion from the standpoint of a Protestant New Testament scholar, has given expression to this letting go as follows:

The "formless self" that transcends the opposition of being and nonbeing, sense and nonsense, realizes its self-abandonment in God when it sees itself bound to God through "Christus." God transcends the opposition of good and evil. He is the one who "causes his sun to rise on bad men as well as good, and his rain to fall on honest and dishonest men alike" (Matt. 5:45). *God is the ground of being and non-being, of integration and disintegration.*

Therefore one cannot say that the "formless self" does not allow for God (Hisamatsu). The reverse seems to me to be the case. Religious existence quite consciously acts in response to integration so long as it exists. Here ethical activity and responsibility are grounded. But their being and non-being lie in the hands of God who transcends the opposition of being and non-being, sense and nonsense.[12]

In his attempts to reach an understanding with the Buddhist participants in the dialogue, Yagi has, to some extent, met with forceful opposition from his colleagues. For instance, Y. Noro has put the question to both Yagi and Takizawa as the Christian Japanese who have been in effect the most outspoken in the dialogue with Buddhism:

> Is their view of God, which is so close to the thought of Kitarō Nishida on absolute nothingness as the ground of being and non-being, Christian *enough?* For instance: Yagi considers God as the ground of being and non-being that exists effectively in the ground of the ego. But is that a very complete explanation of the Christian God? Of course we know the *effects* of God, but God is in my view not to be *equated* with these effects. He is rather the transcendent one who embraces those effects in himself and transcends them.[13]

At the point that mutual suspicions grow up between Buddhists and Christians within Japan, it becomes appropriate to add a few fundamental remarks on the experience of God and the doctrine of God as represented in the realms of Catholic theology.

God: Experience, Belief and Doctrine

Developments within contemporary theology are only comprehensible if one keeps in mind the framework of intellectual history proper to our time. Obviously, a detailed account of that framework lies outside the scope of these pages,[14] but closer inspection will show that significant points of contact between religions appear in common components of a worldwide development.[15]

The breakdown of an objectifying metaphysic, the Copernican shift to the subject, the discovery of the world as history, the concern with the connection between event and interpretation, with history as a linguistic event and with language as an opening up of history—all these are considerations that have had their affect on theology and its talk of

God.[16] Johannes Metz demonstrated in his first book, *Christian Anthropocentricism*, how Aquinas' way of thinking had already paved the way for the transition from a cosmocentric to an anthropocentric view of the world. Later he was to raise objections critical of the fact that in the concrete forms of the shift to anthropocentricism with its transcendental, existential and personalistic orientation, there seems to be a common "trend toward the private" which in turn needs to find its corrective in a "theology of the world" or, rightly understood, in a "political theology."[17]

In the concrete world of today that is characterized, in the West both outside of and partially within organized Christianity, by an alienation from God, agnosticism, indifference to the question of God and the search for God, atheism and anti-theism, and in which similarly the will to live *etsi Deus non daretur*[18] is on the increase, the question of the experience of God and of belief in God comes again into question. In contrast to the questions of the grounding of belief and the proofs for God, this question has come to be given a certain priority, and along with it an interest in the twofold question of describing the experience of God and establishing criteria for judging it.

Interest in a theology "which is not cut off from experience"[19] is not to be ignored. Further inquiry into the historical Jesus and his experience of God, into the experience of God in history, and finally into the experience of God today and approaches to it need also to be mentioned in this connection.[20]

In one of his essays Karl Rahner, whose theology, as Fischer says, "might be called the quest of the mystic to translate his experience for others and to have them share in his grace,"[21] thematizes the "experience of God today." The difficulty of this topic consists for him in the fact that

> we are seeking to reflect upon an experience which is present in every man (whether consciously or unconsciously, whether suppressed or accepted, whether rightly or wrongly interpreted, or whatever the way in which it is present), and which involves the following factors: *on the one hand* it is more basic and more inescapable than any process of rational calculation in which we follow a line of causality leading from the egg to the hen, from the lightning to the thunder, in other words from the world to an originator, but which can also be broken off, leaving the conclusions which might have been arrived at unrecognized. *On the other hand,* however, this experience does not impose itself upon us irresistibly (as does the physical existence of a datum of sense experience or an organic sensation) in such a way that the transition from the experience itself to an explicit recognition of it in which we reflect upon, interpret, and express it, imposes itself upon us irresistibly.[22]

Rahner also speaks initially of the God experience that he has in mind in a negative, limiting sense. For him it is "not the privilege of the individual 'mystic,' but is present in every man even though the process of reflecting upon it varies greatly from one individual to another in terms of force and clarity."[23] (This is perhaps the place to ask whether the doubts of the later Suzuki with regard to "mysticism" cannot be laid to rest from here on.) Rahner goes on to assert that "that which we call 'God,' considered 'as' the object of this experience is not present in a manner which should be thought of as analogous to that in which we view an object immediately confronting us . . . We should say, rather, that God is present as the asymptotic goal, hidden in itself, of the experience of a limitless dynamic force inherent in the spirit endowed with knowledge and freedom."[24] Linked to this is the question whether, in their critique of the "objectification" of God, Nishitani and his colleagues have not more carefully to distinguish between a way of speaking that cannot avoid objectification and that which is being hinted at through objectifying language, even though it is precisely the opposite of what is put forth linguistically and thus ultimately eludes articulation in words.

Furthermore, for Rahner, in the experience of God the "dynamic force which the spiritual subject experiences within itself is experienced not as an autonomous power of this subject, but rather as initiated and sustained by the goal toward which it tends." It is experienced as "grace-given" in that it "includes within itself the powerful hope of achieving a state of ultimate proximity and immediacy to that goal towards which it is tending, so that this goal does not remain merely the power that draws it yet remains eternally asymptotic and remote from it, but really does constitute a goal that can be reached."[25] This makes it clear that even with all due consideration given to the uniqueness of man, it is only in a radical surrender of himself that man experiences what that uniqueness consists in. For this reason then, too, it is "meaningless to subject this experience, in a manner which is, theologically speaking too hasty, to the question of whether it belongs to 'nature' or 'grace.' "[26] For Rahner this is a matter that belongs to the subsequent process of reflection and not to a treatment of the experience itself.

When he goes on, however, to present this same experience by leading into it mystagogically and enveloping it in almost wordless wordiness—a presentation that he himself designates as "extremely abstract"[27]—we meet with a conceptual scheme that has many points of contact with the philosophy of emptiness. The following passage, which we cite at length to demonstrate the point, merits special attention in this regard:

A potent factor in every life is a certain element of the ineffable, namely mystery. This does not signify that part of reality which still remains to be explored, which we have not yet thoroughly understood or achieved or made real to ourselves. Mystery, rather, is the underlying substrate which is presupposed to and sustains the reality we know. For the condition which makes it possible for man to achieve the fulness of his own existence, and which gives it its special character, is precisely a certain prior apphrehension which transcends every particular concrete reality which we conceive of or make real to ourselves, a certain radical limitlessness inherent in every movement of knowledge and freedom—a limitlessness which cannot be pent in by any individual, any definite being, or anything that would mean a definite halt.* We exist, think and act in freedom only in virtue of the fact that we have already all along transcended that which is specific and particular, that which we can comprehend, in a movement which knows no boundaries. The moment we become aware of ourselves precisely *as* the limited being which in so many and such radical ways we are, we have already overstepped these boundaries. Admittedly in doing so we step, as it were, into *emptiness*. But nevertheless we have overstepped them. We have experienced ourselves as beings which constantly reach out beyond themselves towards that which cannot be comprehended or circumscribed, that which precisely as having this radical status must be called infinite, that which is sheer mystery, because as the condition which makes every act of apprehending, distinguishing and classifying possible, it itself cannot in turn be experienced in *that* mode which it itself makes possible and of which it is the condition. It is present as the abiding mystery. This ultimate and original reality, therefore, which has no other basis beyond itself, even though the experience of it is mediated through our apprehension of some concrete object, cannot properly speaking be explained in terms of anything else than itself. It is the experience of that mystery which abides, which has been present all along, and precisely as such is both the inconceivable *and* that which alone is self-evident both at the same time. The dynamism of this limitless movement, and in it the ultimate point of reference towards which it tends, are of course experienced in a *single* act, and at the same time are in this experienced as distinct. But the "ultimate point of reference" of this movement is *per definitionem* precisely *not,* and cannot be, an "object" in the same sense as the object aimed at in acts of knowledge and freedom at other levels, so that it can be brought under the control of the knower as the preliminary stage in this movement in such a way that he can assign it a specific place in a co-ordinated system. Moveover, this ultimate point of reference is experienced *in* the infinite movement of the spirit and *in terms of* it, even though it is also precisely that which in itself initiates and sustains this movement. And for these reasons the question of where this movement culminates is ultimately a secondary one. One man may say that the infinite sphere opened up without bounds or end in this movement is *emptiness* which, in order to be able to exist at all, points on to an infinite fulness, because *nothingness,* if the term is taken seriously, cannot be extended so as to become the sphere within which this movement takes place. Another may say that this ultimate point of reference is the infinite fulness itself which is aimed at. Which of these two alternatives we choose is secondary. Hence too it is also a secondary question whether we decide to speak of an experience of God or of the experience of an orientation towards God. Certainly we must always maintain the distinction between the "objective" and "subjective" sides of the experience in this context (if man is to avoid making himself God), but nevertheless these two sides are, in a unique and radical manner, inseparable one from the other.[28]

Faced with this by no means easy text of Rahner's, the typical objections of the Kyoto School regarding God simply do not hold up. This is all the more so the case if one includes Rahner's brief allusions to the "special characteristics proper to our own times" of this "experience of God":

(1) "This experience of God, precisely as it exists *today* is, much more clearly and radically than in earlier times, an experience of transcendence, a transcendence which eliminates the divine from the world and is thereby enabled to let God be God."[29]

(2) "And it may be conjectured—though perhaps there is some small element of prophecy here—that the mode of existence which is typical precisely of this *present* age, and which is destined gradually to fulfil this role of being the medium in which the experience of God is communicated, is not so much the existence of the saint with his wisdom and contemplation, but rather that of the man whose life does not appeal to our feelings, who bears responsibility for himself in silence and solitude, yet who exists selflessly for the sake of others."[30]

(3) One of the great difficulties here is in the manner of addressing God as "thou": "It is no matter for regret, if we find the courage to address God in this way only by keeping our eyes fixed on Jesus, seeing that even in death he still managed to call this Mystery 'Father,' and to surrender himself into his hands even as, in slaying him, it withdrew itself from him and threw him into the most inconceivable state of dereliction from God."[31]

(4) At first sight "it seems as though there were hardly anything specifically Christian in this experience of God." But Rahner offers the thesis: "Among the religions which *de facto* exist (considered as historical and social phenomena) it is precisely Christianity which makes real

this experience of God in its most radical and purest form, and in Jesus Christ achieves a convincing manifestation of it in history."[32]

Of this last thesis more needs to be said later on. But before we do that, let us offer a few remarks summarily:

For Rahner, who represents a prominent example of the Catholic theology of our day, belief in God is nothing other than the existential appropriation of the experience of God in which man, in trust, lets go of himself and lets himself fall into the unfathomable and unspeakable mystery that is called God. Deductively speaking, then, the doctrine of God, "theo-logy", is *de facto* as well as existentially, a *"reductio in mysterium."* [33] That is, it is "that human activity in which man, even at the level of conscious thought, relates the multiplicity of the realities, experiencies, and ideas in his life to that mystery, ineffable and obscure, which we call God."[34] In this connection our attention turns naturally once again to the question of the peculiarity of theological language:

> The propositions of theology must constantly be referred back to the single indefinable mystery and the ultimate and grace-given experience of this. In fact all of them express, ultimately speaking, nothing else than the fact that this mystery has imparted itself so as to achieve a state of absolute proximity to man, in which it becomes his authentic consummation and the future that lies before him. . . . [These statements] cannot be replaced by an attitude of silent adoration, by a *theologia negativa"** which effectively reduces itself to silence. Nor can we express these statements in a form which suggests that the actual formulation of them in human words is the ultimate goal at which we are aiming. Rather it is the attitude of trembling and silent adoration which is intended to beget these statements, and this belongs to that deathly silence in which man's lips are sealed with Christ's in death. It is, therefore, a very difficult task with which theology has to cope in these statements. They must be expressed in words in order that we can arrive at the authentic silence which we need. They must be borne with in patience and hope in respect both of their necessity and of their incommensurability, in which they attempt to utter the ineffable. I believe that theology today has still very much to learn before it speaks in such a manner that men can achieve a direct, effective, and clear recognition of the special quality of this language.[35]

On Naming God

Statements about theology as a *"reductio in mysterium"* lead us to a final area of consideration that is tied up with Takeuchi's remark cited at the very outset that Western philosophers and theologians line up almost without exception on the side of being, while Eastern thinkers take the side of nothingness.[36] But it is not only the Buddhist and Buddhistically oriented thinkers who bring Western Christians face to face with their basic insight. Japanese Protestant theologians have also made cautious attempts to build bridges, though they have not always found enough of an audience among their Western colleagues.

Tetsutarō Ariga, a Protestant Christian and observer at the Second Vatican Council, and later Professor Emeritus of Christian Thought at the State University of Kyoto until his death in 1977, brought up for consideration the idea that the ontological understanding of God in the West may have come as a necessary result of Greek structures of thought and language, and hence may represent a reshaping of the original understanding of God derived from the Hebraic *"hajah."* Thus to "ontology" Ariga has emphatically set in opposition what he calls "hayatology."[37] The question that he raised from the linguistic perspective of Japanese[37] and brought to the dialogue with Tillich and Brunner, however, was not as such taken notice of at all—a fact that he bemoans in his summary work, *Kirisutokyōshisō ni okeru sonzairon no mondai* ("The Problem of Ontology in Christian Thought").[38]

In opposition to the claim that the understanding of *"hayah"* signifies the dynamic unity of being and becoming, Abe objects that in this case, too, God remains "absolutely other" with regard to man and the world.[39] Ariga's intended dialogue has yet really to be come to grips with, either in the world of Christian theology or in that of the Kyoto School. The reasons for this may lie not least of all in the fact that, on the one hand, too little thought is given to the connection between a language aimed at wordlessness and one making claims in the sense of an ontology: and on the other, that Ariga himself has gone into the intentions behind the statements of the Kyoto School in too little depth.

In Rahner we met with the basic theological aim of a *"reductio in mysterium"* and had it in mind to look at certain points of contact with the intentions of Nishitani. In the Catholic philosopher Leslie Dewart, Professor at St. Michael's College of the University of Toronto, we meet with a critical reflection on the metaphysical foundations of Christian faith.[40] In the age of "ecumenical ecumenism," to use a phrase of Panikkar's, Dewart aims at deepening the foundations of belief in the "meta-metaphysical."[41] From this standpoint Dewart advances a "de-Hellenizing" of Christianity, by which he means:

> the conscious creation of the future of Christian belief, not necessarily through the *adaptation* of non-Hellenic cultural forms, but ideally through the invention of its own concepts and other forms of experience on the basis of an imaginative, creative evolutionary leap ahead. De-Hellenization means the creation of a world that does *not yet* exist, on the basis of the only one that *does* exist.[42]

Essential to his line of thought is, first of all, his conception of language. For Dewart, speaking is not an activity that follows upon intellectual activity. Rather, thinking is "experience of a linguistic form."[43] Consequentially "one cannot very well learn to speak in any language, without that language becoming by that very fact the linguistic form of one's thought."[44] Hence man is also "glossocentric" to the extent that "he uncritically assumes that his selfhood, his culture and his times are the center of reality."[45]

Taking note of the Chinese language and its syntax has taught Dewart to ask to what degree in Indo-European languages, though here too not in all of them, the verb "to be" exercised a definite syntactic function that cannot simply be transferred to other languages without further ado.[46] But once the relativity of the connection between the *copulative* function and the *existence-mediating* function of the verb "to be" is recognized and acknowledged, the necessity of relating the self to reality through the aid of the verb "to be" is allowed to come into question.

Chinese syntax, for Dewart, lends support to the suggestion that

it is perfectly possible to conceive a reality which is relative to being but which is other than being—a reality, therefore, which is not a transcendent being but which transcends being, and which can thus be immanent in being while remaining distinct from being precisely because it is other than being.[47]

This, then, in turn results for him in the further possibility of saying that in the formula "The Tao is a term for Nothing,"

Nothing (or, in my terminology, *non-being*), does not mean the absence or negation of reality: it means the absence or negation of an *existing* reality; it means the absence of being, *(ens).*[48]

The distinction of reality from being leads to corresponding consequences for the understanding of God, which in turn is defined essentially by the new understanding of reality:

Reality, therefore, in which (and in relation to which), man is (and is conscious), is neither essence nor existence nor being—though being, essence and existence are real (which is why reality may both exist and be intelligible). But reality remains: it is *that in relation to which* absolute contingencies can be absolutely contingent upon. In other words, the reality of being is not distinct from the being of real being; but reality as such is not being. Reality as such is that in which being can be real: reality is that in which existence can be and essence can be understood. . . . *God* is, to speak properly, not "ultimate" reality, since he is not the reality which exists "after" immediate reality: he is the reality *in relation to which* any other reality is real. God is reality as such. Thus, whatever is true of any being is true because it is real (and not only because it *is*). On the other hand, reality *as such* does not exist, and therefore, the reality of any given being, or the reality of being as such is not the same as reality as such. Of course, reality exists *as* being, and being as such is real. But existing reality is not reality as such; it is being. Thus, being is real because God is real, but God does not exist simply because being exists.[49]

In this regard Dewart arrives at a new formula for sin and the love of God. God is

if I may so put it, subsistent Relativity. It is only man's reality (and that of other creatures, though unfortunately for them they do not know it) that can *lack* relation. Only man can be consciously un-related. Only man is capable of refusing to relate himself—for instance, refusing to give himself. Thus, the contingency of man is what renders him apt to alienate himself from God; and the ground of this possibility is being, since only beings as such can be contingent . . . to-be-absolutely is the essence of sin. . . .

To love God is to live in function of the awareness of his sub-stantial presence in the world: it is to stake one's future on the belief that man is not, never has been and, above all, never will be, alone in or even with the world. For *Yahweh,* as we believe, will never withdraw himself or his presence from the world of being, and thus will always remain related to us. To love God is to em-body in one's existence and self-disposition the belief that God is so far from being an absolute reality that he can be defined indeed as absolute relativity itself.[50]

This at base extremely revolutionary way of speaking about God, which in turn affects the way one speaks of the economy of salvation and the worship of God, has, sad to say, yet to lead to a foundational discussion in the European world.[51] With good reason non-Europeans may find in this a sign of the provincialism of European theology. Still, there have been two sorts of reactions that give us something to think about.

First, A. Keller locates the weakness of the book "in an overvalu-ation of its redesignations (e.g., replacing 'being' with 'reality' as the su-preme transcendent)."[52] But this argument can easily be turned right back around. Rahner also finally comes to call it "a secondary ques-tion" whether one says that "the infinite sphere opened up without bounds or end . . . is emptiness" or that "this ultimate point of reference is the infinite fullness itself which is aimed at."[53] But in Asia—and in our particular case, in Nishitani's philosophy of emptiness—the "redesignation" not only *seems* important but in fact is important. And if Dewart's concept of reality can, moreover, be coordinated in many respects with "emptiness," then the point needs to be discussed fully as such.

Secondly, L. Scheffczyk, in his 1974 book *Belief in God Without God?* in fact goes into Dewart's "destruction of theism in 'relative belief,' " but does so not in reference to the book we cite but to Dewart's earlier work *The Future of Belief.* Since this book already contained the kernel of Dewart's fundamental thesis Scheffczyk's critique can also serve as a comment on *The Foundations of Belief.* Scheffczyk states succinctly:

> His intention of overcoming for theism the extremes of objectivizing, of a "setting over against" the subject by means of being, and of an anthropomorphic personalizing goes beyond its goal and lands up in an opposite extreme: namely, the extreme of subjectivizing and of a peculiar hominizing of God which makes him an existential phenomenon of man, a function of human openness.[54]

This criticism that views Dewart's thought as a mere shift from an "objectivizing" of God to his "subjectivizing" and hominization, misses the main point he is making. Still it is typical of the lack of attention paid in the premises to the relationship between speech and thought, and of the still widespread ignorance of non-European structures of language and thought and its corresponding uncritical transference of Western habits of thought and language to all forms of language and thought in general. Only this could enable Scheffczyk to ask:

> But what is this God to be then if he is neither to have a being nor to be a nothing? An "in-between" being and nothingness cannot be conceived of.[55]

Only when the copulative function of the verb "to be" and its existence-mediating function are set in the foundations together is it possible to make the claim of a "logical contradiction" between the sentences "God is not, he possesses no being, neither in the sense of existence nor of essence," and "God is a presence, he is present," or to say:

> If one excludes being and existing from God in every sense, one must, consequentially, omit every "is" statement from God altogether.[56]

This should lead us then to ask whether or not Scheffczyk allows for the "is" statement that signals the leap into the unspeakable. Only when one thinks exclusively in terms of a subject-object scheme must

God be located either on the side of the object or on that of the subject, so that a "neither/nor" is inconceivable.

One further consideration may indicate that the result of Dewart's considerations really come closer to the Christian God than at first seemed to be the case. Heidegger has answered the question "How does God come into philosophy?" this way:

God comes into philosophy the first time we decide to give some thought to the regions outlying the essence of the distinction between being and beings. The distinction sets down the main lines for the construction of the essence of a metaphysic. The decision results in the concession that being is the pro-ductive ground which, by virtue of what is grounded by it, itself requires an appropriate grounding or primal materialization through what is primal. This is the primal as *causa sui,* which is the proper name for God in philosophy. Man can neither pray to this God nor make offerings to him. Before the *causa sui* man can neither fall to his knees in awe nor dance and make music.

Accordingly, godless thought which must relinquish the God of philosophy, God as *causa sui,* is perhaps nearer to the godly God.[57]

Regarding the relationship between theology and philosophy, Heidegger had once proposed for consideration:

Whoever has experienced theology, both that of the Christian faith as well as that of philosophy, from its natural birth, prefers today to remain silent in the area of thought about God.[58]

But then he also keeps room available for the distinction:

Christian experience is something so totally other that it has really no need at all to come into competition with philosophy. If theology persists in seeing philosophy as folly, the mysterious nature of revelation is the more easily maintained. When all is said and done, their paths come to a parting.[59]

This brings us to the point where the reconciliation of philosophy and theology is conceivable, so to speak, only through the course of disputation and a new letting go. We recall Pascal's famous outcry:

Not the God of the philosophers, but the God of Abraham, Isaac and Jacob.[60]

These words, which awaken the memory of the burning bush in the desert, make the God experience, together with its naming, the business of concrete man, neither a matter of careful intellectual calculation nor of an intellectual leap. This experience is not a result but a gift, a grace—unearned and unexpected. It leads to the sober simplicity of service as easily as to the drunken abandon of dance. It comes closest perhaps to the "huge laugh" at "entering into the marketplace with open hands."[61] It resounds in the Hallelujah of Mozart of which Van Bragt writes. Indeed one would like to know what answer Nishitani would give to his questions:

> I asked myself: is this feeling of grateful jubilation before the Lord accounted for in *What is Religion?* . . . Then I started wondering: would Mozart's Hallelujah correspond to nothing in Prof. Nishitani's life?[62]

In both cases Van Bragt supposes a negative answer. I myself am not so sure. Several things lead me to suspect that Nishitani could go along with the "metamorphosis" of the "God of philosophy" of which Ratzinger writes:

> a) *The God of philosophy is essentially only self-related,* pure thought contemplating itself. The God of faith is defined fundamentally through the category of relation. It is creative expanse that embraces the whole . . .
> b) *The God of philosophy is pure thinking.* The concept forms his ground; thinking and only thinking is divine. The God of faith is love, as thinking. At the basis of this conception of God is the conviction: love is divine. The logos of the whole world, the creative primal thought, is likewise love. Indeed this thought is creative since it is love as thought and thought as love. A primordial identity of truth and love appears in their full realization, not as two realities standing side by side or face to face, but as one, the only absolute.[63]

10. Jesus Christ:
The Figure of the "Empty" God

Jesus Christ answered the question of the search for God concretely, in the words of the Gospel of John, by pointing to himself:

"Have I been with you all this time, Philip," said Jesus to him, "and you still do not know me? To have seen me is to have seen the Father, so how can you say, 'Let us see the Father'?" (Jn. 14:9).

But to look at Jesus of Nazareth is, in the first place, to look at nothing other than a concrete man in concrete human history.

Here Buddhism, as the "religion of absolute this-sidedness" (see above, Ch. 6, "Nothing and Emptiness"), and Christianity encounter one another in a way that has up until now hardly been considered. Rahner, who on the one hand through his *"reductio in mysterium"* guides the Christian to a new reserve in talking about God, indeed to a silence *in* his reality, on the other tires not of pointing to Jesus Christ as the ful-*fill*-ment of the "otherwise so *empty*" concept of the absolute:

Man is at once a concretely corporeal and historical entity on earth and an absolutely transcendent one. Accordingly he looks out— and looks out in the course of his history—to see whether the supreme fulfillment (however free it may remain) of his being and his expectation is not on its way to meet him: a fulfillment in which his (otherwise so empty) concept of the Absolute is wholly fulfilled and his (otherwise so blind) gaze can "see through" to the absolute God himself. Thus man is he who has to await God's free Epiphany in his history. Jesus Christ is this Epiphany.[1]

This talk of the "otherwise so empty concept of the absolute" is indeed interesting insofar as it has to do not with an "emptiness" without content, not with an emptiness that coincides with a nothingness devalued as nihilistic,[2] but with an emptiness of comprehension. For man's will-to-comprehend passes over into "emptiness" of its own power, and the ground of man opens itself up into the realm of the ground-less, i.e., the "ground" that man believes himself to be resting on eludes his command and can only take a firm hold in the "composure" of letting go and letting fall.

This "so empty concept" receives its "filling" and its "ful-fillment" in the figure of Jesus, as we hope now to show somewhat more clearly.

But before that, let us return once again to Nishitani. From his use of the formula "*nirvāna-sive-samsāra*" to its full extent in defining the relationship between "emptiness" and history, one might have expected him to have accorded similar attention to the fundamental Christian formulation of the relationship between God and world in terms of the God-man Jesus Christ—that is to say, in terms of the dogma of God's incarnation. In fact, however, we find a conspicuous reserve in Nishitani on this point. This "neutrality" towards the key figure of Christian belief admits of various possible interpretations, the most important of which we shall list here.

(1) His reserve could be an indication of a great reverence and awe in the face of an uncomprehended and perhaps even incomprehensible mystery. This possibility ought not be summarily passed over in view of the obvious sympathy that Nishitani shows for one of the greatest and most historically influential figures among the followers of Christ: St. Francis of Assisi, a figure who reappears at the end of *What is Religion?*

(2) It could also be a sign of an inadequate appreciation of the intimate link between the question of God and the question of Christ in Christianity. This possibility is not to be excluded either, inasmuch as Nishitani, like Nishida before him, treats the question of God very much from the historical angle of mysticism. But then, too, the Christian mysticism of the Middle Ages, by virtue of its strong neoplatonic influence, often has failed to articulate clearly enough the particularly Christian or Christ-related aspects of mysticism and its experience of God even where they come into the picture.[3]

(3) Moreover, it could be an indication of an ultimately unconvincing attitude to the world that does not take the world seriously according to "*soku.*" To be sure, one finds in the circles of Nishitani's philosophy a clear criticism of any Buddhist standpoint of emptiness that is transhistorical or ahistorical, and so could hardly lead to an authentic historical consciousness (see above, Ch. 7, "World, History and Man"). And yet at the same time, as usual one misses in the world of Buddhism an attitude toward the world that could be likened to the positive and yet finally unbiased posture that Christianity takes to the world. Therefore neither is the possibility to be excluded that for this reason Nishitani has not recognized the approach to the figure of Christ as the form of approach to the world and its history proper to Christianity.

(4) Finally it could also be a consequence of the fact that he has after all preferred to encounter Christianity in the realms of the modern

Western history of philosophy where the figure of Christ has noticeably retreated behind the Christian worldview and its corresponding doctrinal systems. This possibility is not to be ruled out if one calls to mind the authors to whom Nishitani has given special attention throughout his life: the German idealists, Nietzsche and Heidegger.

Of course, a further possibility is ever present and should not be passed over in silence. Just over a decade ago Hans Fischer-Barnicol reported on an encounter with Nishitani under the title "Questions from the Far East." The central point of his sympathetic essay is the Pauline *"koān"* that Nishitani had placed before the theologians in Basel and Marburg and to which, as he himself has stated, no satisfactory answer was forthcoming:

> I find a statement in Paul which I, coming out of Zen-Buddhism, believe I understand only too well. He says he has suffered a death: "I live now not with my own life but with the life of Christ who lives in me." That makes sense to me immediately. Allow me only to ask you this: Who is speaking here?[4]

Nishitani's European colleagues made no reply to his question arising out of Galatians 2:20. Is it any wonder that he himself has preferred, beyond a few hints (see above, Ch. 6, "I-Thou and Nothingness"), to keep his silence?

Now this is hardly the place to attempt to make up for the responsibility of Christians to proclaim and bear witness to the *"werdend gewordener* Buddhist" and the *"werdender* but not *gewordener* Christian" (see the end of Ch. 5). Let us rather—true to our intentions of laying down a few stepping stones for dialogue—give each side something to think about with regard to the figure of Jesus in the form of two propositions: (1) The Christian confesses Jesus Christ as the "emptiness" of God taken form; and (2) the Christian only follows Jesus as his model when he imitates him by "putting on" Christ his own way.

Jesus Christ and the "Emptiness" of God

The classic passage on the "emptying" of God is found in Paul's letter to the Philippians, 2:5–8:

> In your minds you must be the same as Christ Jesus. His state was divine, yet he did not cling to his equality with God but emptied himself to assume the condition of a slave, and became as men are; and being as all men are, he was humbler yet, even to accepting death, death on a cross.

The interpretation of the kenōsis of God has a long and to some extent rather involved history behind it.[5] Urs von Balthasar has traced that history from the angle of the new image of God which it entailed but has failed to consider the union of mysticism and dogmatics that becomes visible from that aspect.[6] For our own consideration here, we should like therefore to refer back once again to Karl Rahner. In his penetrating reflections on the kenotic passages in Scripture, Rahner arrives at the conclusion that the original phenomenon given to faith is the *"self*-emptying, the coming to be, the kenōsis and genesis of God himself, who can come to be by *becoming* another thing, derivative, in the act of constituting it, without having to change in his own proper reality which is the unoriginated origin."[7] This "other thing" is, *de facto*, man:

> This man is, as such, the self-utterance [*Selbstäusserung*] of God in his self-emptying [*Selbstentäusserung*], because God expresses *himself* when he empties himself. He proclaims *himself* as love when he hides the majesty of this love and shows himself in the ordinary way of men.[8]

Rahner seeks to define man himself, from this "self-emptying" of God, as

> that which ensues when God's self-utterance, his Word, is given out lovingly into the void [*Leere*, emptiness] of godless nothing . . . If God wills to become non-God, man comes to be, that and nothing else, we might say.[9]

The world, then, is the "emptiness" of God and man, in it, is that-which-is-not-God. The end, the high point of the kenōsis of God, is realized in two steps, with the radical and total correspondence of the self-emptying of God and the self-emptying of man. That is precisely what Christian belief confesses in the figure of Jesus Christ and in no other. The self-surrender of God to the world in his Logos corresponds to the radical obedience of Jesus of Nazareth in his total self-surrender to his "other" which he calls "God" and whom he addresses as "Father." In Jesus of Nazareth the self-emptying of God and the self-emptying of man coincide.

This process reaches its final consequences in death—as a historically comprehensible event in the life of Jesus—since only through death are things shown to be what they are.[10] Rightly, therefore, is this death spoken of as the "death of God," which finds expression in the outcry of abandonment by God from Jesus on the cross: "My God, my God, why have you deserted me?" (Mk. 15:34).

The paradox of this outcry consists in that the very absent God who is addressed in these words himself becomes present, so that the distance and proximity of God are in some strange way mutually conditioning. The ambiguity of "emptiness" preserves its unique stamp in this death. For only in the radical letting go of itself *usque ad mortem* is it revealed

> whether the fullness reached in death is the previously only disguised emptiness and nothingness of man, or vice versa, whether the emptiness that shows itself in death is only the appearance (deceiving to us who have not yet died) of a true fullness.[11]

The ambiguity of "emptiness" as a reality without God and, through God's becoming man, as a reality full of God,[12] could perhaps of itself offer a fresh point of contact for further dialogue, in virtue of the fact that even Nishitani himself confronts the simple identification of "emptiness" and God with some degree of reserve.

Decisive for both sides, then, might be to ask what kind of hope death holds out for the Christian and the Buddhist. In this regard, the question of whether man lives his life once and for all or is subject to the law of rebirth is of secondary importance. The Christian answers the question by pointing to the "resurrection of Jesus"—a central formula that we can do no more than mention here. The Buddhist, on the other hand, speaks of "*myō-u*" (wondrous being), as the reverse side of "true emptiness" (see above, Ch. 6, "Being and Nothingness"). But both Christians and Buddhists have to answer for the ground of their hope. The confrontation of the smiling Buddha sitting in a position of meditation with the helpless, mournful Christ hanging on a cross lifted up from the earth—according to Suzuki, a sight almost unbearable to Eastern sensitivities[13]—certainly does not supply sufficient information.

The kind of death that Jesus dies—the death of a criminal and hence a death of solidarity with the most abject of creatures in this world—calls to mind a further theme that should be noted only in passing here, viz., the double interpretation of "godlessness": godlessness as non-divinity, and godlessness as man's self-alienation from and lack of relatedness to God—sin. Abe finds this theme missing in Nishitani.[14] He remarks, in speaking of Christianity and its reconciliation with science:

> The real reconciliation, I think, contrary to Teilhard's view, can be achieved only when Christianity embraces the rational objectivity of modern science within itself without neglecting man's consciousness of sin and death, Christ's redemption for them, and the idea of eschatology.[15]

In the search to build bridges of understanding, themes such as this can be set aside for the moment, but cannot simply be struck from the agenda.

Jesus Christ and the "Emptiness" of Man

The stages[16] of God's "emptying"—creation,[17] incarnation, death, death on a cross—point to an ever greater radicality of the "emptiness" of God. No motivation is given for the kenōsis of God; it happens groundlessly, selflessly. But when God acts groundlessly and selflessly, the highest name we have at our disposal for such a motive is: love.

Ultimately the Christian understands what love is by turning his gaze to the figure of the crucified Jesus of Nazareth:

> the mystery of the world, the overcoming of the terrors which are in the world, that which unifies and embraces, that which transforms, that which liberates and is tender, that which is only realized in its fullness when the one who loves makes a total surrender of everything pertaining to the movement of his own personal history towards its fulfillment. This is achieved when this love of his is pierced through and silently pours out its heart's blood into the futility of the world, and thereby conquers it . . . There is really no word capable of describing this love, because there is nothing else like it which we could use as an external standard in order to define it; also because it is, in itself, the unifying and absolutely original essence of all reality, and therefore there is nothing apart from it except emptiness and nothingness. For it has been written: "But God is love," and in these two words man finds two different ways of expressing the single infinite mystery of his own existence.[18]

The fundamental attribute of the figure of Jesus is that, despite the central significance it possesses for Christian faith, it continually and radically points away from itself. For at some point our gaze turns away from Jesus toward God his Father. Jesus understands himself as one who totally belongs to God in obedience: "The Father and I are one" (Jn. 10:30). As Ratzinger says, Jesus' life is pure relatedness, "non-substantiality."[19]

Hence, in following the self-emptying of God, our eye turns from Jesus to the world, to man, and to all of creation. There is nothing in him to which he holds fast for himself. This attribute finds its expression in the formula: Jesus was without sin. As Jesus himself asks in the Gospel of John, 8:46: "Can anyone convict me of sin?" And in the Letter to the Hebrews we read: "one who has been tempted in every way that we are, though he is without sin" (4:15; cf. 2 Cor. 5:21, 1 Peter 2:22).

The "giving up of his spirit" that takes place in a double sense in the death of Jesus means also the "tradition of his spirit" to the world (John 19:30). The synoptic gospels express this by describing cosmic phenomena that attended the death of Jesus (see especially Matt. 27:51–54).

For the Christian, however, and this cannot be stressed enough in the dialogue with Nishitani and his colleagues, the figure of Jesus is not primarily an *object* of contemplation. An object of contemplation remains something fixed and external that, in our desire to comprehend, we can train ourselves to get ahold of in "theory," in sight, in fantasy. But Christ does not wish so much to be an *ob-jectum* for us as to take form within our very selves.

The aforementioned passage from the second chapter of the Letter to the Philippians begins expressly with the challenge: "In your minds you must be the same as Christ Jesus." Paul describes this share in the mind of Jesus again and again in fresh images of transformation. To list only a few of them: "stripping off your old behavior with your old self" (Col. 3:9, Eph. 4:22); "putting on a new self" (Eph. 4:24, Col. 3:10); "clothing yourselves in Christ" (Gal. 3:27, Rom. 13:14); "imitating Christ in his death" (Rom. 6:5); "reproducing the pattern of his death" (Phil. 3:10).

It is here also that the passage from Galatians 2:20 which Nishitani used as a *kōan* belongs: "I live now not with my own life, but with the life of Christ who lives in me." When no distinction any longer remains between Christ and the one who believes in him, and only then, does the full actualization of what it means to be a Christian take place. When that happens, certain statements are able to be read vice versa:

Paul: "Take me for your model, as I take Christ" (I Cor. 11:1).
Jesus: "To have seen me is to have seen the Father" (Jn. 14:9).
"You must therefore be perfect just as your heavenly Father is perfect" (Matt. 5:48).

A phrase like this last one only makes sense, fundamentally, when in radical self-emptying, every measuring stick has been cast aside. This is what happens when "talk about" passes over into existential completion. Buddhists and Christians alike, each in their own way, must expose their attitudes to scrutiny. The Buddhist will come into genuine dialogue with the Christian only when he understands Christian dogmatics as persistently very complex and yet as a consequential commitment to the freedom of an indescribable God whose unfathomable love man cannot confine and cannot get to the bottom of. And the Christian, on the other hand, will come into genuine dialogue with the Buddhist only when he begins to address himself to the existential completion of his own selflessness and self-emptying, and thus to the selflessness and self-emptying of Christ. The opportunity for both sides rests in and depends on letting go of oneself.

In his own inimitable way Karl Rahner has expressed the opportunity available for all sides this way:

> And the grace of God and Christ are in everything, as the secret essence of all eligible reality: it is not so easy to grasp at anything without having to do with God and Christ—one way or another. Anyone therefore, no matter how remote from any revelation formulated in words, who accepts his existence, that is, his humanity— no easy thing!—in quiet patience, or better, in faith, hope and love—no matter what he calls them, and accepts it *as* the mystery which hides itself in the mystery of eternal love and bears life in the womb of death: such a one says yes to something which really is such as his boundless confidence hopes it to be, because God has in fact filled it with the infinite, that is, with himself, since the Word was made flesh. He says yes to Christ, even when he does not know that he does. For he who lets go and jumps, falls into the depths such as they are, and not such as he has himself sounded. Anyone who accepts his own humanity in full—and how immeasurably hard that is, how doubtful whether we really do it!—has accepted the Son of Man, because God has accepted man in him.[20]

The Buddhist may affirm or deny these statements as they stand. But at bottom he ought not refuse to acknowledge anything that bars his way to radical openness for what it is.

Our reflections cannot come to an end on a note of challenge to dialogue but in the call to take a leap together. Only such a leap can open the eyes of those who risk it so that, finally, "hearing and seeing will pass away": *enlightenment.* And only that leap can bring those who risk it together in selfless, self-surrendering communality: *love.*

Since the time of the enlightenment of the Buddha, enlightenment is the measure of all things for the Buddhist. The Buddhist is one who strives for self-realization in his life and thereby comes to see that he cannot win it without a radical letting go. And true enlightenment calls him back to an engagement in compassion and mercy.

Since the time of Christ's death on the cross, love is the measureless measure of behavior for the Christian. The Christian is one who strives for self-realization in being consumed with a radical commitment to others. True love sees itself driven on by enlightenment through the Spirit of Christ.

Enlightenment that radiates love, and love that is enlightened and gripping, condition one another. And when we have seen that, the question arises for us: Do not *the smile of the enlightened Buddha* and *the tortured countenance of the crucified Jesus* really come face to face when there is a sharing in the depths where the true self resurrects in poverty, death and absolute nothingness?

Notes

Introduction

1. "The Dialogue between Oriental and Occidental Thought," p. 292.
2. "Was ist Metaphysik?" *Wegmarken,* pp. 19, 211.
3. *Systematic Theology,* Vol. 1, p. 186.
4. *Ibid.,* p. 198.
5. *Ibid.,* Vol. 2, p. 11.
6. *Zeit und Geheimnis,* p. 138. See also B. Welte, "Versuch zur Frage nach Gott," J. Ratzinger, ed., *Die Frage nach Gott* (Quaestiones Disputatae 56), Basel, 1972, p. 26.
7. Cf. Herbert Marcuse, *One-Dimensional Man,* Boston, Beacon Press, 1968.
8. "Rationale of the International Institute for Japan Studies," pp. 3f.

Part One: Background

1. The Buddha

1. "Ansprache zum Heimatabend," p. 62.
2. *Ibid.,* p. 63.
3. *Ibid.,* p. 65.
4. *The Collection of the Middle Length Sayings* (Majjhima-Nikāya), trans. by I. B. Horner, London, Pali Text Society, 1967, Vol. 1, p. 207. In the original text, Discourse 26, Section 163 (hereafter cited in parentheses). On the theme of homelessness, see also: Vol. 1, p. 240 (36:240), p. 22 (4:16), pp. 138–40 (17:106–8), p. 263 (31:210), p. 224 (27:179), p. 338 (40:284); Vol. 2, p. 9 (51:344–45), p. 124 (66:452), p. 132 (67:460).
5. *Ibid.,* Vol. 2, p. 9 (51:343–44). See also: D. Schlingloff, *Die Religion des Buddhismus,* Vol. 1, pp. 37, 47ff; Vol. 2, p. 55.
6. "The Awakening of Self in Buddhism," pp. 53f.
7. Y. Takeuchi, "Probleme der Versenkung im Ur-Buddhismus," pp. 1–19; T.R.V. Murti, *The Central Philosophy of Buddhism,* pp. 36–54.
8. For the full text see the Majjhima-Nikāya (note 4 above), Vol. 2, pp. 97–101 (63:426–32). The passage cited here is on p. 100.
9. *Ibid.,* p. 101.
10. Takeuchi, *op. cit.,* p. 65.
11. *Ibid.,* pp. 6, 65.

12. Murti, *op. cit.*, pp. 22f.

13. E. Conze, *Buddhist Thought in India*, pp. 36–39. See also his *Buddhism*, pp. 18–21.

14. H. Oldenberg, *Buddha*, pp. 235, 416, 435; similarly, A. Bareau, *Der Indische Buddhismus*, pp. 37, 153 and *passim*.

15. *Op. cit.*, p. 26.

16. Cf. Oldenberg, *op. cit.*, p. 444; Bareau, *op. cit.*, pp. 9, 40, 71, 92 and *passim;* H. Zimmer, *Philosophie und Religion Indiens*, p. 407.

17. Conze, *Buddhist Thought in India*, p. 37.

18. *Geschichte der indischen Philosophie*, p. 255.

19. *Ibid.*, p. 193.

20. *Christianity Meets Buddhism*, p. 83.

21. Étienne Cornelis, *Valeurs chretiennes des religions non chrétiennes: Histoire du salut et histoire des religions Christianisme et Buddhisme*, Paris, Éditions du Cerf, 1965, p. 146.

22. EB III/1, p. 15.

23. "East-West Religious Communication," pp. 109f.

24. Conze, *Buddhist Thought in India*, p. 156; *Buddhism*, p. 48.

25. Streng, *Emptiness*, p. 37 and *passim*.

26. H. Nakamura, "The Basic Teachings of Buddhism," Dumoulin, *Buddhism in the Modern World*, p. 15; see also Frauwallner, *op. cit.*, pp. 197–214 and Bareau, *op. cit.*, p. 33 and *passim*.

27. Bareau, *op. cit.*, p. 14; Frauwallner, *op. cit.*, p. 197 and *passim*. Oldenberg (*op. cit.*) calls it a "causal nexus of origination" (p. 212), and remarks later: "Causality—or, to render the Indian word *paticcasamuppāda* more precisely, origination (of something) in dependency (on something else)—presents a relation between two elements, neither of which is at any moment identical with itself" (pp. 233f).

28. H. Waldenfels, *Meditation-Ost und West*, p. 62. See also Streng, *op. cit.*, p. 150, where it is referred to as "reciprocal relation to something else."

29. *Op. cit.*, p. 197.

30. Cf. Takeuchi, *op. cit.*, pp. 10f; Frauwallner, *op. cit.*, p. 197; Bareau, *op. cit.*, pp. 33f.

31. Takeuchi, *op. cit.* p. 13.

32. *Ibid.*, p. 13.

33. See Masao Abe's article, "Buddhism and Christianity as a Problem of Today," and the replies published subsequently as "A Symposium on Christianity and Buddhism" in *Japanese Religions*, 3/2, 3/3, 4/1, 4/2.

2. Nāgārjuna

1. For further information on the Mādhyamika School, see Murti, *The Central Philosophy of Buddhism*, pp. 238–49; and for an overview of the relevant literature, see Streng, *Emptiness*, pp. 241–45.

2. *Die Grossen Philosophen*, Vol. 1, pp. 934–56.

3. On this problem see D. F. Casey, *Aspects of the Śūnyatā-Absolute of Nāgārjuna of Second Century A. D. Andhra*, pp. 60–69. At several points in my discussion I have had recourse to this doctoral thesis, which the author has kindly put at my disposal.

4. *Östliche Meditation und christliche Mystik*, p. 106.

5. See on this point A. Bareau, *Der Indische Buddhismus,* pp. 136f; Casey, *op. cit.,* p. 94; Conze, *Buddhist Thought in India,* pp. 238f; Murti, *op. cit.,* pp. 88–91. For a German translation of the "Mahāyānaviṁśikā" see H. Schumann, *Buddhismus,* pp. 92–95 or the same author's *Buddhismus. Ein Leitfaden durch seine Lehren und Schulen,* pp. 149–52.

6. On Stcherbatsky's work, see Bareau, *op. cit.,* pp. 159f; Murti, *op. cit.,* p. 5; Streng, *op. cit.,* pp. 22, 235; on both thinkers, see Casey, *op. cit.,* pp. 59f.

7. Cf. Bareau, *op. cit.,* pp. 160, 173ff, 178ff; A. Govinda, *Foundations of Tibetan Mysticism;* H. Nakamura, *Ways of Thinking of Eastern Peoples,* pp. 187, 197, 245 (China), 340 (Tibet), 556 (Japan).

8. *Die Gemeinschaft des Geistes,* pp. 131–319.

9. *Aporie und Glaube,* pp. 125–51; the passage cited here is on p. 143.

10. See B. Altaner and A. Stuiber, *Patrologie. Leben, Schriften und Lehre der Kirchenväter* (Basel, 1966), pp. 501–5, especially pp. 502f.

11. Otto, *West-östliche Mystik;* Nishitani, *Kami to zettai mu* and *Shimpishisōshi.* Cf. also my presentation, "Das schweigende Nichts angesichts des sprechenden Gottes."

12. See H. Waldenfels, "Absolute Nothingness," pp. 21, 369 and note 55; Conze, *op. cit.,* p. 233; Dumoulin, *Östliche Meditation und christliche Mystik,* pp. 100–119.

13. Murti, *op. cit.,* pp. 123f and *passim.*

14. *Ibid.,* pp. 131f; Conze, *op. cit.,* pp. 239–42; Bareau, *op. cit.,* p. 155.

15. Murti, *op. cit.,* p. 132; Conze, *op. cit.,* p. 241.

16. Conze, *op. cit.,* p. 242; and his *Buddhism,* pp. 135–36.

17. We cite here according to Streng's translation (*op. cit.,* pp. 181–220). The numbers given in parentheses correspond to chapter and verse in the text.

18. See here Murti, *op. cit.,* pp. 129–31; Conze, *Buddhist Thought in India,* pp. 219, 261–69; Bareau, *op. cit.,* pp. 155ff; Zimmer, *Philosophie und Religion Indiens,* pp. 463–67.

19. Murti, *op. cit.,* p. 129.

20. On the meaning of *"prajñā"* see Bareau, *op. cit.,* pp. 145–55; Streng, *op. cit.,* pp. 82–98, 159–63; Murti, *op. cit.,* pp. 209–27.

21. Ch. 24 of the *Kārikās* treats the interpretation of these two truths. On this point see also Bareau, *op. cit.,* pp. 154f, 170; Conze, *Buddhism,* pp. 132ff; Murti, *op. cit.,* pp. 243–55; Streng, *op. cit.,* pp. 39f, 144f.

22. Streng, *op. cit.,* p. 89; cf. also pp. 86f, 162.

23. Conze, *Buddhism,* p. 130.

24. *Ibid.,* pp. 130f; see also Nakamura, *op. cit.,* p. 45.

25. Conze, *Buddhist Thought in India,* p. 61; Streng, *op. cit.,* pp. 76f.

26. See also Murti, *op. cit.,* pp. 50–4.

27. See above, Ch. 1, note 4: Vol. 1, p. 365 (44:302); see also Conze, *Buddhist Thought in India,* pp. 59–69; H. v. Glasenapp, *Die Weisheit des Buddha.* pp. 194–95.

28. Bareau, *op. cit.,* p. 153.

29. *Op. cit.,* p. 7; Bareau, *op. cit.,* pp. 156–68.

30. *Op. cit.,* p. 63.

31. *Op. cit.,* pp. 16f.

32. Murti, *op. cit.,* p. 139.

33. Streng, *op. cit.,* pp. 75f; Conze, *Buddhist Thought in India,* pp. 225–32.

34. Murti, *op. cit.*, p. 234.
35. Conze, *Buddhist Thought in India,* p. 232.
36. *Op. cit.*, pp. 79, 80.

3. Zen Buddhism

1. For the text and a commentary, see H. Dumoulin, *A History of Zen Buddhism,* pp. 67ff.

2. "Zen and Western Thought," p. 538. The original Japanese text is in K. Nishitani, *Kōza Zen,* Vol. 1, pp. 146f.

3. On this matter cf. Conze, *Buddhist Thought in India,* pp. 242–49; Murti, *The Central Philosophy of Buddhism,* pp. 7f, 329ff and *passim.*

4. On the Yogacāra see Bareau, *Der indische Buddhismus,* pp. 161–70; Murti, *op. cit.*, pp. 311–28; Conze, *op. cit.*, pp. 250–60.

5. On the distinction of the two Vasubandhu, see Bareau, *op. cit.*, pp. 86f; Murti, *op. cit.*, p. 107.

6. Bareau, *op. cit.*, p. 161.

7. Murti, *op. cit.*, p. 107.

8. "The Characteristics of Oriental Nothingness," pp. 86–91 and *passim;* and the passages in his *Chosakushū* found in Vol. 2, pp. 222–37 and *passim.* See also S. Yamaguchi, *Bukkyō ni okeru mu to u to no tairon,* which deals expressly with the two great currents in Indian Mahāyāna Buddhism.

9. Cf. H. Nakamura, *Shin-Bukkyōjiten,* "Ishiki," pp. 18f.

10. *Op. cit.*, pp. 34–51.

11. "Basic Thoughts Underlying Eastern Ethical and Social Practice," in C. Moore, ed., *The Japanese Mind,* p. 432 note 5.

12. Cited by Nakamura, *Ways of Thinking of Eastern Peoples,* p. 57; cf. also Dumoulin, *op. cit.*, pp. 42–55. An English translation of the Vimalakīrti, translated by H. Izumi, has been published in the pages of the *Eastern Buddhist* (Vol. 3, 1924/5, pp. 55–191; Vol. 4, 1926–28, pp. 348–66); and a German translation, *Das Sutra Vimalikīrti,* was published in Tokyo in 1944 by Fischer and Yokota. This *sutra* represents one of the clearest embodiments of what is spoken of in Buddhism as "*kyōge betsuden*" ("outside of doctrinal formulations, without tradition"), the transmission of which, when authentic, goes directly from heart to heart. [The passage in Izumi's English translation corresponding to Nakamura's translation differs considerably in its wording though not in its basic sense (Vol. 3, p. 182f). With the author, I have followed Nakamura.—Trans.]

13. *Op. cit.*, p. 46.

14. *Ibid.*, p. 49.

15. *Ibid.*, pp. 81f. See also Thomas Merton, *Mystics and Zen Masters,* pp. 18f. Zimmer (*Philosophie und Religion Indiens,* p. 486) makes reference to the age of the mirror-tradition. [The translator of Dumoulin's book rendered the first line of Hui-nēng's response "The Bodhi is not like a tree" which is both a distortion of the meaning and of the original German translation. I have accordingly corrected it here.—Trans.]

16. Merton, *op. cit.*, p. 23.

17. *Ibid.*, p. 32.

18. In his sympathy for Hui-nēng's attitude, Merton makes it sufficiently clear that he is aware that in Christianity's emphasis on the I-Thou relationship "even the contemplation of the void as described by Hui-nēng has definite affin-

ities with the well-known records of Christian mystical experience . . ." (p. 30). Merton finds a certain confirmation for his emphasis on the difference between Shēn-hsui and Hui-nēng in Enomiya's *Zen-Buddhismus* insofar as this latter also relativizes the difference between the sudden and the gradual in enlightenment. Most recently, Dumoulin has commented on the history of the sixth patriarch in his *Erleuchtungsweg des Zen im Buddhismus,* pp. 52–63.

19. Let it be noted clearly at this point that we are only concerned here with alluding to the problematic, without being able so much as to outline the actual process of mediation itself in broad strokes. For further detail on the introduction and reception of Buddhism in China, the reader should refer to the relevant literature. I mention only a few titles here: Fung Yu-lan, *A History of Chinese Philosophy,* 2 Vols., Princeton University Press, 1952–53; J. Gernet, *Les aspects économiques du Bouddhisme,* Saigon, 1956; E. Zürcher, *The Buddhist Conquest of China,* Leiden, 1959; K. S. Ch'en, *Buddhism in China,* Princeton University Press, 1964; A Wright, *Buddhism in Chinese History,* Stanford, 1965; H. Steininger, "Der Buddhismus in der chinesischen Geschichte," *Saeculum,* No. 13, 1962, pp. 132–65; W. Eichhorn, *Die Religionen Chinas,* Stuttgart, 1973. On the relation between Taoism and Zen and the influence of Chuangtsu, one may refer, in addition to the well known works of Fr. Dumoulin, to: G. Béky, *Die Welt des Tao,* Freiburg im Breisgau, 1972; and H. Welch, *Taoism, the Parting of the Way,* London, 1966.

20. Cf. Nakamura, *Ways of Thinking of Eastern Peoples,* pp. 175f.

21. *Ibid.,* p. 177.

22. Cf., for instance, Nakamura's remarks on the description of *pratītya-samutpāda* in the translation of Kumārajīva (344–413), one of the most important translators in early Chinese Buddhism (*ibid.,* p. 187). For further detail on Kumārajīva, see Ch'en, *Buddhism in China,* Princeton University Press, 1964, pp. 81ff. On his understanding of *śūnyatā,* see Allan Andrews, "Nembutsu in the Chinese Pure Land Tradition," *Eastern Buddhist,* III/2, 1970, pp. 38f.

23. Cf. Nakamura, *op. cit.,* p. 233. See also my remarks in "Das schweigende Nichts angesichts des sprechenden Gottes," pp. 324–27.

24. Nakamura, *op. cit.,* p. 190.

25. *Two Zen Classics: Mumonkan and Hekiganroku,* trans. with a commentary by Katsuki Sekida, New York and Tokyo, Weatherhill, 1977, p. 27.

26. Dumoulin, *A History of Zen Buddhism,* p. 129; Nakamura, *op. cit.,* p. 205.

27. See W. Bauer's summary in *China und die Hoffnung auf Glück. Paradiese, Utopien, Idealvorstellungen,* Munich, 1971, p. 572.

28. Nakamura, *op. cit.,* provides further detail on the science and scholarship of the Chinese (pp. 214–16, 220–25), on their pragmatism (pp. 233–46), esteem for hierarchy (pp. 259–76) and their esteem for nature (pp. 277–83).

29. Nakamura speaks expressly of a "non-development of metaphysics" (*ibid.,* pp. 243–46).

30. Aside from the works of Dumoulin, Enomiya-Lassalle and Suzuki already cited and the respective passages in the various compilations of the history of religions, see also: A. K. Reischauer, *Studies in Japanese Buddhism,* New York, 1925; C.N.E. Eliot, *Japanese Buddhism,* London, 1935; W. Gundert, *Japanische Religionsgeschichte,* Tokyo, 1935; J. Takakusu, *Essentials of Buddhist Philosophy,* Honolulu, 1947; W. K. Bunce, ed., *Religions in Japan. Buddhism, Shinto, Christianity,* Tokyo, 1955; M. Anesaki, *History of Japanese Religion,* To-

kyo, 1963; E. D. Saunders, *Buddhism in Japan,* Philadelphia, 1964; J. M. Kitagawa, *Religion in Japanese History,* New York, 1966; J. H. Kamstra, *Encounter or Syncretism? The Initial Growth of Japanese Buddhism,* Leiden, 1967; K. Morioka and W. H. Newell, eds., *The Sociology of Japanese Religion,* Leiden, 1968; H. B. Earhart, *Japanese Religion, Unity and Diversity,* Belmont, 1969; A. Matsunaga, *The Buddhist Philosophy of Assimilation;* S. Watanabe, *Japanese Buddhism.* See also Dumoulin in his *Buddhism in the Modern World.* A description of the contemporary situation through statistical details has been published by the Agency for Cultural Affairs under the title *Japanese Religion* (ed. by I. Hori *et al.,* Tokyo, 1974).

31. See the interesting dispute between Suzuki and Hu Shih reported by Dumoulin, *A History of Zen Buddhism,* p. 52.

32. See the special edition of the *Eastern Buddhist* dedicated to him, II/1, 1969.

33. *Either* the historical treatment comes to the fore (as in Dumoulin) *or* else practice is given preference (as in Enomiya-Lassalle and Kapleau), *or,* finally, a systematizing of history and practice is attempted (as with Suzuki and not a few researchers in Kyoto).

34. Cf. Nakamura, *op. cit.,* p. 449.

35. *Ibid.,* pp. 400ff. Nakamura writes expressly: "Hampered by their own inclination to accentuate the social nexus and their alogical mentality, the Japanese are often lacking in the radical spirit of confrontation and criticism" (p. 402).

36. *Ibid.,* pp. 386f. See also Saunders, *Buddhism in Japan,* pp. 94–100; S. Hanayama, "Prince Shōtoku and Japanese Buddhism," *Philosophical Studies of Japan,* IV, 1966, pp. 23–48.

37. The Japanese word *"shū"*—as in *shūkyō,* religion—can refer as well to the doctrines of religion as to religious groups. The English word "sect" is an altogether inappropriate translation.

38. The three treatises are (1) the Mūlamadhyamakakārikā or Madhyamakaśāstra (Jap., *Chūron);* (2) the Dvādaśadvārśāstra ("Treatise on the Twelve Gates," Jap., *Jūnimonron)* which in any case is attributed to Nāgārjuna; and (3) the Śatakaśastra ("One Hundred Verse Treatise," Jap., *Hyakuron)* of Āryadeva, the first disciple of Nāgārjuna. Cf. Saunders, *op. cit.,* pp. 114–19; Bareau, *op. cit.,* pp. 136f.

39. Dumoulin, *A History of Zen Buddhism,* p. 138.

40. *Ibid.,* pp. 112–22. See also his "Die Entwicklung des chinesischen Ch'an nach Hui-nēng im Lichte des Wu-mēn-kuan."

41. Dumoulin, *A History of Zen Buddhism,* p. 151. For further details on Dōgen, see *ibid.,* pp. 151–74 and also his "Die religiöse Metaphysik des japanischen Zen-Meisters Dōgen"; O. Benl, "Der Zen-Meister Dōgen in China," *Nachrichten der Deutschen Gesellschaft für Natur- und Völkerkunde Ostasiens,* 79/80, 1956, pp. 67–77; O. Benl, "Die Anfänge der Sōtō-Mönchsgemeinschaft, *Oriens Extremus,* 7, 1960, pp. 31–50; R. Heinemann, *"Shu-shō-ittō* und *Genjōkōan";* Heinemann, "Zokugo in Dōgens Shōbōgenzō," *Oriens Extremus,* 15, 1968, pp. 101–19; K. Tsujimura, "Dōgens Lehre von Sein-Zeit," G. Condrau, ed., *Festschrift für Medard Boss,* Bern, 1973; pp. 172–201.

42. Cf. Nakamura, *op. cit.,* pp. 352ff, 454, 569ff.

43. On the classic texts of Japanese Buddhism see Y. Takeuchi and T. Umehara, *Nippon no Butten,* pp. 237–50. The *Fukanzazengi* and *Shōbōgenzō zazengi* have been translated into English by N. Wadell and M. Abe and published

in the *Eastern Buddhist* (VI/2, 1973, pp. 115–28) as have the *Bendōwa* (IV/1, 1971, pp. 124–57) and selections from the *Shōbōgenzō* (IV/2, 1971, pp. 108–18; V/1, 1972, pp. 70–80; V/2, 1972, pp. 129–40; VII/1, 1974, pp. 118–23; VIII/2, 1975, pp. 94–112. Dumoulin has published a German translation of the *Fukan-zazengi* in his "Allgemeine Lehre zur Förderung des Zazen von Zen-Meister Dōgen."

44. Dumoulin *A History of Zen Buddhism,* pp. 242–68.

45. On the *Wu-mēn-kuan,* see Dumoulin's translation in German, and the English translation by K. Sekida (note 25 above). A German translation of the *Pi-yen-lu* has been done by W. Gundert and a translation of selected passages by S. Ohasama.

46. On Zen art, see Seckel, *Buddhistische Kunst Ostasiens,* pp. 225–54; H. Munsterberg, *The Arts of Japan;* E. Herrigel, *Zen in the Art of Archery* and *Der Zen-Weg;* G. L. Herrigel, *Der Blumenweg,* Weilheim, 1956; H. Hammitzsch, *Chadō, der Tee-Weg,* Weilheim, 1958. On Bashō cf. W. Gundert, *Die japanische Literatur,* Wildpark-Potsdam, 1929, pp. 121–23; D. T. Suzuki *Zen and Japanese Culture,* New York, 1959, pp. 252–62; Dumoulin, *A History of Zen Buddhism,* pp. 213–24.

47. Cf. S. Hisamatsu, *Zen and The Fine Arts* (Vol. 5 of his *Chosakushū*).

4. Kitarō Nishida (1870–1945)

1. Cf. K. Nishida, *Die intelligible Welt,* Berlin, 1943.

2. *Intelligibility and the Philosophy of Nothingness,* Tokyo, 1958.

3. See Y. Takeuchi's article in the 1967 edition of the *Encyclopaedia Britannica* on "Japanese Philosophy: Modern Japanese Philosophy."

4. "How to Read Nishida," an introduction to the English translation of Nishida's *A Study of Good,* p. iii.

5. "Absolute Nothingness," p. 359. I have drawn on this earlier work considerably in the composition of the present chapter.

6. *Loc. cit.,* p. iii; cf. also pp. i–vi; Shimomura, *Nishida Kitarō,* pp. 216–29.

7. The translations currently available have been listed together by Yagi and Luz, eds., *Gott in Japan,* pp. 94f. Cf. also G. Piovesana, *Recent Japanese Philosophical Thought,* 1862–1962, p. 93.

8. We deliberately use the term *"Buddhist*-Western" and not *"Asiatic*-Western" in reference to the dialogue since a pan-Asiatic treatment would in all cases have to take note of the East-West discussion in India.

9. The current edition (Tokyo, 1965–) is based on an earlier edition of the collected works (Tokyo, 1947–53). On this point, see Piovesana, *op. cit.,* pp. 97f.

10. The peculiar interweaving and dialectics of Zen Buddhism and Amidism that we have observed in the representatives of the Kyoto School, as well as in Suzuki and earlier on already in Hakuin, expressly in the *Ōbaku-shū* and in the beginnings of classical Japanese Zen, deserve to be made the subject of studies in their own right.

11. We cite this work, which first appeared in 1911, according to its later version edited by K. Nishitani and published in *Kitarō Nishida.* Corresponding references to the English translation are added, in parentheses. Concerning the work as a whole, see Nishitani's introduction, pp. 7–64; T. Shimomura, *Nishida Kitarō,* pp. 47–114 and his afterword to the English translation, pp. 191–217; Y. Takeuchi, "The Philosophy of Nishida," pp. 4–10; M. Kōsaka, *Nishida Kitarō,* pp. 45–70; Piovesana, *op. cit.,* pp. 86–97.

Express mention should be made of the fact that the *"zen"* of *Zen no ken-kyū* and the *"zen"* of Zen Buddhism are not the same word.

12. Nishitani, *Nishida Kitarō,* p. 145 (Eng., p. 33).

13. "East-West Synthesis in Kitarō Nishida," p. 347.

14. Nishitani, *op. cit.,* pp. 441f.

15. Cf. here Shimomura, *Nishida Kitarō,* pp. 9–114; Kōsaka, *op. cit.,* pp. 24–52, 283–95; L. Knauth, "Life is Tragic. The Diary of Nishida Kitarō."

16. See Z. Shibayama, *Zen Comments on the Mumonkan,* pp. 19–31; P. Kapleau, *The Three Pillars of Zen,* pp. 63–83; Dumoulin, *Mumonkan,* pp. 37ff.

17. Shimomura, *Nishida Kitaro,* p. 60; S. Ueda, "The Logic of Locus and the Worldview of Religion" (introductory remarks), Nishitani, *op. cit.,* p. 90.

18. *Loc. cit.,* p. 345.

19. Ueda, *loc. cit.,* p. 95.

20. Nishitani, *op. cit.,* p. 251 (Eng., p. 189).

21. *Ibid.,* p. 122 (Eng., p. 1).

22. On Nishida's understanding of "pure experience," cf. Nishitani, *op. cit.,* pp. 7–23; T. Shimomura, "Nishida Kitarō and Some Aspects of his Philosophical Thought," pp. 200–07; Takeuchi, "The Philosophy of Nishida," pp. 10–17; Kōsaka, *op. cit.,* pp. 45–70; Piovesana, *op. cit.,* pp. 94–97.

23. Nishitani, *op. cit.,* p. 180 (Eng., p. 84).

24. Cf. Nishida's presentation of God as creator in *Zen no kenkyū,* especially, Part 2, Ch. 10 and all of Part 4, particularly Chs. 3 and 4.

25. Nishitani, *op. cit.,* pp. 183f (Eng., pp 88f). How far in fact the intentions of Nishida coincide with those of Cusanus would, of course, have to be studied more carefully.

26. Nishitani, *op. cit.,* p. 244 (Eng., pp. 178f).

27. *Ibid.*

28. M. Matsumoto has commented on the question of *"creatio ex nihilo"* in his article "Mu kara no sōzō," which appeared in a Festschrift honoring Fr. Dumoulin edited by K. Okada, *Nippon no fūdo to Kristokyō,* pp. 85–104.

29. Interestingly enough, neither Nishida nor any of his followers seem to have come to consider yet the connection between "utopia" and "absolute nothingness." His thoughts on locus define Nishida's later thought from "Hataraku mono kara miru mono e" (From working on to seeing) in 1927 up to such works as "Tetsugaku no komponmondai" ("The fundamental problems of philosophy." In this regard, cf. the English translation of D. A. Dilworth, Tokyo, 1970, written from 1933–34, up until his last essay. The thin line of distinction betwen locus *(basho)* and field *(ba)* is due to the fact that in illustrating his teachings Nishida had referred not only to Aristotle's "hypokeimenon" but also to Plato's "topos" and Lask's "field theory." Cf., e.g., Nishitani, *op. cit.,* pp. 72–81; Kōsaka, *op. cit.,* pp. 118–68. M. Kuroki's "Die Frage nach Gott in der modernen japanischen Philosophie" draws on the presentations of Piovesana *(op. cit.,* pp. 103–22), of T. A. Imamichi *(Betrachtungen über das Eine,* pp. 153–61), and of Paul Lüth *Die japanische Philosophie)* without recourse to the texts of Nishida or the relevant secondary literature in Japanese.

30. "Nishida Kitarō and Some Aspects of his Philosophical Thought," pp. 211ff.

31. Nishitani, *op. cit.,* pp. 98ff.

32. Let it be observed, in this context, that logical and ontological categories do not always admit of a clear-cut distinction.

33. Schinzinger translates and illustrates the Japanese notion of *"urazu-keru"* through the example of the "lining" of the kimono: "The Japanese kimono has a precious silk lining which shows at the ends. So the lining envelops, in a way, the kimono. Nishida uses this word "lining" to indicate the progress from the natural world to the psychological world and finally to the intelligible world. The higher sphere is like an enveloping lining of the lower sphere. The natural world is "lined" with the world of psychology, and this conscious world is again lined with the intelligible world. The innermost "lining" is the all-enveloping Nothingness" (*Intelligibility and the Philosophy of Nothingness,* Glossary, p. 248).

34. It is worth noting that in many Western languages "being" and "beings" cannot be adequately distinguished.

35. This insight also results when one combines the thought of absolute nothingness with the Bodhisattva ideal. Compare the description of the "way" found in the ancient Chinese story of the ox and his herdsman, translated by Tsujimura and Buchner and rendered in English by M. H. Trevor.

36. Nishida, *Intelligibility and the Philosophy of Nothingness,* p. 139.

37. *Ibid.,* p. 133.

38. *Ibid.,* p. 135.

39. *Ibid.,* p. 137.

40. *Ibid.,* p. 138. The text of this note does not appear in the Japanese edition. Prof. Nishitani informs me that Schinzinger's reference to the author of the story as a known Japanese Zen Buddhist named Kanemitsu Kogun has probably confused the name with a Chinese author. In any case, a Japanese Buddhist named Kanemitsu Kogun is unknown.

41. In distinction to the Western notions of "absolute" and "relative," the Japanese notions of *"zettai"* (absolute) and *"sōtai"* (relative) imply one another etymologically. That is to say, *"zettai"* is spoken of in connection with *"sōtai"* as that which is free of, separated from and cut off from *"tai"* (ob-jectum). In contrast to the Japanese notion, this "ob-jectum" can no longer be expressed in the Western notion of "absolute."

42. This passage appears in the German translation provided by Yagi and Luz, *op. cit.,* pp. 95–109 and corresponds in the original text to Nishitani, *op. cit.,* pp. 391f. [The present English version for this and the following quotation is made from the original.—Trans.] Concerning the notion of "inverse correspondence" (i.e., the way in which relative and absolute correspond to one another *insofar as* they negate one another), see Yagi and Luz, p. 94.

43. Yagi and Luz, *op. cit.,* p. 98; Nishitani, *op. cit.,* p. 392.

44. Nishitani, *op. cit.,* p. 374.

45. Ueda, "Nishida Kitarō and Some Aspects of his Philosophical Thought," p. 114.

46. The Japanese conjunctive *"soku"*, which we shall meet again in the course of our deliberations, should be seen in the context of *pratītyasamutpāda.* It showed up already, indirectly, in Suzuki's version of the famous formula *"shiki soku zekū"* and its inverse, *"kū soku zeshiki"* ("form and color, all is emptiness," "emptiness, all is form and color"), with the only real difference being that Suzuki had substituted the sign of mathematical equation "=" (see above, Ch. 3, "Theory and Praxis in Zen Buddhism") for the copula *"soku."* But the type and form of equating is the key to this relationship.

In the discussion between a Japanese and his questioner that Heidegger had recourse to in his *Unterwegs zur Sprache* (pp. 83–55), only half of the formula is cited: "We say *iro*, i.e., color, and *kū*, i.e., emptiness, openness, the heavens. We say: without *iro*, no *kū*" (p. 101).

On Buddhist logic, see the respective sections on China and Japan in Nakamura, *Ways of Thinking of Eastern Peoples*, pp. 185–95, 531–76. Concerning the contrast of Eastern and Western logic, see also T. Yamauchi, "Problems of Logic in Philosophy East and West; Piovesana, *op. cit.*, pp. 247–50.

47. In this regard see the second part of Nishida's last essay already referred to, in Yagi and Luz, *op. cit.*, pp. 95–109.

48. Cf. *ibid.*, p. 99. From his notion of "panentheism" one may gather that the essential point Nishida was making was that he did not wish for his position to be qualified as "pantheistic."

Part Two: Keiji Nishitani and the Philosophy of Emptiness

5. Stimuli

1. Cf. also Kapleau, *The Three Pillars of Zen*, pp. 301–13. In the edition of Zen texts that he has edited together with S. Yanagida, Nishitani has also produced a new translation of the ten stages of the ox path (*Zengakuroku*, pp. 152–60).

2. See his letter on "Humanism" in *Wegmarken*, p. 172.

3. Trevor, *op. cit.*, p. 23.

4. See Nishitani's essay, "Watakushi no tetsugakuteki hossokuten" (My philosophical starting-point), as well as his introductions to *Nihirizumu* and *Kami to zettai mu*.

5. See Introduction, note 8.

6. "Watakushi no tetsugakuteki hossokuten," p. 229, cited here according to the translation of Van Bragt, "Nishitani on Japanese Religiosity," pp. 271f. Already in his *Kongenteki shutaisei no tetsugaku*, especially in *Nihirizumu* and finally in remarks made in passing throughout *Shūkyō to wa nanika*, Nishitani shows his concern with Nietzsche. On his interest in Dostoyevsky, see his *Dosutoefusuki no tetsugaku*. M. Heinrichs has gathered together Nishitani's passages on Francis of Assisi from *Shūkyō to wa naniki* and published them in his *Der grosse Durchbruch;* his introduction and commentary are, however, not very impressive as a whole. Natsume Sōseki (1867–1916) was a leading Japanese author at the turn of the century; Hakuin (1685–1768; see Ch. 3, "Japanese Zen Buddhism") and Takuan (1573–1645) were famous Zen masters.

7. *Jiyū ishiron* ("On Free Will"), Tokyo, 1927; *Ningenteki jiyū no honshitsu* ("On Human Freedom"), Kyoto, 1948.

8. Cf. *Shimpi shisōshi; Kami to zettai mu; Shimpishugi no rinri shisō* ("The ethical notions of mysticism"), Tokyo, 1951; *Shūkyōtetsugaku* ("The philosophy of religion"), Tokyo, 1950.

9. Cf. *Kongenteki shutaisei no tetsugaku*, pp. 433–81, where Nishitani offers his reflections on the critiques of Nishida made by Yamauchi, Takahashi and Tanabe; and *Nishida tetsugaku* ("The philosophy of Nishida"), Tokyo, 1950, Vol. 2, pp. 191–218; *Kitarō Nishida.*

10. "Tanabe tetsugaku ni tsuite."

11. The first part of this work was republished in 1969 under the title *Shū-kyō to bunka* ("Religion and culture").

12. *Ibid.*, chapter entitled "Shūkyō, rekishi, bunka" (Religion, history, culture).

13. "Eine buddhistische Stimme zum Thema der Entmythologisierung."

14. "Nishitani Hakasecho *Shūkyō towa nanika* o yomite," pp. 84f.

15. "On Modernization and Tradition in Japan," p. 69.

16. *Shūkyō,* p. 53 (Eng., EB III/1, p. 1). ·

[The author explains that he has made frequent reference to the English translation because of the numerous insertions and revisions that Prof. Nishitani made in reviewing the translation. (These are noted in pointed brackets < > here.) For reasons explained in the Translator's Note, I have kept strictly to the English version as published.—Trans.]

17. *Ibid.,* p. 87. (Eng., EB IV/2, p. 30).

18. "Science and Zen," p. 79.

19. Cf. the following remark: "The world was no longer looked upon as having its ground in what may be called a pre-established harmony of the "internal" and "external"; rather, it came to be looked upon as an "external" world having its own laws in itself and existing only by itself" *(ibid.).*

20. Cf. *Shūkyō,* pp. 54f and *passim* (Eng., EB III/1, pp. 2f); *ibid.,* pp. 89ff (Eng., EB IV/2, pp. 32ff).

21. "Christianity and Buddhism. Centering around Science and Nihilism," p. 38.

22. Nishitani, "On Modernization and Tradition in Japan," p. 75; *idem., Shūkyō,* pp. 89ff (Eng., EB IV/2, pp. 32ff).

23. *Idem., Shūkyō,* pp. 55f (Eng., EB III/1, p. 3).

24. *Ibid.,* p. 57 (Eng., EB III/1, p. 5).

25. "On Modernization and Tradition in Japan," pp. 77f.

26. Cf. *Shūkyō,* p. 55 (Eng., EB III/1, p. 3). Compare also Kant's *Der einzig mögliche Beweisgrund zu einer Demonstration des Daseins Gottes,* Part 2, Sec. 3, *Werke,* Vol. 2, Darmstadt, 1967, pp. 667–69. [No serviceable English translation exists.—Trans.]

27. *Shūkyō,* p. 57 (Eng., EB III/1, p. 5).

28. "On Modernization and Tradition in Japan," pp. 70, 95.

29. *Shūkyō,* p. 96 (Eng., EB IV/2, pp. 38f).

30. "On Modernization and Tradition in Japan," pp. 82f.

31. *Shūkyō,* pp. 96f (Eng., EB IV/2, pp. 39f).

32. *Ibid.,* p. 97 (Eng., p. 40).

33. *Nihirizumu,* p. 3.

34. In the revised edition of the book, Nishitani has included a chapter, originally published separately, on nihilism in Russia.

35. *Ibid.,* p. 4.

36. Cf. *Shūkyō,* pp. 61–65 (Eng., EB III/1, pp. 8–13).

37. *Ibid.,* pp. 62f (Eng., p. 10).

38. *Ibid.,* p. 64 (Eng., p. 12).

39. *Ibid.,* pp. 65f (Eng., p. 13).

40. Cf. Nietzsche, "Aus dem Nachlass der Achtzigerjahre," *Werke,* Vol. 3, Darmstadt, 1966, p. 634; Nishitani, *Nihirizumu,* pp. 55–63.

41. *Ibid.*, p. 557.
42. Cf. *Shūkyō,* pp. 66ff (Eng., EB III/1, pp. 13ff).
43. "On Modernization and Tradition in Japan," pp. 83f.
44. *Ibid.,* p. 85.
45. *Ibid.,* pp. 85ff.
46. "Eine buddhistische Stimme zum Thema der Entmythologisierung," pp. 253–62.
47. *Ibid.,* p. 257.
48. With this last reference to "breakthrough" we come to grips with a word from the mysticism of Eckhart that Nishitani and his colleagues use a great deal. Cf. Ueda, *Die Gottesgeburt in der Seele und der Durch-bruch zur Gottheit,* pp. 119–39. M. Heinrichs falls short of understanding this concept in the Kyoto School in seeing the "great breakthrough" as a "Buddhistic break-through" which is not to be seen "as a breakthrough to the transcendent, but as a breakthrough into a greater depth, a greater interiorization and hence a great-er immanence" (*Durchbruch,* p. 188; cf. also pp. 102, 221).
49. The relevant allusions are widely strewn through Nishitani's work. We mention only a few noteworthy passages:
   a) on the kenotic theology of the cross: *Shūkyō,* pp. 66–70 (Eng., EB III/1, pp. 14–18).
   b) on Gal. 2:20: *Kongenteki shutaisei no tetsugaku,* pp. 112–28.
   c) on Francis of Assisi: *Shūkyō,* pp. 310–15 (German, Heinrichs, *op. cit.,* pp. 210–15): "On Modernization and Tradition in Japan," pp. 78f.
   d) on the Rhine mystics, see above, note 5.
   e) on "God-is-dead" theology, cf. Abe, "Christianity and Buddhism," pp. 53–62.
50. "Japan in the World," p. 8.
51. *Ibid.*
52. "Rationale of the International Institute for Japan Studies," p. 5.
53. "Science and Zen," p. 108.
54. Van Bragt, *loc. cit.,* p. 279.
55. *Shūkyō,* pp. 1f. This Foreword has not yet appeared in English.
56. *Ibid.,* pp. 3f.
57. In his essay, "Nipponjin no shūkyō no mondai," written in reply to J. Roggendorf's essay on "Religiosity in Japan," Nishitani defines his standpoint in quite similar fashion. He wishes to represent an aim somewhat divergent from that of Roggendorf: "I do not wish to have this understood from a Bud-dhistic standpoint so much as from the standpoint of a Japanese who lives in modern-day Japan. In other words, it has to do not so much with a confronta-tion between religions as rather with a dialogue on the religiosity of the Japa-nese as that problem is treated in general."
58. Kuyama *et al., Sengo Nihon seishinshi,* p. 194 (Eng., Van Bragt, *loc. cit.,* pp. 280f.) The italicized German phrases are Nishitani's own.

6. From Nihilistic Despair to the Emptiness of "Open Hands"
   1. For a comprehensive look at the problematic of "nothingness" from a Western viewpoint, see K. Riesenhuber, "Nichts." The notes to this essay pro-vide additional information on the principal relevant literature.
   2. When we speak here of being and beings, we wish to emphasize the point that there is a double tradition: *"u"* in the Eastern-Buddhist tradition of being,

and "bhāva" or *"yū"* in the Western tradition. The widely used *Philosophical Dictionary* published by Heibonsha of Tokyo seeks to master this complicated situation by devoting one article on *"u"* to the Eastern notion and then following it by another piece on *"yū"* to cover the history of being in the West (K. Mori, pp. 90f, 1191f). Cf. also Waldenfels, "Das schweigende Nichts angesichts des sprechenden Gottes," pp. 325ff. On the relationship between "absolute" and "relative," see Ch. 4, note 41 above.

3. Trevor, *The Ox and His Herdsman,* p. 24.

4. "Science and Zen," p. 102.

5. Nishitani, *Shūkyō,* p. 11 (Eng., PSJ II, p. 27).

6. *Ibid.,* p. 21 (Eng., p. 35).

7. *Ibid.,* pp. 21, 24 and *passim* (Eng., pp. 35, 37).

8. *Ibid.,* pp. 21f (Eng., p. 35).

9. *Ibid.,* pp. 23f (Eng., p. 37).

10. *Ibid.,* p. 26 (Eng., p. 41).

11. PSJ II, p. 40; the quotation of this sermon is lacking in the original Japanese text.

12. The passage comes originally from Hakuin's *Orategama,* Hakuin Oshō Zenshū, Vol. 5, Tokyo, 1935, p. 232; we cite here the translation of Dumoulin, *A History of Zen Buddhism,* p. 258.

13. *Ibid.,* pp. 221–23 and Dumoulin, pp. 257f.

14. *Shūkyō,* p. 39 (Eng., PSJ II, p. 52).

15. In this connection, see *ibid.,* pp. 35–41 (Eng., pp. 49–54).

16. We may recall once again here as before (see Ch. 1, "Anātman and Pratītyasamutpāda") the difficulties involved in translating the terms *anātman* and *muga.* The English translation of the opening essay of *Shūkyō* uses "non-self" (PSJ II, p. 52).

17. *Ibid.,* p. 39 (Eng., p. 52).

18. "Nishitani Hakasecho *Shūkyō towa nanika* o yomite," pp. 85f.

19. *Wegmarken,* p. 9.

20. *Ibid.,* pp. 12, 18.

21. Abe points out that at the time that Nishitani was drafting the first four chapters of the book, certain important works of Heidegger, such as *Was heisst Denken?* and the collection entitled *Vorträge und Aufsätze* had not yet been published (*loc. cit.,* p. 85).

22. "Buddhism and Christianity as a Problem of Today" and its ensuing symposium, together with Abe's final rejoinder and its ensuing discussion have all been published in the pages of *Japanese Religions.* Cf. also his essays "Zen and Western Thought," "Zen and Compassion," and "Zen and Nietzsche."

23. "Non-Being and Mu: The Metaphysical Nature of Negativity in the East and the West."

24. *Systematic Theology,* Vol. 1, p. 186.

25. *Ibid.,* Vol. 1, p. 189.

26. *Ibid.,* Vol. 1, p. 235.

27. *Ibid.,* Vol. 2, p. 11.

28. "Non-Being and Mu," p. 181.

29. Heidegger, *Wegmarken,* p. 16; see also Tillich, *op. cit.,* Vol. 1, p. 188.

30. Tillich, *op. cit.,* Vol. 1, pp. 188ff, 252ff and *passim.*

31. Abe, "Non-Being and Mu," p. 183.

32. *Ibid.,* pp. 183, 187.

33. Lao-tsu, *Tao te ching*, trans. with an introduction by D. C. Lau, Middlesex: Penguin, 1976, p. 101. On the meaning of *"tao"*, cf. G. Béky, *Die Welt des Tao*, Munich, 1972.

34. *Ibid.*, p. 54.

35. Abe considers Chuang-tsū as even more radical than Lao-tsu (*ibid.*, p. 184).

36. *Ibid.*, pp. 184ff.

37. *Ibid.*, pp. 186ff.

38. See note 2 above.

39. Abe, *op. cit.*, p. 188.

40. *Ibid.*, p. 181.

41. *Ibid.*, pp. 188f.

42. Cf. Riesenhuber, *loc. cit.*, pp. 1000–05.

43. Cf. Abe, *loc. cit.*, pp. 190f. Abe points expressly to the existential and soteriological meaning of negativity in Buddhism.

44. *Ibid.*, pp. 191f.

45. *Shūkyō*, p. 124 (Eng., EB V/2, p. 97).

46. *Ibid.*, p. 125 (Eng., p. 98).

47. *Ibid.*, p. 126 (Eng., p. 99).

48. *Ibid.*, p. 126 (Eng., pp. 99–100). The English text has been greatly reworked and expanded at this point.

49. On the discussion of "substance" see the rest of Ch. 3 as well as the relevant passages scattered through Ch. 4. We shall take up the question of intersubjectivity in Ch. 6, "I-Thou and Nothingness."

50. See his *Kami to zettai mu* and his comparison of Eckhart and Nietzsche, in his *Shūkyō to bunka* (Cf. Ch. 5, note 11 above), pp. 3–38. The Western reader may get a feel for the concern with Eckhart that is present already in the early Kyoto School from: Suzuki, *Mysticism: Christian and Buddhist;* M. Nambara, "Die Idee des absoluten Nichts in der deutschen Mystik und seine Entsprechungen im Buddhismus"; and Ueda, *Die Gottesgeburt in der Seele und der Durchbruch zur Gottheit.* Regarding this latter work, we may observe that unfortunately Ueda fails to bare his Japanese sources to the Western reader. The introductory remarks by E. Benz (pp. 11–20) do not suffice. See my book review, "Ein japanisches Eckhartbuch," *Hochland,* 60, 1967–68, pp. 166–69. Recently Ueda has taken up again, this time in Japanese, the relationship of Zen and mysticism in his *Zenbukkyō.*

Finally, one should note that the interpretation of Eckhart in Japan continues as before to draw its life from the image of Eckhart prevalent in the latter half of the nineteenth century, and only gradually makes room for more recent scholarship in the area. Cf. A. Dempf, *Meister Eckhart,* pp. 37–42; H. Fischer, *Meister Eckhart,* pp. 142–58; J. Degenhardt, *Studien zum Wandel des Eckhartbildes,* Leiden, 1967; T. Schaller, *Die Meister-Eckhart-Forschung von der Jahrhundertwende bis zur Gegenwart,* Freiburg im Breisgau, 1969; B. Welte, *Meister Eckhart.*

51. See Ueda, *Die Gottesgeburt in der Seele und der Durchbruch zur Gottheit,* p. 113. [Eckhart did not share the preoccupation of medieval philosophy with drawing clear distinctions between *esse, ens* and *essentia,* with the result that *"wesen"* can perform the function of any of these notions for him. The ambiguity that modern German can reflect only with difficulty by using the same word is not possible at all in English.—Trans.]

52. *Shūkyō,* p. 70 (Eng., EB III/2, p. 71).

53. *Op. cit.,* p. 116 cited from F. Pfeifer, *Deutsche Mystiker des 14. Jahrhunderts* II, Göttingen, 1924, pp. 319:3f; see also Meister Eckehart, *Deutsche Predigten und Traktate,* ed. and trans. by J. Quint, Munich, 1955, p. 407: 16f.

54. Ueda, *op. cit.,* pp. 117f.

55. *Shūkyō,* p. 72 (Eng., EB III/2, pp. 73f).

56. *Ibid.,* p. 75 (Eng., p. 77).

57. *Wegmarken,* p. 10.

58. *Ibid.,* p. 17.

59. *Holzwege,* p. 104.

60. "Nishitani Hakasecho *Shūkyō towa nanika* o yomite," p. 85.

61. *Wegmarken,* p. 239.

62. *Ibid.,* p. 247.

63. *Ibid.,* p. 249.

64. *Shūkyō,* p. 109 (Eng., EB V/1, p. 57).

65. See above, Ch. 4, note 46. Since Heidegger cites only half the formula, it is dubious whether he was conscious of its reciprocity.

66. *Shūkyō,* p. 123 (Eng., EB V/2, p. 96).

67. *Wegmarken,* p. 15; cf. also p. 12.

68. *Ibid.,* p. 107.

69. *Shūkyō,* pp. 108f (Eng., EB V/1, p. 56).

70. Abe, *loc. cit.,* p. 86.

71. "On Modernization and Tradition in Japan," pp. 77, 78.

72. *Ibid.,* pp. 78f.

73. *Shūkyō,* p. 79 (Eng., EB III/2, p. 80).

74. *Ibid.,* p. 79 (Eng., p. 80).

75. *Ibid.,* Eng., pp. 80f. This passage does not appear in the original Japanese text.

76. *Ibid.,* p. 80 (Eng., p. 81). Cf. S. Schlossman, *Persona und* ΠΡΟΣΩ-ΠΟΝ *im Recht und im christlichen Dogma,* 1968; M. Nédoncelle, "Prosopon et persona dans l'antiquité classique, *Revue de science et de religion* 22, 1948, pp. 277–99.

77. Cf. Migne, *Patres Latini,* 64, 1343, C.

78. Cf. for example, *In Sent.,* 30, 4: *Summa Theologiae* I, q. 40 a. 1 ad 1; I, q. 29, a. 1; and see A. Halder, "Person," *Lexikon für Theologie und Kirche,* Vol. 8, pp. 287–89.

79. W. Pannenberg, "Person," *Die Religion in Geschichte und Gegenwart,* third edition, ed. by K. Galling, 1957–65, Vol. 5, p. 231.

80. Cf. Waldenfels, *Glauben hat Zukunft,* pp. 58ff; and my observations in W. Böld *et al., Kirche in der ausserchristlichen Welt,* pp. 134–41. On Pannenberg, see the article referred to in the previous note, pp. 230–35; *Grundzüge der Christologie,* pp. 249–57, 182ff etc. On H. Ott, see the second volume of his *Wirklichkeit und Glaube,* Göttingen, 1969. On H. Mühlen, see *Das Vorverständnis von Person und die evangelisch-katholische Differenz* and *Die abendländische Seinsfrage als der Tod Gottes und der Aufgang einer neuen Gotteserfahrung.* Finally, cf. also W. Kasper, *Jesus the Christ,* pp. 240–52.

81. *Einführung in das Christentum,* pp. 146f; cf. also pp. 142–44. These words are echoed in Kasper's remark: "What is known as functional theology . . . is itself a form of ontic Christology. 'Being' however is understood here not as mere existence but as realization, not as substance but as personal relation.*

Jesus' being is realized as proceeding from the Father to men. Thus it is precisely functional Christology which gives expression to God's nature as self-giving love" (*Jesus the Christ*, p. 166; the phrase marked with a * was ommitted by the English translator). Kasper also points out in general that in modern times, "prepared both by medieval Scotism and Nominalism and by thinkers like Meister Eckhart and Nicholas of Cusa, the concept of God was desubstantialized" (pp. 181f).

Cf. also Ratzinger's "Zum Personverständnis in der Theologie," in his *Dogma und Verkundigung*, Munich, 1973, pp. 205–23.

82. *Shūkyō*, pp. 80f (Eng., EB III/2, pp. 81–2).

83. *Loc. cit.*, p. 71; cf. also W. Gundert, *Bi-yän-lu*, Vol. 3, pp. 105f.

84. *Ibid.*, p. 73.

85. *Ibid.*, pp. 75–6.

86. See the commentary of Engo (Chin., *Yüan-wu*), *ibid.*, pp. 79f.

87. *Ibid.*, p. 80.

88. *Ibid.*, pp. 80f.

89. *Ibid.*, p. 81.

90. *Ibid.*, p. 82.

91. *Ibid.*, p. 82.

92. *Wegmarken*, p. 162.

93. *Shūkyō*, Eng., EB III/2, p. 74. This passage was added to the English text and is not in the original Japanese.

94. "God, Emptiness and the True Self," p. 28.

95. *Shūkyō*, p. 78 (Eng., EB III/2, pp. 79–80).

96. *Ibid.*, pp. 71f (Eng., p. 72).

97. *Ibid.*, p. 67 (Eng., EB III/1, p. 15).

98. *Ibid.*, pp. 44f (Eng., PSJ II, p. 57).

99. *Ibid.*, p. 46 (Eng., PSJ II, pp. 58f).

100. *Ibid.*, p. 47 (Eng., p. 59).

101. Compare the following remark: "In this sense, within God's perfection is included a characteristic to be spoken of as a kind of trans-personality or impersonality—not an impersonality which is in simple contradistinction to personality, but as mentioned above, a personal impersonality" (*Ibid.*, Eng., EB III/1, pp. 16f). While the key word *chō-jinkakusei* (transpersonality) is found in the original Japanese text (p. 70), the English text has been considerably expanded at this point. Dumoulin has good grounds for connecting this choice of terminology with Tillich (*Christianity Meets Buddhism*, p. 190, note 53); cf. also Abe, "Christianity and the Encounter of the World Religions," pp. 116–19.

102. *Wahrheit als Begegnung*, Zurich, 1963. Cf. Nishitani, *op. cit.*, pp. 76ff (Eng., III/2, pp. 77ff).

103. *Shūkyō*, p. 78 (Eng., EB III/2, p. 79).

104. *Ibid.*, pp. 77f (Eng., p. 79).

105. See Josef Hochstaffl, *Negative Theologie*.

106. Denzinger and Schönmetzer, eds., *Enchiridion Symbolorum Definitionum et Declarationum de Rebus Fidei et Morum*, 33rd Ed., Barcelona, 1965, n. 806.

107. It remains to be shown still at what points and on what basis Eckhart was condemned. The condemnatory passages can be found in Denzinger, *op. cit.*, nn. 950–80.

108. See Abe, "Nishitani Hakasecho *Shūkyō towa ninika* o yomite," p. 98.

109. Karl Rahner, *Theological Investigations*, Vol. 1, p. 176, note 1.

110. *Ibid.,* Vol. 4, pp. 114f.
111. Cf. *Ibid.,* Vol. 4, pp. 77–102; the quotation appears on p. 87.
112. *Shūkyō,* pp. 116–22 (Eng., EB V/1, pp. 63–69).
113. *Ibid.,* p. 118 (Eng., p. 65).
114. *Ibid.,* p. 119 (Eng., p. 66).
115. *Ibid.,* pp. 119f (Eng., pp. 66f).
116. *Ibid.,* pp. 119f (Eng., p. 67).
117. *Ibid.,* p. 147 and *passim* (Eng., EB VI/1, p. 79).
118. *Ibid.,* p. 140 (Eng., EB VI/1, p. 73).

Emptiness and the Appreciation of World, History and Man
1. M. H. Trevor, *The Ox and His Herdsman,* pp. 23f.
2. *Ibid.,* pp. 91, 92. In this connection, see also L. Kolakowski, "The Priest and the Jester," in his *Marxism and Beyond,* London, Paladin, 1971, pp. 31–58.

Johannes Metz writes: "Jesus was neither clown nor rebel, but apparently close enough to be mistaken for both of them. Before Herod he was mocked as a clown; and by his own countrymen he was sent to the cross as a rebel. Whoever would follow him, whoever is not ashamed of his words, must count on falling prey to this mistake and falling out with every front—again and again, without reprieve" (J. Metz and J. Moltmann, *Leidensgeschichte. Zwei Meditationen zu Markus 8:31–38,* Freiburg-im-Breisgau, 1974, pp. 53f).

3. Trevor, *op. cit.,* p. 92.
4. *Ibid.,* p. 94.
5. Cf. S. Yamaguchi, "The Concept of the Pure Land in Nāgārjuna's Doctrine," p. 42.
6. *Shūkyō,* p. 149 (Eng., EB VI/1, p. 81).
7. "Nishitani Hakasecho *Shūkyō towa nanika* o yomite," pp. 93f.
8. "Der Buddhismus und das Problem der Säkularisierung," pp. 269, 274, 270.
9. "Zen and Western Thought," p. 538 (Jap., pp. 146f).
10. "Buddhism and Christianity as a Problem of Today," pp. 29f. It is striking that in this connection Abe refers to the doctrine of *karma* only in a footnote, and there claims that the doctrines of *karma* and Bodhisattva, if properly presented, can offer an answer to the question.
11. Abe, "Christianity and Buddhism," p. 40.
12. See the translation of the *Fukanzazengi* published by Waddell and Abe (Ch. 3, note 43 above) in which the following appears: "You should therefore cease from practice based on intellectual understanding, pursuing words and following after speech, and learn the backward step that turns your light inwardly to illuminate your self. Body and mind of themselves will drop away, and your original face will be made manifest. If you want to attain suchness [*tathatā*], you should practice suchness without delay" (*loc. cit.,* p. 122).
13. Shūkyō, p. 221. (Eng., EB X/2, pp. 10–11).
14. *Ibid.,* p. 112 (Eng., EB V/1, p. 60).
15. *Loc. cit.,* p. 40.
16. Cf. H. Nakamura, *Shin-Bukkyōjiten,* pp. 412f; Yamaguchi, *loc. cit.,* pp. 35, 43; Y. Takeuchi, *Probleme der Versenkung im Ur-Buddhismus,* pp. 6, 67, 86f; also E. Conze, *Buddhism,* p. 36.
17. Yamaguchi, *loc. cit.,* p. 43.
18. On the three-body doctrine, see Conze, *op. cit.,* pp. 35–8, 188–91; H. W. Schumann, *Buddhismus* (1963), pp. 60–65 and *Buddhismus* (1973), pp. 76–

83; E. Benz points out that this doctrine deserved to be compared to the Christian doctrine of "*corpus Christi*" in his "Buddhism and Christianity," pp. 14f.

19. Nishitani, *Shūkyō*, Eng., EB III/1, pp. 15f, note 3. This passage was added to the English version.

20. *Ibid.,* p. 221.

21. "Der Buddhismus und das Problem der Säkularisierung," p. 264.

22. Waldenfels, "Unfähigkeit und Bedürfnis zu glauben," pp. 9–20.

23. Abe, "Buddhism and Christianity as a Problem of Today," p. 28, note 20. Cf. also Ueda, *loc. cit.,* p. 271; Nakamura, *op. cit.,* pp. 229, 241.

24. "On Modernization and Tradition in Japan," pp. 89f.

25. *Ibid.,* p. 91.

26. *Ibid.,* p. 92.

27. *Shūkyō,* p. 141 (Eng., EB VI/1, p. 74).

28. *Ibid.,* pp. 141f (Eng., p. 74).

29. *Ibid.,* p. 164 (Eng., EB VI/2, p. 63).

30. *Ibid.,* p. 165 (Eng., p. 64). Compare this with No. 17 of the *Summarium Constitutionum Societatis Jesu:* " . . . in omnibus quaerant Deum, exuentes se, quantum fieri potest, amore omnium creaturarum, ut affectum universum in ipsarum Creatorem conferant, eum in omnibus creaturis amando, et omnes in eo, iuxta sanctissimam ac divinam ipsius voluntatem."

31. On this point, see M. Schmaus, "Perichorese," *Lexikon für Theologie und Kirche,* Vol. 8, pp. 274–76.

32. This note can be found in the *Eastern Buddhist,* VI/2, p. 66, note 1. Meantime, Professor Nishitani has provided the following additional clarification in a letter dated May 2, 1976: "The word *'ego'* is a Zen word used since olden times. It was made use of in the *Sandōkai* and other works, through the 'five degrees' of Tōzan, and in the Zen of China and Japan. One speaks of the *'shōhen ego'* of Tōzan. His five degrees are also extremely highly esteemed as a *kōan* with Hakuin in later Rinzai Zen. (The formula *'egoteki kankei'* is of course a constructed word that I have used for reasons of convenience.) From the characters we obtain the meaning:

  e = circum, around

  go = one another, mutually

  egoteki = back-and-forth around one another."

The *"Sandōkai"* is the Japanese transliteration of an ancient poem by an early Chinese Zen master of the T'ang Dynasty, Shih-t'ou Hsi-ch'ien (Jap., Sekitō Kisen) who lived from 700–790. Cf. Nakamura, *Shin-Bukkyōji-ten,* pp. 209, 315.

Tung-shan Liang-chieh (Jap. Tōzan Ryōkai) (807–869) is one of the two founders of Chinese Ts'ao-tung-Zen (Jap., Sōtō Zen). The "five degrees" (Jap., *goi*) of enlightenment go back to him. In Japanese, they are: (1) shō-chū-hen, (2) hen-chū-shō, (3) shō-chū-rai, (4) hen-chū-shi, and (5) ken-chū-to. The key concepts are those that Nishitani gives in citing the formula *"shōhen ego,"* viz., *shō* and *hen.* Following the sequences just given, they can be associated with the following pairs of words: (1) absolute-relative, (2) emptiness-form and color, (3) like-different, (4) one-many, and (5) absolute self-relative self. The copulative *chū* means "in," "within," "in the midst of," "between," "among," and the like, and reflects the relative opposition of *shō* (literally precise, upright) and *hen* (literally twisted, awry). Cf. Kapleau, *The Three Pillars of Zen,* pp. 330f; Dumoulin, *A History of Zen Buddhism,* pp. 112–18.

Nishitani's historical allusion leads therefore to the result that what he means by *"egoteki kankei"* in Japanese through the use of a linguistic form from Zen Buddhist tradition, is being rendered in English through the use of a linguistic form from Christian tradition, so that it comes to settle in a no-man's-land between Buddhism and Christianity. One will readily understand that this delicate situation still needs further clarity, and for the moment should not be made more difficult by the addition of another translation.

33. See the quotation referred to in note 27 above. At this point let it be noted that the major world philosophies, and above all the phenomenology of Husserl and his disciples, deserve to be questioned, with due reserve for the particular conditions of this problematic, on the possibility of their offering help in building a bridge for communicating in realms where linguistic and rational formulation are no longer possible. In the field of ethics, A. Deeken, taking off from Max Scheler, has made such an attempt; cf. his *Process and Permanence in Ethics: Max Scheler's Moral Philosophy,* New York, 1974.

34. Cf. *Shūkyō,* p. 168 (Eng., EB VI/2, p. 66).

35. *Ibid.,* p. 168 (Eng., p. 66).

36. Cf. *Ibid.,* pp. 181f (Eng., pp. 79f).

37. Nishitani, "On Modernization and Tradition in Japan," pp. 95f, note 9, writes *"Muge* means to penetrate or participate in without hindrance. Thus, *rijimuge* means the unhindered interpenetration of the noumenal and phenomenal. *Jijimuge* means the unhindered interpenetration of all phenomena." In our description we have followed the somewhat clearer formulation of S. Hisamatsu that DeMartino quotes during a conversation with Paul Tillich: " . . . I prefer to render *'ri'* not so much as 'universal' as 'non-particular.' *'Rijimuge'* would thus be 'between non-particular and particular no contraposition.' For precisely on the basis of this nonduality of any thing and its own negation *(riji-muge)* rests the non-duality of any thing and any 'other' thing *(jiji-muge)"* ("Dialogues, East and West," p. 106).

These two basic formulas both find their place of origin in the speculations of Kegon (Chin., Hua-yen) of which Suzuki says in reference to their relation to Zen: "the philosophy of Zen is Kegon and the teaching of Kegon bears its fruit in the life of Zen" (cited in Dumoulin, *op. cit.,* p. 38). Abe sees at work in them and in parallel formulas the struggles with the standpoint of emptiness or non-ego (Jap., *kū, muga):* "We may say that such post-Nāgārjuna concepts as the 'absolute middle' of the San-lun School, the 'perfect true nature' of the Vijñaptimātra School, the 'perfect harmony among the three truths of the empty, the provisionally-real, and the mean' of the T'ien-t'ai Sect, and 'the realm of unhindered mutual interpenetration of phenomena and phenomena' of the Hua-yen Sect, while differing in their respective positions, each endeavored to fathom the standpoint of Emptiness and non-ego essential to Buddhism" ("Zen and Western Thought," p. 520; Jap., I, p. 130). For further clarification of the formula, see Nakamura, *Shin-Bukkyōjiten,* "Sangan" (p. 200) and "Hokkai" (pp. 478f), and also the discussion between Hisamatsu, Tillich and DeMartino referred to earlier in this note.

38. Nishitani, "Science and Zen," p. 104, uses the term "homo-centric"; Abe does the same in "Dōgen on Buddha Nature," pp. 32, 38f, 44f and *passim;* and again in "Man and Nature in Christianity and Buddhism," *passim.*

39. Cf. "On Modernization and Tradition in Japan," pp. 84f.

40. "Science and Zen," pp. 103f.

41. *Ibid.,* pp. 104–6.

42. *Shūkyō,* p. 197 (Eng., EB IX/1, p. 50).

43. A. Bertholet and E. Lehmann, eds., *Lehrbuch der Religionsgeschichte,* Tübingen, 1925, Vol. 2, p. 85; cf. also p. 110, and E. Frauwallner, *Geschichte der indischen Philosophie,* pp. 291ff, 307, 371ff, 351ff, etc.

44. See above all, Nishitani, *Shūkyō,* pp. 189–221 (Eng., EB IX/1, pp. 42–71; X/2, pp. 1–11).

45. *Ibid.,* p. 190 (Eng., EB IX/1, p. 43). See also Dumoulin, "Die religiöse Metaphysik des japanischen Zen-Meisters Dōgen," pp. 208–12 with textual references.

46. Abe, "Dōgen on Buddha Nature," p. 31.

47. *Ibid.,* pp. 31f.

48. *Ibid.,* p. 38.

49. *Ibid.,* p. 44.

50. *Ibid.,* p. 39.

51. Nishitani includes *"gō"* (Skt., *karma*) among those fundamental Buddhist concepts that he chooses to use without giving the priority to a definite Buddhist usage nor to argue from such a basis; see his introductory remarks to *Shūkyō,* p. 3. A complete evaluation of the reinterpretation of understanding this involved would require a detailed consideration of the sort that falls outside the scope of these pages.

52. *Japanese Religions* 4/2, p. 23.

53. "Man and Nature in Christianity and Buddhism," p. 4.

54. Abe, "Dōgen on Buddha Nature," p. 34.

55. *Ibid.,* p. 35.

56. Abe, "Man and Nature in Christianity and Buddhism," p. 7.

57. *Shūkyō,* pp. 173f (Eng., EB VI/2, p. 72).

58. Cf. Abe, "Dōgen on Buddha Nature," pp. 44–64.

59. Suzuki and S. Ueda, "The Sayings of Rinzai," p. 93; Jap., Nishitani and Suzuki, *Kōza Zen,* Vol. 1, p. 281. A fuller treatment can be found in Vol. 3 of Suzuki's *Zenshū* (Complete Works), Tokyo, 1968, "Rinzai no kihonshisō," pp. 339–560.

60. Ueda and Suzuki, "The Sayings of Rinzai," p. 93; Jap., Nishitani and Suzuki, *Kōza Zen,* Vol. 1, p. 281.

61. Nishitani, *Shūkyō,* p. 179 (Eng., EB VI/6, p. 78).

62. *Ibid.,* p. 179 (Eng., p. 78).

63. *Ibid.,* pp. 243f.

64. Cf. *ibid.,* p. 204; *"hibi kore kōjitsu"* or *"nichinichi kore kōnichi."* Cf. also Abe, "Dōgen on Buddha Nature," p. 67.

65. *Shūkyō,* p. 181 (Eng., EB VI/2, p. 79).

66. On the reinterpretation of *saṃsāra,* cf. *Ibid.,* pp. 190–99 (Eng., EB IX/1, pp. 43–52).

67. *Ibid.,* p. 243.

68. *Ibid.,* pp. 221–38 (Eng., EB X/2, pp. 11–30), 245–68 and *passim;* see also *idem, Shūkyō to bunka,* pp. 39–123.

69. Cf. *Shūkyō,* p. 275.

70. *Ibid.,* p. 276. Compare also Abe's comment: "Heidegger discusses *'Sein und Zeit'* (Time and Being) emphasizing *'Ergebnis'* as a 'gift' of 'it' *(Es gibt)* in which time and being are inseparable" ("Dōgen on Buddha Nature," p. 69, note 82).

71. Cf. *Shūkyō*, p. 275.
72. See above note 26 and accompanying quotation.
73. Cf. *ibid.*, pp. 292ff, 298.
74. On this "trinitarian" formula, cf. *ibid.*, p. 300; on the significance of *"soku"*, *ibid.*, p. 200 and note 37 above, especially H. Nakamura, "Sangan," p. 200. On the function of *"chū"* see B. Waldenfels, *Das Zwischenreich des Dialogs* (The Hague 1971), which takes Husserl as its starting point.
75. Nishitani, *Shūkyō*, pp. 299f.
76. For formulations of this sort, see K. Nishitani, "Die religiös-philosophische Existenz im Buddhismus," *passim.*
77. *Ibid.*, p. 387.
78. Cf. M. Heinrichs, *Der grosse Durchbruch*, pp. 211–25. His translation needs reworking at some points.
79. *Ibid.*, p. 221, also pp. 102, 188.
80. Cited in Waldenfels, "Anmerkungen zum Gespräch der Christenheit mit der nichtchristlichen Welt," p. 133.
81. Nishitani, "Die religiös-philosophische Existenz im Buddhismus," p. 398.
82. " 'Life and Death' and 'Good and Evil' in Zen."
83. Cf. above, Ch. 3, note 12.
84. Cf. notes 8 and 9 above.
85. Abe, "Zen and Western Thought," p. 533; Jap., Nishitani and Suzuki, *Kōza Zen*, Vol. 1, p. 142.
86. "Nishitani Hakasecho *Shūkyō towa nanika* o yomite," p. 104.
87. *Shūkyō*, p. 177 (Eng., EB VI/2, p. 76).

Part Three: Stepping Stones For Dialogue

8. Mystical Experience and Philosophical Reflection
1. "Zen Buddhismus und Christentum im gegenwärtigen Japan," p. 156. Biographical and bibliographical details on Takizawa are given at the beginning of his essay.
2. Waldenfels, "A Symposium on Christianity and Buddhism," pp. 13f; *idem.*, "Absolute Nothingness," p. 366; see also Abe's reply, "Answer to Comment and Criticism," pp. 26–29.
3. "Notulae on Emptiness and Dialogue," pp. 53–55. Although tendency (3) has to be stated in simple terms, it should not be taken without further ado as a mere reproach. There are a variety of reasons for this lamentable fact. And it remains lamentable even when one contrasts it with the fact that for a long time in the West Buddhism was identified with Theravada Buddhism, and that today Mahāyāna Buddhism is widely associated exclusively with Zen.
4. Nishitani, *Shūkyō*, p. 174 (Eng., EB VI/2, p. 72).
5. Cf. above, Ch. 4, notes 38 and 39 for references to Nishida; for Nishitani, see Ch. 7, note 27.
6. Narayanrao Appurao Nikam, "Sein und Freiheit in der indischen Philosophie," in Wisser, ed., *Sein und Sinn*, pp. 255–69; the quotation appears on p. 256.
7. See above, Ch. 6, note 108.
8. See for example Nishitani's description of the three religious standpoints in *Shūkyō to bunka*, pp. 45–55.

9. *Truth and Method,* p. 317. On the question of experience, see also K. Lehmann, "Erfahrung," *Sacramentum Mundi,* Vol. 1, pp. 1117–23; A. S. Kessler, A. Schöpf and C. Wild, "Erfahrung," *Handbuch der philosophischen Grundbegriffe,* Vol. 2, pp. 373–86.

10. Gadamer, *op. cit.,* p. 319.

11. *Ibid.,* p. 320.

12. *Ibid.,* p. 320f.

13. *Shūkyō,* pp. 183f (Eng., EB VI/2, pp. 82f).

14. See the entries given above in Ch. 5, note 8.

15. Cf. Dumoulin, *A History of Zen Buddhism,* pp. 282–90; also his *Östliche Meditation und christliche Mystik.*

16. *Zen-Buddhismus,* pp. 223–374. In reference to J. B. Lotz and others, he makes the claim: "We have seen that *satori* is religious experience of a high level which one can characterize as mysticism, at least in the sense of a natural mysticism" (*ibid.,* p. 410; cf. also pp. 386, 397, 412). Cf. also *idem., Meditation als Weg zur Gotteserfahrung.*

17. *The Eastern Buddhist* I/1, p. 124.

18. "The Sayings of Rinzai," p. 102; Jap., Nishitani, *Kōza Zen,* Vol. 1, p. 288.

19. K. P. Fischer, *Der Mensch als Geheimnis,* p. 406.

20. "Zur Ortsbestimmung christlicher Mystik," in Beierwaltes *et al., Grundfragen der Mystik,* pp. 37–71: the quotation appears on pp. 46f.

21. See his *Psychologie des mystischen Bewusstseins; Das mystische Erkennen;* and the posthumously published *Das mystische Wort.*

22. *Psychologie des mystischen Bewusstseins,* p. 254.

23. *Ibid.,* p. 106.

24. *Ibid.,* p. 215.

25. *Ibid.,* p. 218.

26. *Das mystische Erkennen,* p. 267.

27. *Ibid.,* p. 264.

28. *Ibid.,* p. 329.

29. *Ibid.,* p. 360.

30. *Ibid.,* p. 369.

31. *Ibid.,* pp. 375f.

32. A Brunner, *Der Schritt über die Grenzen,* pp. 13–46.

33. "Self the Unattainable," p. 5.

34. *Die Gottesgeburt in der Seele und der Durchbruch zur Gottheit,* p. 169.

35. *Zenbukkyō,* pp. 65–133. On p. 70 he speaks expressly of the *"un-wortlichen Urwort,"* using the German phrase.

36. *Ibid.,* pp. 119ff.

37. Cf. H. Waldenfels, *Unfähigkeit und Bedürfnis zu glauben,* pp. 51–60.

38. In *Die Gottesgeburt in der Seele* Ueda offers several attempts in this direction worth considering.

39. Ueda, *Zenbukkyō,* pp. 134–87, especially pp. 135–38.

40. "On the I-Thou Relationship in Zen Buddhism," pp. 71–87; see also above, Ch. 6, "I-Thou and Nothingness: The Interpersonal."

41. Ueda, *Zenbukkyō,* pp. 166–72.

42. *Ibid.,* pp. 172–87, especially pp. 184–86.

43. See above, note 36.

44. See A. M. Haas, "Die Problematik von Sprache und Erfahrung in der

deutschen Mystik," in Beierwaltes *et al., Grundfragen der Mystik,* pp. 73–104, especially p. 80.

In not a few of the following quotations, the Japanese reader should be asked once again to avoid too quickly passing judgment on the texts for the objectivizing and dualism he disdains. Only one who approaches the various statements free of prejudice will be able to peer behind (in the Asiatic sense) clumsy and censurious statements to see the real sense contained in them.

45. *Ibid.,* pp. 86f.

46. On this problem, see Vol. 5, No. 9 of *Concilium* (May 1973) entitled "The Crisis in the Language of Faith."

47. Cf. A. M. Haas, *loc. cit.,* pp. 87–97.

48. *Ibid.,* p. 88.

49. J. Maritain, *The Degrees of Knowledge,* p. 311.

50. *Ibid.,* p. 326.

51. *Ibid.,* p. 327.

52. Cf. *ibid.,* pp. 331–37.

53. Compare the famous concluding sentence of Wittgenstein's *Tractatus logico-philosophicus:* "What we cannot speak about we must consign to silence," which R. Spaemann has taken for the starting point of his essay, "Mysticism and Enlightenment," *Concilium* V/9, May 1973, pp. 70–83. See also A. Grabner-Haider, "Wittgenstein und das 'Mystische': Folgerungen für die Theologie."

54. Maritain, *op. cit.,* p. 332.

55. *Ibid.,* p. 336.

56. See above, Ch. 7, note 8.

57. Spaemann, *loc. cit.,* pp. 82–83.

58. See above, Ch. 8, notes 4 and 13.

59. Maritain, *op. cit.,* pp. 236ff.

60. *Ibid.,* pp. 237ff, note 3.

61. From the translation of A. C. Pegis, London, University of Notre Dame Press, 1976, pp. 96f.

62. Maritain, *op. cit.,* pp. 237–8.

63. *Ibid.,* p. 238, note 3.

64. *Ibid.,* p. 238.

65. *Ibid.,* p. 240. See also Hochstaffl, *Negative Theologie,* I. 1/5, 2/3–5, 3.

66. Cf. Josef Pieper, *Unaustrinkbares Licht,* especially pp. 73–79.

67. K. Rahner, *Theological Investigations,* Vol. 9, pp. 193–94. On this point see also K. P. Fischer, *op. cit.,* pp. 381–88.

68. Rahner, *op. cit.,* p. 194.

9. God and Emptiness

1. A differentiated treatment of the problematic would have to give some attention to the fact that within the Kyoto School there is to be found a more Zen oriented group of thinkers (Nishida, Nishitani and Hisamatsu, Abe and Ueda, Tsujimura) and a more Amidistic oriented group of thinkers (Tanabe, Takeuchi), and these differences also affect their treatment of the God question.

2. "Harmony as Guide," p. 35; cf. also above, Ch. 4.

3. *Ibid.,* p. 35.

4. "East-West Religious Communication," p. 105.

5. *Ibid.,* p. 109.

6. "Christianity and the Encounter of the World Religions," p. 118.

7. "God, Emptiness and the True Self," p. 28.

8. *Ibid.*, pp. 22f. The comment on Pseudo-Dionysius would, of course, need to be demonstrated more carefully. On this point, see J. Hochstaffl, *Negative Theologie*, pp. 120–55.

9. "The Characteristics of Oriental Nothingness."

10. Cf. above, Ch. 6, "Being and Nothingness: Neither Object-Substance nor Subject" and "I-Thou and Nothingness: God and Man."

11. *Shūkyō*, p. 47 (Eng., PSJ II, pp. 59f).

12. S. Yagi and U. Luz, eds. *Gott in Japan*, pp. 182f.

13. *Ibid.*, p. 205. On K. Takizawa see above all his *Bukkyō to Kirisutokyō;* and *idem.*, "Was hindert mich noch, mich taufen zu lassen?" and "Zen-Buddhismus im gegenwärtigen Japan."

14. For an introduction to the newer developments, see H. Vorgrimler and R. Vander Gucht, eds., *Bilanz der Theologie im 20 Jahrhundert* and the accompanying volume *Bahnbrechende Theologen*, Vienna, 1970; H. J. Schultz, ed., *Tendenzen der Theologie im zwanzigsten Jahrhundert*, Stuttgart, 1970; C. Geffré, *Die neuen Wege der Theologie. Erschliessung und Überblick*, Vienna, 1973.

15. It is precisely on this point that the Kyoto School has made its significant contribution.

16. At this point we recall what Kasper says of the modern "desubstantialization of the concept of God" (see above, Ch. 6, note 81).

17. *Zur Theologie der Welt*, especially pp. 99ff.

18. This phrase of H. Grotius has been brought back chiefly through the thought of D. Bonhoeffer; cf. his *Widerstand und Ergebung*, Siebenstern-Taschenbuch, pp. 176ff, 158ff. On the historical classification of the phrase, see E. Feil, *Die Theologie Dietrich Bonhoeffers. Hermeneutik, Christologie, Weltverständnis*, Munich, 1971, p. 361.

19. Geffré, *op. cit.*, p. 56.

20. Hans Küng's book *On Being a Christian* is a prominent example of this approach (Garden City, Doubleday, 1976).

21. Cf. Fischer, *Der Mensch als Geheimnis*, p. 21.

22. *Theological Investigations*, Vol. 11, p. 150.

23. *Ibid.*, p. 153.

24. *Ibid.*, p. 153.

25. *Ibid.*, p. 153.

26. *Ibid.*, p. 154.

27. *Ibid.*, p. 157.

28. *Ibid.*, pp. 155–56. [The italicizing of emptiness—which I have substituted for "void," used by Rahner's translator—and nothingness has been added by the author.] The sentence marked with a * seems to have been misunderstood by Rahner's translator; it has been corrected accordingly.—Trans.]

29. *Ibid.*, p. 161.

30. *Ibid.*, p. 162.

31. *Ibid.*, p. 163.

32. *Ibid.*, p. 164.

33. See Rahner's essay "Reflections on Methodology in Theology," *Theological Investigations*, Vol. 11, pp. 68–114, especially Part III and pp. 101, 103, 111–12.

34. *Ibid.,* p. 102.
35. *Ibid.,* pp. 111–12. [*I have corrected the error of Rahner's English translator who misread *"negativa"* as *"meditativa."*—Trans.]
36. See above, Introduction, note 1.
37. See above all his summary work *Kirisutokyō shisō ni okeru sonzairon no mondai.*
38. *Ibid.,* p. 450.
39. See his remarks in *Japanese Religions* 3/5, pp. 13–16.
40. Cf. *The Foundations of Belief;* and my review of the work in *Theologie und Philosophie* 47/1, 1972, pp. 135–39 and 48/1, pp. 121–26.
41. Dewart, *op. cit.,* pp. 18–19.
42. *Ibid.,* p. 114.
43. *Ibid.,* p. 127.
44. *Ibid.,* p. 133.
45. *Ibid.,* p. 137.
46. *Ibid.,* pp. 139–50. These reflections need to be gone into more deeply still, all the more since the formulations of ancient Buddhism reach back into the realms of the Indogermanic.
47. Cf. *ibid.,* pp. 413–25; the quotation appears on p. 420.
48. *Ibid.,* pp. 418f.
49. *Ibid.,* pp. 492–93, 495.
50. *Ibid.,* pp. 497, 498.
51. See chiefly *ibid.,* pp. 472–90.
52. See *Philosophische Rundschau,* 21/1–2, 1978, pp. 114–16.
53. *Theological Investigations,* Vol. 11, p. 156.
54. *Gott-loser Gottesglaube? Grenzen und Überwindung der nichttheistischen Theologie,* Regensburg, 1974, p. 168; cf. Dewart, pp. 171–88 especially.
55. *Op. cit.,* p. 159.
56. *Ibid.,* p. 159.
57. *Identität und Differenz,* pp. 64f.
58. *Ibid.,* p. 45.
59. Cited in O. Pöggeler, *Der Denkweg Heideggers,* Pfullingen, 1963, p. 194. On the relationship of Heidegger to Theology, see J. M. Robinson and J. B. Cobb, Jr., eds., *New Frontiers in Theology,* Vol. 1, *"The Later Heidegger and Theology,"* New York, 1963; H. Danner, *Das Göttliche und der Gott bei Heidegger,* Meisenheim, 1971; A Gethmann-Siefert, *Das Verhältnis von Philosophie und Theologie im Denken Martin Heideggers,* Freiburg-im-Breisgau, 1974; W. Strolz, "Differenz von Seins- und Gotteserfahrung," *Herder-Korrespondenz* 29/2, 1975, pp. 96–98.
60. On this point see Ratzinger, *Einführung in das Christentum,* pp. 103–14; W. Strolz, *Menschsein als Gottesfrage. Wege zur Erfahrung der Inkarnation,* Pfullingen, 1965, especially pp. 225–40; G. Picht, *Der Gott der Philosophen und die Wissenschaft der Neuzeit,* Stuttgart, 1966.
61. See the tenth station of the ox path cited at the opening of Ch. 7 above.
62. "Notulae on Emptiness and Dialogue," pp. 63f.
63. Ratzinger, *op. cit.,* p. 112.

10. Jesus Christ: The Figure of the "Empty" God
1. *Theological Investigations,* Vol. 1, p. 187; cf. K. Fischer, *Der Mensch als Geheimnis,* pp. 278–89.

2. See the passage referred to in note 18 below.

3. Cf. A. Brunner, *Der Schritt über die Grenzen,* pp. 97–99; P.-G. Gieraths, "Deutsche Mystik," *Sacramentum Mundi,* I, pp. 845–50.

4. Cf. Fischer-Barnicol, *Hochland* 58, 1966, pp. 210.

5. Cf. P. Henry, "Kenose," *Dictionnaire de la Bible,* Supplément, V, Paris, 1957, pp. 7–161.

6. Cf. "Die Kenosis und das neue Gottesbild," *Mysterium Salutis* III/2, pp. 143–54.

7. Cf. Rahner, *Theological Investigations,* Vol. 4, pp. 105–20; the quotation appears on p. 114. [The misspelling of a Greek word in the English has been corrected here.—Trans.]

8. *Ibid.,* p. 116.

9. *Ibid.,* p. 116.

10. Cf. on this point H. Waldenfels, *Offenbarung,* pp. 260–65. On the discussion referred to here, W. Kasper has offered some extremely relevant comments in his book *Jesus the Christ.* For example, in speaking of the obedience of Jesus, he writes: "He is totally an empty mould giving form to God's self-communicating love" (p. 110). Poverty and emptiness also appear in the prayer of Jesus: " . . . by being totally open to God, he is also totally open to us. Being petitioner makes him at the same time Lord. If making a request is the mark of poverty and powerlessness, being able to make a request is proof of a power and potential which must be given by another. Poverty and wealth, power and helplessness, fullness and emptiness, receptiveness and completion are embodied in Jesus" (p. 110). The death of Jesus is, ultimately, emptiness and fullness in one: "This death is the form in which the Kingdom of God exists under the conditions of this age; the Kingdom of God is in human powerlessness, wealth in poverty, love in desolation, abundance in emptiness, and life in death" (p. 119). As a starting point for dialogue, it may be significant first of all to perceive that the fundamental fulfillment of belief for man rests in a letting be, which is the realizing of a "totally empty mould," and that this is for the Christian the call to the imitation of Christ (cf. p. 82).

11. Rahner, *Zur Theologie des Todes,* p. 39.

12. Both "godless" and "full of God" can be interpreted in two senses. Regarding the former, see the comments that follow. On the latter, it may be observed that the "fullness of God" realized in the incarnation would have to be considered along with the "fullness of God" revealed in creation, i.e., the fundamental immanence of God that is of eminent importance in the dialogue with Asia.

13. Cf. Suzuki, *Mysticism: Christian and Buddhist.*

14. See above, Ch. 6, note 103.

15. Cf. Abe, "Christianity and Buddhism," p. 42.

16. In speaking here of "stages" we should note that Catholic theology does not understand this in such a way that each of the following stages can be said to result *necessarily* from the one preceding. Rather it stands firm on the absolute freedom and the operation of grace in creation, incarnation, and death as death on the cross.

17. The problematic of belief in creation is one which we cannot go into further here without departing from our general framework. Of course, we should not overlook the fact that new stimuli from contemporary theology have resulted in a number of new points of view that would be of help in laying the

ground for and giving direction to discussion of belief in creation. Cf. here Waldenfels, *Offenbarung*, pp. 208–17.

18. Rahner, *Theological Investigations,* Vol. 8, pp. 239f.

19. See above, Ch. 6, note 81.

20. *Theological Investigations,* Vol. 4, p. 119.

Bibliography

The following is intended as a selective bibliography and as such does not pretend to present an exhaustive list either of the works of Prof. Nishitani nor of the secondary publications relevant to the themes of this book. By the same token, not all the works referred to in the notes are included here; in such cases, the full bibliographical information is supplied in the notes themselves.

The following abbreviations have been adopted in this bibliography and occasionally in the notes:

EB=*The Eastern Buddhist*, New Series
JR=*Japanese Religions*
Mon. Nipp.=*Monumenta Nipponica*
PSJ=*Philosophical Studies of Japan*
ZRGG=*Zeitschrift für Religions- und Geistesgeschichte*

1. Works by Keiji Nishitani

The Philosophy of Fundamental Subjectivity, Tokyo, 1940. The first part was reissued as Religion and Culture, Tokyo, 1973.
A History of the Ideas of Mysticism, Tokyo, n.d.
Nihilism, Tokyo, 1946; reissued 1973.
God and Absolute Nothingness, Tokyo, 1949; new edition, 1971.
With T. Watsuji *et al.*, *The Philosophy of Dostoyevsky*, Tokyo, 1950; new edition, 1967.
"The Problem of the Religiosity of the Japanese," *Kokoro* X/8, 1957, pp. 2–11; X/9, pp. 10–24.
"The Problem of Time in Shinran," *Shinran Zenshū* (Gendaigoyaku), Vol. 10, Tokyo, 1958, pp. 76–86. English translation: EB XI/1, 1978, pp. 13–26.
"The Problem of Myth," *Religious Studies in Japan*, Tokyo, 1959, pp. 50–61.

"Die religiös-philosophische Existenz im Buddhismus," R. Wisser (*q.v.*), pp. 381–98.

"Die religiöse Existenz im Buddhismus," *Proceedings of the Eleventh International Congress for the History of Religions, Tokyo and Kyoto, 1958*, Tokyo, 1960, pp. 577–83.

"Der Buddhismus und das Christentum," *Nachrichten der Gesellschaft für Naturund Völkerkunde Ostasiens* 88, 1960, pp. 5–32.

"Eine buddhistische Stimme zum Thema der Entmythologisierung," ZRGG XIII, 1961, pp. 244–62, 345–56.

What Is Religion? Tokyo, 1961. The English translation, insofar as it has been published: Ch. 1, "What Is Religion?" PSJ II, Tokyo, 1960, pp. 21–64; Ch. 2, "The Personal and the Impersonal in Religion," EB III/1, 1970, pp. 1–18; III/2, pp. 71–88; Ch. 3, "Nihilism and Śūnyatā," EB IV/2, 1971, pp. 30–49; V/1, 1972, pp. 55–69; V/2, pp. 95–106; Ch. 4, "The Standpoint of Śūnyatā," EB VI/1, 1973, pp. 68–91; VI/2, pp. 58–86; Ch. 5, "Emptiness and Time," EB IX/1, 1976, pp. 42–71; X/2, 1977, pp. 1–30.

With M. Kōsaka *et al., Christianity in Modern Japan*, Tokyo, 1961.

With M. Kōsaka *et al., An Intellectual History of Post-War Japan*, Tokyo, 1961.

"The Problem of Evil," *Shinrinri Kōza*, Vol. 2, Tokyo, 1961, pp. 1–27.

"Buddhism and Western Intellectual History," *Kōza Kindaibukkyō*, Vol. 3, Kyoto, 1962, pp. 7–32.

"My Philosophical Starting Point," *Kōza tetsugaku taikei*, Vol. 1, Tokyo, 1963, pp. 221–30.

"Rationale of the International Institute for Japan Studies," *Japan Studies* I/1, 1964, pp. 1–8.

"Japan in the World." *Japan Studies* I/2, pp. 2–9.

"Japan in the Contemporary World," *Japan Studies* I/13, pp. 1–6.

"On the Philosophy of Tanabe," *Tetsugaku kenkyū* 42/7, Kyoto, 1964, pp. 547–77.

"Science and Zen," EB I/1, 1965, pp. 79–108.

"The Awakening of Self in Buddhism," EB I/2, 1966, pp. 1–11.

Lectures on Zen, ed., 8 vols., Tokyo, 1967–68.

With R. Mutai *et al., What Is Philosophy?* Tokyo, 1967.

Gendai Nippon Shisōtaikei No. 2, ed., Tokyo, 1968.

"A Buddhist Philosopher Looks at the Future of Christianity," *The Japan Christian Yearbook*, Tokyo, 1968, pp. 108–11.

"On the I-Thou Relationship in Zen Buddhism," EB II/2, 1969, pp. 71–87.

"On Modernization and Tradition in Japan," N. Kobayashi and Y. Kuyama, eds., *Modernization and Tradition in Japan*, Nishinomiya, International Institute for Japan Studies, 1969, pp. 69–96.

With H. Yanagida (eds.), *Zenkagoroku* II, Tokyo, 1974.

2. Works by Other Authors

Abe Masao, "Reading Dr. Nishitani's *What Is Religion?*" *Tetsugaku kenkyū* 42/1, Kyoto, 1962, pp. 83–104.

———, "Buddhism and Christianity as a Problem of Today," JR 3/2, 1963, pp. 11–22; 3/3, pp. 8–31. See also the following "Symposium on Christianity and Buddhism: A Reply to Professor Abe," JR 4/1, 1964, pp. 5–52; 4/2, 1966, pp. 3–25; 8/4, 1975, pp. 10–53; 9/1 and 2, 1976.

———, "Christianity and the Encounter of the World Religions," EB I/1, 1965, pp. 109–22.

———, "Answer to Comment and Criticism," JR 4/2, 1966, pp. 26–57.

———, "Zen to seiyōshisō," K. Nishitani, ed., *Kōza Zen*, Vol. 1, pp. 113–48. English translation: "Zen and Western Thought," *International Philosophical Quarterly* X/4, 1970, pp. 501–41.

———, "Zen and Compassion," EB II/1, 1967, pp. 54–68.

———, "Christianity and Buddhism—Centering around Science and Nihilism," JR 5/3, 1968, pp. 36–62.

———, "God, Emptiness, and the True Self," EB II/2, 1969, pp. 15–30.

———, " 'Life and Death' and 'Good and Evil' in Zen," *Criterion*, Autumn, 1969.

———, "Dōgen on Buddha Nature," EB IV/1, 1971, pp. 28–71.

———, "Man and Nature in Christianity and Buddhism," JR 7/1, 1971, pp. 1–10.

———, "Zen and Nietzsche," EB VI/2, 1973, pp. 14–32.

———, "Religion Challenged by Modern Thought," JR 8/2, 1974, pp. 2–14.

———, "Non-Being and *Mu*. The Metaphysical Nature of Negativity in the East and the West," *Religious Studies* II, pp. 181–92.

———, "The Crucial Points: An Introduction to the Symposium on Christianity and Buddhism," JR 8/4, 1975, pp. 2–9.

Adorno, Theodor, *Negative Dialectics*, Seabury, New York, 1973.

Albrecht, Carl, *Psychologie des mystischen Bewusstseins*, Bremen, 1951.

———, *Das mystische Erkennen. Gnoseologie und philosophische Relevanz der mystischen Relation*, Bremen, 1958.

———, *Das mystische Wort. Erleben und Sprechen in Versunkenheit*, ed. by Hans A. Fischer-Barnicol, Mainz, 1974.

Arendt, Dieter, (ed.). *Der Nihilismus als Phänomen der Geistesgeschichte in der wissenschaftlichen Diskussion unseres Jahrhunderts*, Wege der Forschung CCCLX, Darmstadt, 1974.

Ariga Tetsutarō, *The Problem of Ontology in Christian Thought*, Tokyo, 1969.

Awakawa Yasuichi, *Zen Painting*, Tokyo, 1979.

Balthasar, Hans Urs von, *Herrlichkeit. Eine theologische Asthetik*, 3 vols., Einsiedeln, 1961–1969.

———, *Glaubhaft ist nur Liebe*, Einsiedeln, 1963.

———, "Mysterium Paschale," J. Feiner and M. Löhrer, eds., *Mysterium Salutis*, III/2, Einsiedeln, 1969, pp. 133–326.

Bareau, André, "Der indische Buddhismus," A. Bareau *el al., Die Religionen Indiens*, Vol. 3 (Die Religionen der Menschheit, ed. by C. M. Schröder, No. 13), Stuttgart, 1964, pp. 1–215.

Beierwaltes, Werner *et al., Grundfragen der Mystik*, Einsiedeln, 1974.

Benz, Ernst, "Mystik als Seinserfüllung bei Meister Eckhart," R. Wisser (*q.v.*), pp. 319–413.

———, "Buddhism and Christianity," JR 8/4, 1975, pp. 10–18.

Berlinger, Rudolph, *Das Nichts und der Tod*, Frankfurt, 1972.

Bernhart, Josepf, *Meister Eckhart und Nietzsche. Ein Vergleich für die Gegenwart*, Kevelaer, n.d.

Böld, W. *et al., Kirche in der ausserchristlichen Welt*, Regensburg, 1967.

Bochenski, J. M., *Formale Logik*, Frankfurt am Main, 1970.

Bragt, Jan Van, "Notulae on Emptiness and Dialogue. Reading Professor Nishitani's *What Is Religion?*" JR 4/4, 1966, pp. 50–78.

———, "Nishitani on Japanese Religiosity," J. Spae (*q.v.*), pp. 271–84.

Brüll, Lydia, and Ulrich Kemper, eds., *Asien. Tradition und Fortschritt*, Festschrift für Horst Hammitzsch zu seinem 60, Geburtstag, Wiesbaden, 1971.

Brunner, August, *Der Schritt über die Grenzen. Wesen und Sinn der Mystik*, Würzburg, 1972.

Casey, David F., *Aspects of the Śūnyatā-Absolute of Nāgārjuna of Second Century A.D. Andhra*, Harvard University, 1960 (doctoral dissertation).

———, "Nāgārjuna and Candrakirti. A Study of Significant Differences," *Transactions of the International Conference of Orientalists in Japan* IX, Tōhō Gakkai Tokyo, 1964, pp. 34–45.

Conze, Edward, *Buddhism. Its Essence and Development*, New York, Harper and Row, 1951.

———, *Buddhist Thought in India. Three Phases of Buddhist Philosophy*, University of Michigan Press, Ann Arbor, 1973.

Cuttat, Jacques-Albert, *Begegnung der Religionen*, Einsiedeln, 1956.

———, *Asiatische Gottheit-Christlicher Gott. Die Spiritualität der beiden Hemisphären*, Einsiedeln, 1971.

Dempf, Alois, *Meister Eckhart*, Vienna, 1960.

Dewart, Leslie, *The Future of Belief. Theism in a World Come of Age*, New York, Herder and Herder, 1966.

———, *The Foundations of Belief*, London, Herder and Herder, 1969.

Dumoulin, Heinrich. "Die Entwicklung des chineschen Ch'an nach Hui-nēng im Lichte des *Wu-men-kuan,*" *Monumenta Serica* VI, 1941, pp. 40–72.

————, "Boddhidharma und die Anfänge des Ch'an Buddhismus," Mon. Nipp. VII, 1951, pp. 67–83.

————, (trans.), *Wu-men-kuan. Der Pass ohne Tor*, Mon. Nipp. Monographs No. 13, Tokyo, 1953.

————, "Das Merkbuch für die Übung des Za-Zen des Zen-Meisters Keizan," Mon. Nipp. XIII, 1957, pp. 329–46.

————, "Allgemeine Lehre zur Förderung des Zazen von Zen-Meister Dōgen," Mon. Nipp. XIV, 1958, pp. 429–36.

————, *A History of Zen Buddhism*, New York, Random House, 1963.

————, "Die religiöse Metaphysik des japanischen Zen-Meisters Dōgens," *Saeculum* XII/3, 1961, pp. 205–36.

————, "Der Buddhismus," *Weltgeschichte der Gegenwart* II, Bern, 1963, pp. 626–46.

————, *Östliche Meditation und christliche Mystik*, Frankfurt-am-Main, 1966.

————, *Christlicher Dialog mit Asien*, Munich, 1970.

————, (ed.), *Buddhism in the Modern World*, London, Collier, 1976.

————, *Christianity Meets Buddhism* (Religious Encounter: East and West), LaSalle, Ill., 1974.

————, *Mumonkan. Die Schranke ohne Tor*, Mainz, 1975.

————, *Der Erleuchnungsweg des Zen im Buddhismus*, Frankfort, 1976.

Eliot, Charles, *Japanese Buddhism*, London, 1935.

Enomiya, Hugo M., *Zen-Buddhismus*, Cologne, 1966.

———— Lassale, Hugo M., *Meditation als Weg zur Gotteserfahrung. Eine Anleitung zum mystischen Gebet*, Cologne, 1972.

————, *Zen-Meditation. Eine Einführung*, Cologne, 1975.

Fischer, Heribert, *Meister Eckhart*, Frankfort-am-Main, 1974.

Fischer, Klaus P., *Der Mensch als Geheimnis. Die Anthropologie Karl Rahners*, Basel, 1974.

Fischer-Barnicol, Hans, "Fragen aus Fernost. Eine Begegnung mit dem japanischen Philosophen Nishitani," *Hochland* 58, 1966, pp. 205–18.

Frauwallner, Erich, *Geschichte der indischen Philosophie* I, Salzburg, 1953.

Gadamer, Hans-Georg, *Truth and Method*, New York, Seabury, 1975.

Gardet, Louis, *Mystische Erfahrungen in nicht-christlichen Ländern*, Colmar, 1956.

Glasenapp, H. V., *Die Weisheit des Buddha*, Wiesbaden, n.d.

Gonda, Jan, *Die Religionen Indiens*, I and II (Die Religionen der Menschheit, ed. by C. M. Schröder, Nos. 11/12), Stuttgart, 1960, 1963.

Govinda, Anagarika, *The Psychological Attitude of Early Buddhist Philosophy and Its Systematic Representation According to Abhidhamma Tradition*, New York, S. Weiser, 1969.

————, *Foundations of Tibetan Mysticism According to the Esoteric Teachings of the Great Manta Om Mani Padme Hum*, New York, S. Weiser, 1969.

Guardini, Romano, *Der Gegensatz. Versuch zu einer Philosophie des Lebendigen-Konkreten*, Mainz, 1925.

————, *Unterscheidung des Christlichen. Gesammelte Studien*, Mainz, 1935.

————, *Welt und Person. Versuche zur christlichen Lehre vom Menschen*, Würzburg, 1939.

————, *Die Sinne und die religiöse Erkenntnis. Zwei Versuche über die christliche Vergewisserung*, Würzburg, 1950.

Gundert, Wilhelm, *Japanische Religionsgeschichte*, Tokyo, 1935.

————, *Bi-yän-lu. Meister Yüan-wu's Niederschrift von der Smaragdenen Felswand* ... verdeutscht und erläutert, 3 vols., Munich, 1964–1973.

Heidegger, Martin, *Sein und Zeit*. Tübingen, 12th ed., 1972.

————, *Holzwege*, Frankfort, 1950.

————, *Identität und Differenz*, Pfullingen, 4th ed., 1957.

————, *Gelassenheit*, Pfullingen, 1959.

————, *Nietzsche* I and II, Pfullingen, 2nd ed., 1961.

————, *Unterwegs zur Sprache*, Pfullingen, 3rd ed., 1965.

————, *Wegmarken*, Frankfort, 1967.

————, "Two Addresses: 'Ansprache zum Heimatabend' and 'Über Abraham a Santa Clara'" (with preliminary remarks by K. Nishitani), EB I/2, 1966, pp. 48–77.

Heinemann, Robert, "*Shushō-ittō* und *Genjō-kōan*. Welterkenntnis und Verworklichung bei Dōgen," Brüll and Kemper (*q.v.*), pp. 184–92.

Heinrichs, Maurus, *Katholische Theologie und asiatisches Denken*, Mainz, 1963.

————, *Der grosse Durchbruch. Franziskus von Assisi im Spiegel japanischer Literatur*, Werl, 1969.

Herrigel, Eugen, *Zen in the Art of Archery*. New York, Random House, 1971.

————, *Der Zen Weg. Aufzeichnungen aus dem Nachlass*, together with Gusty L. Herrigel, ed. by H. Tausend, Weilheim, 1958.

Hisamatsu Shin'ichi, "The Characteristics of Oriental Nothingness," PSJ II, 1960, pp. 65–97.

————, (trans.), *Die Fülle des Nichts. Vom Wesen des Zen*, Pfullingen, 1975.

————, "Zen: Its Meaning for Modern Civilization," EB I/1, 1965, pp. 22–47.

————, *Works*: Vol. 2, *The Way of Absolute Subjectivity*; Vol. 3, *Awakening and Creativity;* Vol. 5, *Zen to geijutsu*. English translation, *Zen and the Fine Arts*, Tokyo, 1971.

————, "Ultimate Crisis and Resurrection," EB VIII/1, 1975, pp. 12–29; VIII/2, pp. 37–65.

Hochstaffl, Josef, *Negative Theologie. Ein Versuch zur Vermittlung des patristischen Begriffs*, Munich, 1976.

Honda, Masaaki, "The Buddhist Logic of "Soku" and Christianity," *Katorikku kenkyū* XII/1, 1973, pp. 1–25. (See Kadowaki's discussion also.)

Hori Ichirō *et al.* (eds.), *Japanese Religion*, A Survey by the Agency for Cultural Affairs, Tokyo and Palo Alto, 1972.

Imamichi Tomonobu, *Betrachtungen über das Eine. Gedanken aus der Begegnung der Antipoden*, Institute of Aesthetics of the Faculty of Philosophy, Tokyo University, 1968.

Inoue Eiji *et al.* (eds.), *A Dialogue of Religions: Christianity and the Religions of Japan*, Tokyo, 1973.

Ital, Gerta, *Der Meister, die Mönche und ich. Im zen-buddhistischen Kloster.* Weilheim, 1972.

———, *Auf dem Weg zu Satori. Übersinnliche Erfahrungen und das Erleuchtung*, Weilheim, 1971.

Jaspers, Karl, *Die grossen Philosophen*, Vol. 1, Munich, 1959.

Johnston, William, *The Mysticism of the Cloud of Unknowing. A Modern Interpretation*, New York, 1967.

———, *The Still Point. Reflections on Zen and Christian Mysticism*, New York, Harper and Row, 1971.

Kadowaki Kakichi, "Ways of Knowing," A Buddhist-Thomist Dialogue, *Japanese Missionary Bulletin* XXIII/8, 1969, pp. 467–74; XXIII/9, pp. 515–30.

———, "Towards a Better Understanding of Zen Buddhism," *Japanese Missionary Bulletin* XXIII/10, 1969, pp. 611–19.

———, "A Review of Honda's Article on "Soku" (*q.v.*), Katorikku Kenkyū XII/2, 1973, pp. 153–59; a continuation of the discussion appears *ibid.*, XIII/2, 1974, pp. 149–72.

———, *The Ignatian Exercises and Zen. An Attempt at Synthesis*, Jersey City, N.J., 1974.

Kapleau, Philip, *The Three Pillars of Zen. Teaching, Practice, Enlightenment*, Boston, Beacon, 1965.

Kasper, Walter, *Jesus the Christ*, New York, Paulist Press, 1976.

King, Winston L., *Buddhism and Christianity. Some Bridges of Understanding*, London, 1962.

———, "The Personal Note, Divisive but Unitive," JR 4/1, 1964, pp. 41–46.

———, "East-West Religious Communication," EB I/2, 1966, pp. 91–110.

———, "*Śūnyatā* as a Master-Symbol," *Numen* XVII, Leiden, 1970, pp. 95–104.

———, "The Impersonal Personalism and Subjectivism of Buddhist 'Nihilism,' " JR 8/4, 1975, pp. 37–53.

Kitagawa, Joseph M., *Religion in Japanese History*, New York, 1966.

Knauth, Lothar, "Life Is Tragic: The Diary of Nishida Kitarō," Mon. Nipp. XX, 1965, pp. 335–58.

Kobayashi Kōichi and Miura Masashi, *The Japanese Nihilum and the Japanese Nothingness*, Tokyo, 1970.

Korvin-Krasinski, Cyrill von, *Mikrokosmos und Makrokosmos in religions-geschichtlicher Sicht*, Darmstadt, 1960.

Kōsaka Masaaki, *Nishida Kitarō. The Life and Thought of the Master*, Tokyo, 1971.

Küng, Hans, *Menschwerdung Gottes. Eine Einführung in Hegels theologisches Denken als Prolegomena zu einer künftigen Christologie*, Vienna, 1970.

———, *On Being a Christian*, Garden City, Doubleday, 1976.

Kuroki Mikio, "Die Frage nach Gott in der modernen japanischen Philosophie: Nishida Kitarō und Tanabe Hajime," *Verbum SVD* 16/3–4, 1975, pp. 273–305.

Kuyama Yasushi and Kobayashi Nobuo (eds.), *Modernization and Tradition in Japan*, International Institute for Japan Studies, Nishinomiya, 1969.

Lüth, Paul, *Die japanische Philosophie*, Tübingen, 1944.

Maritain, Jacques, *The Degrees of Knowledge*, New York, Scribner's Sons, 1959.

Matsunaga, Alicia, *The Buddhist Philosophy of Assimilation. The Historical Development of the Honji-Suijaku Theory*, Tokyo, 1969.

Mensching, Gustav, *Buddhistische Geisteswelt. Vom historischen Buddha zum Lamaismus*, Baden, n.d.

———, *Buddha und Christus. Ein Vergleich*. Stuttgart, 1978.

Merton, Thomas, *The Ascent to Truth*, New York, 1951.

———, *Mysticism and Zen Masters*, New York, 1967.

Metz, Johannes, *Christliche Anthropozentrik. Über die Denkform des Thomas von Aquin*, Munich, 1962.

———, *Zur Theologie der Welt*, Mainz, 1968.

Miura Isshū and Ruth Fuller Sasaki, *The Zen Kōan*, New York, 1965.

Moore, Charles (ed.), *The Japanese Mind. Essentials of Japanese Philosophy and Culture*, Honolulu, 1967,

———, *Philosophy and Culture East and West. East-West Philosophy in Practical Perspective*, Honolulu, 1968.

Mori Kōichi *et al.* (eds.), *Philosophical Dictionary*, 10th ed., Tokyo, 1964.

Mühlen, Heribert, *Das Vorverständnis von Person und die evangelisch-katholische Differenz*, Marburg, 1965.

———, *Die abendländische Seinsfrage als der Tod Gottes und der Aufgang einer neuen Gotteserfahrung*, Padderborn, 1968.

Munsterberg, Hugo, *The Arts of Japan. An Illustrated History*, Tokyo, 1972.

Muralt, Raoul von, *Meditations-Sutras des Mahāyāna-Buddhismus*, 2 vols., Oberhain, 1973.

Murti, T. R. V., *The Central Philosophy of Buddhism. A Study of the Mādhyamika System*, London, Allen and Unwin, 1970.

Nakamura Hajime, *New Dictionary of Buddhism*, Tokyo, 1962.

————, *Ways of Thinking of Eastern Peoples: India, China, Tibet, Japan*, Honolulu, 1964.

Nambara Minoru, "Die Idee des absoluten Nichts in der deutschen Mystik und seine Entsprechungen im Buddhismus," *Archiv für Begriffsgeschichte* VI, 1960, pp. 143–277.

Nietzsche, Friedrich, *Werke*, 3 vols., Darmstadt, 1966.

Nishida Kitarō, *Complete Works*, 18 vols., Tokyo, 1947–1953; new edition, 1965- .

————, *Intelligibility and the Philosophy of Nothingness*, Tokyo, 1958.

————, *A Study of Good*, Tokyo, 1960.

————, *Fundamental Problems of Philosophy. The World of Action and the Dialectical World*, Tokyo, 1970.

————, "Towards a Philosophy of Religion with the Concept of Pre-Established Harmony as Guide," EB III/1, 1970, pp. 19–46.

Noda, Matao, "East-West Synthesis in Kitarō Nishida," *Philosophy East and West* (Hawaii), 1954–55, pp. 345–59.

Nyanaponika, (ed.), *Die Lehrreden des Buddha aus der Angereihten Sammlung*, 5 vols., Cologne, 1969.

Obata Yoshinobu, "Japanese Buddhism and Its Problems, Seen in the Light of Modern Christian Theological Methodology," *Katorikku kenkyū*, XIII/2, 1974, pp. 78–102.

Ohasama, Schūej, *Zen. Der lebendige Buddhismus in Japan*, Darmstadt, 1968.

Okada Jun'ichi (ed.), *Christianity and the Spiritual Climate of Japan*, Tokyo, 1972.

Oldenberg, Hermann, *Buddha. Sein Leben, sein Lehre, sein Gemeinde*, Munich, 1961.

Onodera Isao, "The Logic of Locus and the Christian Worldview. An Essay on Topographical Theology," *Katorikku kenkyū*, XIII/1, 1974, pp. 48–83.

Ott, Heinrich, *Wirklichkeit und Glaube*, Vol. 2: *Der Persönliche Gott*, Zurich, 1969.

Otto, Rudolf, *Mysticism East and West*, New York, Macmillan, 1960.

Pannenberg, Wolfhart, *Grundzüge der Christologie*, Gütersloh, 1966.

Picht, Georg, *Der Gott der Philosophen und die Wissenschaft der Neuzeit*, Stuttgart, 1966.

Pieper, Josef, *Über das Ende der Zeit. Eine geschichtsphilosophische Meditation*, Munich, 1953.

————, *Unaustrinkbares Licht. Das negative Element in der Weltansicht des Thomas von Aquin*, Munich, 1963.

Piovesana, Gino, *Recent Japanese Philosophical Thought 1862–1962*.

A Survey, Tokyo, 1963.

Pöggeler, Otto, *Der Denkweg Heideggers,* Pfullingen, 1963.

Radhakrishnan, S., *Die Gemeinschaft des Geistes. Östliche Religionen und westliches Denken,* Darmstadt, n.d. (ca. 1952).

Rahner, Karl, *Theological Investigations,* Vols. I-XIV, New York, Seabury, 1971- .

———, *Zur Theologie des Todes* (Quaestiones Disputatae No. 2), Freiburg, 1958.

———, *Betrachtungen zum ignatianischen Exerzitienbuch,* Munich, 1965.

Ratzinger, Joseph, *Einführung in das Christentum. Vorlesungen über das apostolische Glaubensbekenntnis,* Munich, 1968.

Riesenhuber, Klaus, "Nichts," *Handbuch philosophischer Grundbegriffe,* ed. by H. Krings *et al.,* Munich, 1973-4, Vol. 4, pp. 991-1008.

——— (trans.), *Risō* 9/484, 1973, pp. 58-75.

Salaquarda, J. (ed.)., *Philosophische Theologie im Schatten des Nihilismus,* Berlin, 1971.

Saunders, E. Dale, *Buddhism in Japan. With an Outline of Its Origin in India,* Tokyo, 1962.

Schinzinger, Robert, "Der Denkstil Ostasiens," *Nachrichten der Deutschen Gesellschaft für Natur- und Völkerkunde Ostasiens,* No. 73, 1952, pp. 13-23.

———, "Der Grund und das Nichts. Zum Problem einer japanischen Weltanschauung," Brüll and Kemper *(q. v.),* pp. 508-22.

Schlette, Heinz Robert, *Aporie und Glaube. Schriften zur Philosophie und Theologie,* Munich, 1970

Schlingloff, Dieter, *Die Religion des Buddhismus,* 2 vols., Berlin, 1962-63.

Schultz, Hans Jürgen (ed.), *Wer ist das eigentlich - Gott?* Munich, 1969.

Schumann, Hans Wolfgang, *Buddhismus. Philosophie zur Erlösung,* Bern, 1963.

———, *Buddhismus. Ein Leitfaden durch seine Lehren und Schulen,* Darmstadt, 1973.

Schüttler, Günter, *Die Erleuchtung im Zen-Buddhismus. Gespräche mit Zen-Meistern und psycho-pathologische Analyse,* Munich, 1974.

Schwan, Alexander (ed.), *Denken im Schatten des Nihilismus,* Darmstadt, 1975.

Seckel, Dietrich, *Buddhistische Kunst Ostasiens,* Stuttgart, 1957.

Shibayama Zenkei, *Zen Comments on the Mumonkan* (the authoritative translation, with commentary, of a basic Zen text), New York, 1974.

Shimomura Toratarō, *Nishida Kitarō: The Man and His Thought,* Tokyo, 1965.

———, "Nishida Kitarō and Some Aspects of His Philosophical

Thought," *Nishida, A Study of the Good*, pp. 191–217.

Spae, Joseph J., *Japanese Religiosity*, Oriens Institute for Religious Research, Tokyo, 1971.

Stcherbatsky, T., *The Central Conception of Buddhism and the Meaning of the Word "Dharma,"* Calcutta, 1961.

————, *The Conception of Buddhist Nirvāṇa*, The Hague, 1965.

————, *Buddhist Logic*, S'Gravenhage, 1958.

Streng, Frederick J., *Emptiness. A Study in Religious Meaning*, New York, 1967.

Suzuki Daisetz, *Essays in Zen Buddhism*, Vols. 1–3, London, 1958.

————, *Studies in the Lankāvatāra Sūtra*, London, 1957.

————, *Zen and Japanese Culture*, Princeton University Press, 1970.

————, *Introduction to Zen Buddhism*, New York, 1949.

————. "On the Hekiganroku (The Blue Cliff Records)," EB I/1, 1965, pp. 5–21; cf. I/2, 1966, pp. 12–20.

————, *Zenshū: Complete Works*, 31 vols., Tokyo, 1968–70.

————, "Self the Unattainable," EB III/2, 1970, pp. 1–8.

————, "Infinite Light," EB IV/2, 1971, pp. 1–29.

————, "The Seer and the Seen," EB V/1, 1972, pp. 1–25.

————, *Erfülltes Leben aus Zen. Mit einer Einführung in die Texte von Wei-Lang (Hui-nēng)*, Munich, 1973.

————, *Mysticism Christian and Buddhist*, New York, Harper, 1957.

————, "Zen Buddhism and a Commonsense World," EB VII/1, 1974, pp. 1–18.

————, "The Buddhist Conception of Reality." EB VII/2, 1974, pp. 1–21. N.B.: For further bibliographical information on the works of Suzuki, see H. Rzepkowski, *Das Menschenbild bei Daisetz Teitaro Suzuki*, St. Augustine, 1971, pp. viii–xii; EB II/1, 1967, pp. 216–29; III/2, 1970, pp. 146ff.

———— and T. N. Callaway, "A Dialogue," EB III/1, 1970, pp. 109–22.

———— and S. Ueda, "The Sayings of Rinzai," EB VI/1, 1973, pp. 92–110.

Takakusu Junjirō, *The Essentials of Buddhist Philosophy*, Honolulu, 1947.

Takeuchi Yoshinori, "The Basic Motivation for Speculation in the Doctrine of Pratītyasamutpāda," *A Festschrift for Dr. Yamaguchi on Indian Buddhism*, Kyoto, 1955, pp. 136–44.

————, "The Problem of Dependency in the Doctrine of Pratītyasamutpāda," *A Collection of Essays Commemorating the 50th Anniversary of the Faculty of Letters of Kyoto University*, Kyoto, 1956, pp. 153–81.

————, "Buddhism and Existentialism: The Dialogue between Oriental and Occidental Thought," W. Leibrecht, ed., *Religion and Culture: Essays in Honor of Paul Tillich*, New York, 1959, pp. 291–365.

————, "Das Problem der Eschatologie bei der Jōdo-Schule des japanischen Buddhismus und ihre Beziehung zu seiner Heilslehre," *Oriens Extremus* 8, 1961, pp. 84–94.

————, "Buddhism and Nihilism," *Kōzakindaibukkyō*, Vol. 3, Kyoto, 1962, pp. 72–103.

————, "Hegel and Buddhism," *Il Pensiero* VII/1–2, 1962, pp. 5–46.

————, "The Philosophy of Nishida," JR 3/4, 1963, pp. 1–32.

————, "Die Idee der Freiheit von und durch Kausalität im Ur-Buddhismus," *Akten des XIV. Internationalen Kongresses für Philosophie*, Vienna, 1972, pp. 145–58.

————, "Probleme der Versenkung im Ur-Buddhismus," *Beihefte der ZRGG* XVI, 1972.

————, "The Enlightenment of the Buddha," *Chūokōron* 89/5, 1974, pp. 300–310.

———— and Umehara Takeshi, *Japan's Buddhist Texts*, Tokyo, 1969.

Takizawa Katsumi, "Was hindert mich noch, mich taufen zu lassen?: Antwort," *K. Barth zum 70. Geburtstag am 10.5.1956*, Zollikon, 1956, pp. 911–25.

————, "Buddhism and Christianity," Kyoto, 1964.

————, "Nachwort," W. Böttcher, *Rückenansicht. Perspektiven japanischen Christentums*, Stuttgart, 1973, pp. 154–73.

————, "Zen-Buddhismus und Christentum im gegenwärtigen Japan," Yagi and Luz *(q.v.)*, pp. 139–59.

Thelle, Notto R., "A Barthian Thinker Between Buddhism and Christianity: Takizawa Katsumi," JR 8/4, 1975, pp. 54–86.

Tillich, Paul, *Systematic Theology* (three volumes in one), University of Chicago Press, 1967.

———— and Hisamatsu Shin'ichi, "Dialogues, East and West," EB IV/2, 1971, pp. 89–107; V/2, 1972, pp. 107–28; VI/2, 1973, pp. 87–114.

Trevor, M. H. *The Ox and His Herdsman* (based on the translation of Kōichi Tsujimura and Hartmut Buchner), Tokyo, 1969.

Tsujimura Kōichi, "Dialectics and Time," *Tetsugaku kenkyū* XLII/7, 1964, pp. 645–60.

————, "Bultmann and Heidegger: Belief and Thought," *Tetsugaku kenkyū*, XLII/11, pp. 1031–50.

Ueda Shizuteru, *Die Gottesgeburt in der Seele und der Durchbruch zur Gottheit. Die mystische Anthropologie Meister Eckharts und ihre Konfrontation mit der Mystik des Zen-Buddhismus*, Gütersloh, 1965.

————, "Der Buddhismus und das Problem der Säkularisierung. Zur gegenwärtigen geistigen Situation Japans," O. Schatz, ed., *Hat die Religion Zukunft?* Cologne, 1971, pp. 255–75.

————, *Zen Buddhism. Original Man*, Tokyo, 1973.

Ui Hakuju, *A Concise Dictionary of Buddhism*, Tokyo, 1953.

Vorgrimler, Herbert and Robert Vander Gucht (eds.), *Bilanz der Theologie im 20. Jahrhundert. Perspektiven, Strömungen, Motive in der christlichen und nichtchristlichen Welt*, 3 vols., Vienna, 1969–70.

Waldenfels, Hans, "Absolute Nothingness. Preliminary Considerations on a Central Notion in the Philosophy of Nishida Nitarō and the Kyoto School," Mon. Nipp. XXI/3–4, 1966, pp. 354–91.

———, "Anmerkungen zum Gespräch der Christenheit mit der nichtchristlichen Welt," W. Böld *(q.v.)*, pp. 95–141.

———, "Vom Schweigen des Buddha und den Geistlichen Übungen des Ignatius von Loyola," H. Schlier *et al.*, *Strukturen christlicher Existenz. Beiträge zur Erneuerung des geistlichen Lebens* (F. Wulf-Festschrift), Würzburg, 1968, pp. 139–51.

———, *Offenbarung. Das Zweite Vatikanische Konzil auf dem Hintergrund der neueren Theologie* (Beiträge zur Ökumenischen Theologie, ed. by H. Fries, Vol. 3, Munich, 1969.

———, *Glauben hat Zukunft. Orientierungspunkte*, Vienna, 1970.

———, "Das schweigende Nichts angesichts des sprechenden Gottes. Zum Gespräch zwischen Buddhismus und Christentum in der japanischen Kyoto-Schule," *Neue Zeitschrift für Systematische Theologie und Religionsphilosophie* 13, 1971, pp. 314–34.

———, *Unfähigkeit und Bedürfnis zu glauben*, Cologne, 1972.

———, "Religionen und Christentum und der Säkularisierungsprozess in Asien," *Zeitschrift für Missionswissenschaft und Religionswissenschaft* 58, 1974, pp. 81–112.

———, "Der Absolutheitsanspruch des Christentums und die grossen Weltreligionen," J. Beutler and O. Semmelroth, eds., *Theologische Akademie XI*. Frankfort, 1974, pp. 38–64.

———, *Meditation—Ost und West*, Cologne, 1975.

———, "Das Gebet im japanischen Buddhismus," *Studia Missionalia* 24, 1975, pp. 103–26.

———, "Wort und Wortlosigkeit im Buddhismus," *Concilium* XII/2, 1976, 89–98.

Watanabe Shōkō, *Buddhism*, Tokyo, 1956.

———, *The Buddhism of Japan*, Tokyo, 1958.

——— (trans.), *Japanese Buddhism. A Critical Appraisal*, Tokyo, 1970.

Watsuji Tetsurō, *A Climate. A Philosophical Study*, Tokyo, 1961.

———, "Japanese Literary Arts and Buddhist Philosophy," EB IV/1, 1971, pp. 88–115.

Wei-Lang, *Das Sutra des sechsten Patriarchen*, ed. by R. von Muralt, Zurich, 1958.

Weischedel, Wilhelm, *Philosophische Grenzgänge. Vorträge und Essays*, Stuttgart, 1967.

———, *Der Gott der Philosophen. Grunglegung einer Philosophischen Theologie im Zeitalter des Nihilismus*, 2 vols., Munich, 1971–72.

Welte, Bernhard, *Auf der Spur des Ewigen. Philosophische Abhand-*

lungen über verschiedene Gegenstände der Religion und der Theologie, Basel, 1965.

——, *Heilsverständnis des Christentums*, Vienna, 1966.

——, *Zeit und Geheimnis. Philosophische Abhandlungen zur Sache Gottes in der Zeit der Welt*, Vienna, 1975.

——, *Meister Eckhart. Gedanken zu seinen Gedanken*, Freiburg, 1979.

Wisser, R. (ed.), *Sinn und Sein. Ein philosophisches Symposium*, Tübingen, 1960.

Yagi Seiichi and Ulrich Luz (eds.), *Gott in Japan. Anstösse zum Gespräch mit japanischen Philosophen, Theologen, Schriftstellern*, Munich, 1973.

Yamaguchi Susumu, *The Opposition of Being and Nothingness in Buddhism*, Tokyo, 1964.

——, "The Concept of the Pure Land in Nāgārjuna's Doctrine," EB I/2, 1966, pp. 34–47.

Yamauchi Tokuryū, "Problems of Logic in Philosophy East and West," JR 3/3, 1963, pp. 1–7.

Zimmer, Heinrich, *Philosophie und Religion Indiens*, Zurich, 1961.

Zaehner, R. C., *Mysticism Sacred and Profane. An Inquiry into Some Varieties of Praeternatural Experience*, Oxford, 1961.

The Collection of Middle-Length Sayings ("Majjhima-Nikāya"), 3 vols., London, The Pali Text Society, 1967.

Index

Abe, M., 24, 50, 52, 53, 69–75, 77, 79, 86, 89, 94, 96, 97, 102, 106, 108–09, 115–16, 123, 139–42, 149, 159, 164, 168, 174–83, 185.
abhāva, see bhāva.
Abraham, 153.
absolute, 21, 65, 83, 84, 89, 139, 154, 155.
affirmation and negation, 17, 42, 72, 78, 83, 86, 88, 90, 94, 115, 136, 141.
agnosticism, 144.
Albrecht, C., 127–29.
Altaner, B., 165.
anātman, 10–14, 20–45, 69, 72, 87, 94, 100, 113, 175; *see also* non-self.
Andrews, A., 167.
Anesaki, M., 167.
anitya, 20.
anthropocentricism, 106, 108, 109, 113, 137, 144, 152; *see also* homocentricism.
anxiety, 1, 13, 17, 68–69, 130.
appearance and disappearance, 108.
apophatic and cataphatic, 28, 123, 135–37.
Aquinas, T., 81, 135, 144.
argument, 86, 110.
Ariga, T., 16, 149.
Aristotle, 37, 170.
art, 33–34, 38, 134, 169.
Aryadeva, 168.
Asaṅga, 25.
asat, see sat.
Asia/Asian, vii, 2, 3, 7, 24, 29, 31, 32, 35, 37, 61, 72, 121, 151, 169, 185.
atheism, 2, 52, 58, 68, 144.
ātman, see anātman.
attachment, 57, 73, 75, 78, 79, 90, 94, 110, 142.
Augustine, 37, 82.
autonomy, 12, 97, 105; *see also* freedom.
Avatamsaka Sūtras, 26.
avidya, see ignorance.
awakening, 9, 12, 56, 99, 100, 109, 116; *see also* enlightenment.
awareness, 67, 89, 112.

ba, see field.
Bareau, A., 20, 164, 165, 166, 168.
basho, see locus.
Barth, K., 51, 82, 121.
Bauer, W., 30, 167.
Bashō, 34, 169.
Beierwaltes, W., 185.
being, 30, 45, 49, 55, 57, 69, 82, 83, 84, 102–06, 146, 150–51, 153, 171, 174, 181; and non-being, 1, 15, 17–18, 41, 51, 65, 66, 70–77, 79, 88, 91–92, 94, 108, 109; in the world, 107, 129; in time, 111.
Béky, G., 167, 176.
belief, *see* faith.
Benl, O., 168.
Benz, E., 176, 180.
Bergson, H. 37.
Bertholet, A., 182.
bhāva/abhāva, 21, 30, 72, 175.

204